Liure nouueau/dict
patrõs de lingerie:
cestassauoir a deux
endroitz/a point croise/poit
couche ꝗ point picque/en fil
dor/dargẽt/de soye/ou aul-
tre/en quelque ouurage que
ce soit: en cõprenant lart de
broderie et tissuterie.

¶On les vend a Lyõ en la
maison de Claude nourry/
dict Le prince.

In memoriam Larry Salmon

French Textiles

From the Middle Ages through the Second Empire

Edited by Marianne Carlano and Larry Salmon

Essays by Jean-Michel Tuchscherer, Marianne Carlano, Anne Kraatz, and Jacqueline Jacqué

Wadsworth Atheneum · Hartford, Connecticut · 1985

Cover:
Antependium, detail. Late seventeenth or early eighteenth
century. Glass beads, wool, silk, parchment wrapped with silk;
linen ground. 35 x 71 (89 x 180). Collection of Daniel and
Josiane Fruman.

Frontispiece:
Illustration from a sixteenth-century pattern book for lace,
embroidery and weaving by Claude Nourry, called "the prince,"
Lyons.

Library of Congress Catalog Card Number: 84-51324
ISBN 0-918333-02-4

Funded in part by the National Endowment for the Arts
and the Women's Committee of the Wadsworth Atheneum

Contents

As all art was more or less applied art, the distinction between artists and craftsmen did not arise. The great masters in the service of the courts of Flanders, or of Berry, or of Burgundy, each of them an artist of very marked personality, did not confine themselves to painting pictures or to illuminating manuscripts; they were not above coloring statues, painting shields or staining banners; or designing costumes for tournaments and ceremonies.

Johan Huizinga, The Waning of the Middle Ages

Note to the Reader

The complex nature of this manuscript required special copy editing. For the sake of clarity technical terms are italicized the first time they appear in the essays. These terms are defined in the glossary located at the back of the book. Names of publications such as books and plays are also italicized. Non technical foreign words are in quotation marks.

A bibliography for technical terms follows the glossary.

Dimensions are given inches first, centimeters in parentheses; height precedes width unless otherwise noted. H. = height; L. = length. Max. signifies that measurement taken at the point of greatest width or height in an unevenly shaped textile.

Preface

The idea for this publication was first discussed by Marianne Carlano, Jacqueline Jacqué, and Véronique de Bruignac in 1980. It was crystallized later that year over dinner during an international conference in Como, Italy, which is, appropriately, that country's silk production center. At that time Malitte Matta added her very special words of wisdom and advice.

Although the museum has published several works in the past which made significant contributions to textile scholarship, beginning with *Two Thousand Years of Tapestry Weaving* in 1953, and continuing with *Bed Ruggs* in 1972, and in 1976 a handbook on our permanent collection entitled *Three Centuries of Costumes*, none has been as ambitious as the present publication.

The fact that there was no general work on the history of French textiles, coupled with the special skills and the great enthusiasm for the subject possessed by our own Curator of Costume and Textiles, led to the Atheneum taking on the formidable task of producing a book much beyond the scope of just an exhibition catalogue.

The forthcoming exhibition has been inspired by the extensive French holdings in our own collection of textiles, the large population of people of French heritage in our area, and the historical tradition of the Cheney silk mills of nearby Manchester, whose first weavers were trained in Lyons, France. Because it intends to survey French textiles in a comprehensive manner, the show includes a very broad range of types of textiles and the various forms in which they were used. It does not include tapestries and rugs, but it does cover the gamut from the very finest of courtly styles to quilts and regional costume. These objects are united by a common sensibility which has made France a leader in taste since the Middle Ages.

On behalf of the Wadsworth Atheneum, I would like to thank the French Ministry of Culture for their belief in this project and for their assistance with this book, which chronicles the history of some of the most splendid textile treasures of all time.

My very special thanks as well to Marianne Carlano, who has been the leading spirit behind this enterprise and who has achieved such notable results.

Tracy Atkinson
Director

Acknowledgments

This book is the result of the steadfast dedication and hardwork of many individuals. Anne Kraatz, Jacqueline Jacqué, Jean-Michel Tuchscherer, Larry Salmon, and Marianne Carlano are responsible not only for their own contributions but also for assisting each other in countless ways. This collaborative effort has, it is hoped, assured the accuracy and integrity of the written word.

Beyond this list of authors, a number of people helped with the research for this project. In Europe we thank Madeleine Beaufort, American College of Paris; the staff of the Bibliothèque de la Ville de Paris; the staffs of the manuscript room, photographic services department, and print room, Bibliothèque Nationale, Paris; M. Guibert, Comédie Française; M. Schutz, Ecole Nationale Supérieure des Industries Textiles, Mulhouse; Chantal Gastinel-Coural and Jean Coural, Mobilier National, Paris; Elizabeth Taburet and Dominique Thibaudat, Musée de Cluny, Paris; Josette Brédif, Musée de Jouy; Monique Drosson and Philippe de Fabry, Musée de l'Impression sur Etoffes, Mulhouse; Guillaume Garnier and Madeleine Delpierre, Musée de la Mode et du Costume de la Ville de Paris; Monique Blanc, Véronique de Bruignac, Nadine Gasc, and Micheline Viseux, Musée des Arts Décoratifs, Paris; Pierre Arrizoli-Clementel, Marie-Dominique Frieh, Evelyne Gaudry and Monique Jay, Musée Historique des Tissus, Lyons; M. Alcouffe and Danielle Gabordit-Chopin, Musée du Louvre; Bernard Jacqué, Musée du Papier Peint, Rixheim; Marie-José Beaumelle, Musée du Vieux-Marseilles; Jean Rivière, Musée National de Blérancourt; Daniel Meyer and Beatrice Saule, Palace at Versailles; Bernard Tassinari, Tassinari et Chatel SARL, Lyons; Abbé Ledit, Treasury of the Cathedral at Troyes; Marie-Nöelle de Gary and Françoise Magny, Union Centrale des Arts Décoratifs, Paris; Michael A. Zaccaria, University of London; B. Heitz, University of Strasbourg.

On this side of the Atlantic, our gratitude is extended to Elizabeth Ann Coleman, Brooklyn Museum; Gillian Moss, David Revere McFadden, and Milton Sonday, Cooper-Hewitt Museum; Laila Gross, Fairleigh Dickinson University, New Jersey; Kay and Bill Robertson, Lowei-Robertson, Inc., Los Angeles; Edward Maeder, Los Angeles County Museum of Art; Michael Hall, Jr. and his associates at Michael Hall Fine Arts, Inc., New York; Paul M. Ettesvold, Mary Meyers, Edith Standen, and Alice Zrebiec, Metropolitan Museum of Art; Lotus Stack, Minneapolis Institute of Arts; Deborah Kraak, Jeffrey H. Munger, and Marsha Waldman, Museum of Fine Arts, Boston; Susan Anderson-Hay, Kathryn Hiesinger, and Joseph Rischel, Philadelphia Museum of Art; Zoe Annis-Perkins and Louisa Bartlett, Saint Louis Art Museum; Patsy Orlofsky and her staff, Textile Conservation Workshop, South Salem, New York; Sarah Bremser, University of California, Berkeley.

There are certain persons whose special efforts beyond the call of duty must be noted. Charlotte Lacaze's encyclopedic knowledge of the museums and libraries of Paris and her general all around sound advice deserve mention here. Daniel and Josiane Fruman were kind enough to share their collection and love of embroideries, but kinder still to introduce us to other collectors. Maurice Deramaux allowed us to study his fine embroideries. Véronique Monier acted as liason for a variety of transcontinental arrangements from ordering photographs to the analysis of technical information concerning the textiles from the Fruman and Deramaux collections.

Textiles are among the most difficult objects to photograph because of their often complex structures and surface ornamentation. Joseph Szaszfai's insistence on both technical and aesthetic excellence in his work has resulted in stunning photographs that substantially increase the beauty and informational quality of this book. Jean-Luc Bureau has provided equally fine photographs of lace, perhaps the finest ever published. Robert Hennessey has taken care to incorporate and enhance this photographic information in the halftone printer's negative. Bill Glick, of Meriden-Stinehour Press, saw that the printing of this book received special attention. Robin Bledsoe and Elise K. Kenney copyedited and proofread the essentially bilingual texts with a relentless commitment to perfection. Our deep appreciation goes to Catherine Waters, designer of this book, not only for her skills at visually organizing the material, but also for her boundless enthusiasm, and to John Gambell as consultant, for his careful and discerning eye. Sonia Lee, Mary Schipa, and Françoise Weaver translated the texts by Jean-Michel Tuchscherer and Jacqueline Jacqué with the utmost attention to detail.

Among the Atheneum staff members, Carolyn Bogli and John Teahan's word processor instructions were essential to the production of the manuscript. Gertrud Bourgoyne coordinated the secretarial activities carried out by herself, Jeannette Harrison, Irene Heublein, and Gloria Schroeder. Lynn Ritland, Catherine Knapp, and John Teahan verified many of the tedious details in the manuscript. Christy Anderson, however, must be singled out for her special contribution to this book. She assisted with research, edited the bibliographies, and in the final stages of this project, during my absence, took charge of those inevitable last minute changes. I thank Tracy Atkinson, Director, and Gregory Hedberg, Chief Curator, for their belief in this book.

Finally, I wish to thank the National Endowment for the Arts, a Federal Agency, The Women's Committee of the Wadsworth Atheneum, United Technologies Corporation, Susan and Herbert Meller and their colleagues in the textile industry, and the Costume and Textile Society of the Wadsworth Atheneum for providing the support which made this publication possible.

Marianne Carlano
Curator, Costume and Textiles
Wadsworth Atheneum

Introduction

The publication of this collection of essays about French textiles, organized by the Wadsworth Atheneum, raises an interesting but difficult question: just what makes *these* objects French? Certainly very few of them can be proven by documentation to have been produced in that country, for textiles—more than the objects of any other field of art history—lack the painter's signature, the cabinetmaker's label, the porcelain factory's imprint, in short any identifying artists' marks. Moreover, what archival material exists for these textiles still awaits systematic organization. The study of textiles, therefore, relies heavily on attribution through design, technique, and intuition. Success in this endeavor requires experience and sensitive scholarship, fortunately amply provided by the contributors to this book. In many ways they succeed in establishing a sense for what is French about these embroideries, laces, woven textiles and printed cottons, and by so doing create a cumulative statement about French art in a broader sense.

In addition to the advantage realized through the joint publication of these articles, the authors have strived to include information from original documents either previously unpublished or never before presented in English translation. Organized as a collection of essays on the embroidery, lace, woven, and printed textile arts, this book is intended to serve as a reference tool for students of textile history, design, decorative arts, and related fields. The overview presented here should be useful to the specialist, for these reasons and for the extensive documentation. It is hoped that the nonspecialist as well will find the copious illustrations and the carefully organized texts both enticing and educational.

A truly encyclopedic survey of French textiles would have to include rugs and tapestries, which are missing here. This is in part because these fields have received attention in many other publications, but more relevantly because the objects could not be physically present in the exhibition at the Wadsworth Atheneum.

The decision to close this study of French textiles with the year 1870 was agreed upon from the start. The textile design traditions that began their development in the Middle Ages follow a continuum to the close of the Second Empire. The succeeding decorative styles were consciously conceived as breaks with tradition in the "modern" spirit, and their story is more properly that of the beginning of the history of contemporary textiles.

One of the great pleasures of working in the field of textiles is the variety of valid approaches to the subject. Although technique is a constant underlying current, this study is primarily an art historical one. One will find in the text in-depth technical information for certain more significant textiles, but for the most part this information is in the bibliography, notes, and glossary. This organization is intended to provide a guide to technical material for the specialist without overwhelming the reader with cumbersome details. The textiles are of such breathtaking beauty that they often speak most eloquently for themselves, providing they are properly placed in their art historical background. The people who made them and coveted them understood this well, and it is our goal to bring this appreciation to today's reader.

Marianne Carlano
Larry Salmon

Woven Textiles ❖ Jean-Michel Tuchscherer

Much of the Western world still regards France as the symbol of civilization in the arts and in whatever constitutes good taste and refinement. In fact, France continues to represent a certain quality and a certain aristocratic attitude toward life. For several centuries, especially since the mid-seventeenth century reign of Louis XIV, the Sun King, French art has had a profound influence on all of Europe. Good taste was French then and has remained so almost until today. The art of dress, of personal adornment, the creation of fabrics, ribbons, *passementerie*, even the fabrication of lace, buttons, shoelaces, shoes, and purses—in short what are called today by the ambiguous terms of fashion and its accessories—are foremost among the art forms in which France has traditionally been the stylistic leader.

If French fabrics, as the expression of a civilization, are a relatively new creation, the diverse populations who occupied French territory as it is defined today engaged very early in the art of weaving. At first the only aim was simple bodily protection. The digs on the prehistoric site of Lake Paladru between Lyons and Grenoble, for example, unearthed fragments of primitive weaves made mostly of vegetable fibers, thus proving the existence of weaving in France several centuries before recorded history.[1]

Gallic civilization is unfortunately still mainly unknown despite recent spectacular findings.[2] One can, however, affirm that refined cloth, artistically and technically sophisticated, did not exist in Gaul before the Roman invasion, and the Romans themselves imported their fabrics from the Orient. Very early the wearing of silk, imported exclusively from the East, provoked in the empire the violent reactions of people like Cicero and Pliny who considered the use of silk by men as a sign of decadence. Under Tiberius the senate forbade men to wear silk. Such decrees were regularly delivered during the Roman Empire. Furthermore, economists of the day viewed the silk trade as prejudicial because of the currency drain that it created.

These sumptuary laws and regulations controlling the use of diverse types of cloth in the empire of course applied to Roman Gaul. The latter very quickly conformed to Roman taste, then to that of Constantinople, due to the considerable commercial exchange that flourished thanks to the increasingly efficient imperial administration. Lyons, Vienne, Autun, Saintes, Nimes, Paris, Arles, Nice, and Marseilles were not only demographically important Gallo–Roman cities; they were also centers of civilization laying the foundation for the future.

This future included the establishment of Christianity as early as the second century in Vienne, then in Lyons and Marseilles. Christianity, like other religious and commercial innovations, was imported from the East. Very early on it was a decisive influence on the appreciation of fabrics in the empire. In fact, the trading of relics, which became very important during the Middle Ages, introduced in the West diverse fabrics, for the most part silk, of an unprecedented luxuriousness. These fabrics, signifying supreme luxury and absolute perfection, were considered the only ones worthy of receiving relics. In a Western world obviously still hardly touched by civilization, they were the precursor of oriental taste long before the Crusades. The treasury of the cathedral of Sens, south of Paris, is the most obvious example, among many others, of this massive importation of oriental silks, mostly from Syria. Antioch in Syria was both a brilliant silk weaving center and the point of origin of the intense relic trade.[3]

The importation of oriental silks to the West continued for a long time, first under Charlemagne, then under his successors; the Ottonian emperors further accelerated the trade in the eleventh and twelfth centuries.[4] However, judging from certain texts, one can surmise that for its part the West also created an interesting textile art, using the raw material available. We know that in Antioch goods offered by Western merchants included woolens and fine linen garments, as well as dyeing products. All this makes it possible to follow the evolution of the taste for quality cloth, a taste that became further refined throughout the centuries.

It would be interesting to determine the role played by the Crusades in the evolution and development of this infatuation for silk. In addition to certain spices, vegetables, flowers, gunpowder, and livestock, fabrics were a significant import. A specific study of medieval texts would most likely yield new information on the subject.[5] For the moment, however, the study of textile art in France before the fourteenth century remains limited to vague or incomplete hypotheses. One can assume the existence of diversified crafts, which had probably reached a certain perfection, judging from what already existed in the related field of tapestry. The itinerant weavers wandering throughout the country surely had an impact on the production and consumption of quality fabrics. The medieval chronicles and songs of deeds frequently mention sumptuous cloths displayed on windows[6] to honor the arrival of a dignitary, and silk, gold, or silver draperies were used to cover the walls of bedrooms and other important rooms. All these rich fabrics were, and would be for a long time to come, imported from the Orient, and later from Italy through the intermediary of Venetian or Lombard merchants.

History tells us a bit more about the production of luxurious textiles, for the simple reason that this output was intended for the upper class. Because the fabrication required specialized workers and the raw material was usually extremely expensive, it needed important financial backing. Silk remained what it had been since Roman times—the mark of extreme refinement and luxury. As early as the high Middle Ages, silk was everywhere: draperies, rugs, bed sheets, bed curtains, dresses, coats, and shirts. At about the same time sumptuary laws appeared in order to halt the excesses of luxury.

From the thirteenth century onward silk was made in Paris, Rouen, Montpellier, Avignon, and Nimes.[7] The French industry, unable to compete with foreign imports, limited itself to small items of clothing. Nevertheless, corporative rules were already beginning to regulate silk manufacture. Etienne Boileau, provost of the Paris merchants, tells us in his mid-thirteenth-century book of guilds that in that town the cloth workers and the velvet and *bourserie en lisse* makers were organized into guilds whose production was reserved for the king, the queen, and the royal family.[8] It took six years to learn the profession if the student paid a fee; eight years if the schooling was free. In 1290 Rouen's weavers and ribbon manufacturers formed a guild that a century later, in 1403, numbered nearly two hundred masters, all of them French.

In the south of France, the silk industry of Montpellier was so developed that in 1232 Henry III of England ordered twenty rolls of silk and four rolls of scarlet wool cloth. Likewise, silk manufacture flourished in the fourteenth century in Avignon, then the papacy's temporary seat.[9] In 1399 Lyons's consuls bought ten rolls of red satin from Avignon for their ceremonial robes. In the thirteenth and fourteenth centuries the fabrication of silk was in fact well established throughout most of southern France.

From the Middle Ages to the nineteenth century the wool, linen, and hempen cloth manufacturers made great strides in all of France. The clothiers' guilds were among the most powerful, and they contributed to the economic, and often artistic, development of many cities. (Colbert, one of the great administrators of the kingdom in the seventeenth century showed a special interest in cloth production and in fact came from the rich family of a Reims draper.) However, the manufacture of these fabrics was mostly for everyday use, and therefore very rarely of any artistic interest.

In the fifteenth century France was still a very unstable country, barely recovered from a bloody and endless war with England, the Hundred Years' War. However, the kingdom was slowly but surely becoming unified, notably under the leadership of several kings who managed to annex principalities and dukedoms such as Burgundy, Brittany, and Bourbonnais.

Louis XI (ruled 1461–1483), one of the great French kings, whose role is not yet fully appreciated, had a major influence on the establishment of the silk industry in France. Although he was a very sober individual and dressed very simply, he quickly grasped the considerable economic possibilities that the silk trade offered in the Europe of his time. The aristocracy and the princely and royal courts were literally ruining themselves to acquire these precious fabrics, at exorbitant prices, because the wearing of silk was more honorific than the most splendid title of nobility.[10] France and many other countries were pouring astonishing sums of currency into Italy for the most part, but also into southern Spain, Sicily, and the Orient. A flourishing market had developed around the silk trade, stretching from Venice to Milan, Florence, Lucca, throughout northern Italy, crossing the Alps to supply all of the Spanish, Portuguese, Flemish, German, and English courts. Lyons was the center of this axis. All the important Venetian, Florentine, Milanese, and Lucchese merchants opened important branches and ware-houses there. The silk trade was followed by the financial trade, and the most prestigious European banks established themselves in Lyons, which became, as early as the fifteenth century, an international business community. The Medicis, several of their Florentine colleagues, the Fuggers of Augsburg, and bankers from Nuremberg and Antwerp all had establishments in Lyons. The city on the Rhone enjoyed an unprecedented business boom, especially because, since 1450, it had held an enormous and exclusive right to customs tariffs. All of the silks, raw or figured, that entered the kingdom had to go through Lyons.[11] Five hundred thousand gold crowns (écus) left the country each year for Italy. The most important centers of supply were Florence, Bologna, Venice, Lucca, Genoa, and Milan, where a great variety of fabrics were made: famous *velvets*, *damasks*, *satins*, *taffetas*, *serges*, and many others. Milan was also famous for its silk stockings.[12]

Louis XI, besides seeking to unify and enlarge the kingdom, also considered the development of diverse industries, in particular the manufacture of silks, which were the cause of such a prejudicial loss of gold and silver. Because of its highly developed commercial and banking network, and its advantageous geographical situation, Lyons seemed to him the ideal site for attempting the venture. By the Orléans Ordinance of 23 November 1466 the king first asked the consulate of Lyons to raise two thousand royal pounds to start up the new silk industry.[13] Despite royal promises, such as the declaration of total freedom from corporative regulations and certain substantial privileges, this new trade met the resistance of the people of Lyons, who wanted no part of it. There was a good reason for this. The king had not taken into account the strong, though hidden, opposition of all the Italians established in Lyons, who had no interest in welcoming competition in their own territory. The procrastinations and the obvious bad will dragged matters out so long that, tired of the whole situation, Louis XI decided on 12 March 1470 to transfer the entire colony of Italian weavers to his favored city of Tours, on the Loire River, some 250 miles west of Lyons. Thus Lyons avoided both the problem of competition and the threat of royal interference.

Tours was not so lucky at keeping its independence. The king spent a good deal of time at his residence of Plessis-les-Tours, a few miles to the north, and imposed on the city a first levy of twelve hundred royal pounds, although this was accompanied by numerous privileges: exemption from taille and of the militia, from certain taxes, and ease in borrowing money. But the outcome seems to have been positive, judging from documents of the period. In 1490 it is mentioned that about forty masters and about a hundred looms were manufacturing some "plain and solid color satin," some velvet, and some figured satin. To encourage further the young industry, Charles VIII, Louis XI's successor, added other privileges: exemption from tolls and foreign taxes, and no entrance fees on the raw silk bought outside of the kingdom. Thus Tours superseded Lyons as a silk weaving center.[15]

Moreover, the trade was becoming organized. An apprenticeship lasted five years, with specialization in one of four fabrics: satin, damask, velvet, or gold brocade. In 1498 Louis XII promulgated the first articles of trade that concerned the working of silk in France. To become a master, a candidate had to create a masterpiece in one of these four fabrics. It was forbidden to mix linen or cotton with silk. Each roll of silk, before being allowed on the market, was subjected to official inspection and marked if considered good. Furthermore, and in order to ensure the quality of the manufacturing, four master jurors, elected for three years by the community of masters and workers, inspected the workshops and workrooms. The number of looms permitted per workshop was regulated. However, masters were exempted from this regulation, except for makers of taffeta, who were limited to two looms. Another article dealt with a subject that recurs throughout the history of the silk trade in France—the exploitation of the trade. In this case, the regulations demanded that a merchant, heretofore untrained in weaving, first be an apprentice, then a worker. In other words, the craftsman was still the sole ruler of his trade. But this situation would change a century and a half later.

These articles of trade were not, however, the first regulations concerning the French textile industry. In 1483 Charles VIII had issued for the drapers' guild of Montpellier a very comprehensive set of rules that addressed most of the problems of textile manufacturing. They were confirmed by Louis XII in 1498, the same year that Tours received its trade articles.

Although many other French towns made some efforts to establish within their walls this aristocratic silk industry, it took more than royal or princely whims, even when accompanied by privileges and subsidies, to transform a trade, a new craftsmanship, into a flourishing industry.[16] Even Tours, then the only silk center of the kingdom, had great difficulty holding onto its position. In 1546 the Venetian ambassador, Marino Cavalli, whose information about French mores of the time is very valuable, attributed the creation of Tours silk manufacturing to Louise de Savoie (1476–1531), the mother of François I; this implies a much more recent creation and a rather restricted activity. Moreover, it would be surprising, for example, if luxurious fabrics such as the velvets, gold and silver brocades, and satins that the Cardinal d'Amboise used to decorate his château at Gaillon near Rouen, had by that time (ca. 1506–1510) a French origin.[17] According to his *Théâtre français*, printed in Tours in 1594, Jacques de Beaune, lord of Semblançay, financial secretary of the royal treasury and great lover of art, in the first half of the sixteenth century also brought workers and silk from Italy to begin production in Tours. Many similar comments, detailing the arrival of weavers from Venice, Genoa, and Lucca, can be found all through the sixteenth century. Silk manufacture most likely had achieved a certain development in Tours. It is, however, just as certain that the city's production was not able to satisfy the luxurious tastes of courts as refined as those of François I or Henri II. For a long time to come, the French market remained a tributary of Italy, France being able to manufacture only simple fabrics. Even these were, nevertheless, very much in demand, which explains the relative prosperity of Tours.

Around 1543 about four hundred to five hundred masters worked in Tours, with, according to contemporary sources, very few foreigners among them. This would correspond to some two or three thousand looms, at a generous estimate. The articles of trade and other documents regulating the industry shed a bit more light on the silk trade in Tours in the mid-sixteenth century. The standards of apprentice, "compagnon" (journeyman), and

master were more tightly controlled. The quality of the materials used and the width of the woven fabrics were watched very closely. In fact, freedom of work became more and more restricted. These regulations were applied not only to silk weavers but also to the passementerie and ribbon makers with whom François I ratified articles in December 1542. To facilitate the now very difficult practice of the trade, Tours was exempted from Lyon's monopoly on the purchase of raw silks.

Another considerable privilege took effect in 1545: the creation of two open fairs. The city seemed well equipped to insure a satisfactory, if not a brilliant, future to the French silk industry.

The city of Lyons, which had been the first to attract royal favors, tried to recapture what it had rejected a few decades earlier. In April 1528 the city consulate presented grievances to François I and complained about the poverty that existed in the city. One complaint concerned the considerable profit that foreign merchants were making from the silk trade, especially at fairs, to the detriment of the city's own bourgeoisie. The former repugnance toward the silk industry seemed forgotten in the new desire to establish the industry in the city. This was done in two stages. First, on 2 May 1536, the consulate secured the confirmation of the old 1450 privilege that made the city the mandatory and exclusive customs clearing post and the only warehouse in the kingdom authorized to stock raw or manufactured silks from Italy, Spain, the Orient, and even Provence. This maneuver, which has always provoked the strongest reprobation from other French silk cities, was a fiscal measure intended to stop by royal power the numerous smuggled fabrics from escaping the entry seal.

The second stage occurred a few months later in September 1536, upon François I's victorious return from Provence where he had debated the Holy Roman emperor, Charles V. Two Piedmontese, Etienne Turquet and Barthélemy Nariz, persuaded the municipal magistrates of Lyons to solicit the king for the same favorable privileges as those held by Tours. The weavers were to come from Genoa and elsewhere. The patent letters were granted in October. Soon afterward some masters in velvet making from Avignon established themselves in Lyons; the consulate had granted them a three-hundred-gold crown gratuity as an incentive. The workers' community, specializing in gold brocade, silver cloth, and silk, was definitely established in 1538, having as inspectors Turquet and Raoulet Viard. Turquet was a rich merchant who had earned his fortune in the herring trade and orphans' labor,[18] but who had no knowledge whatever of the silk trade. Viard, a master manufacturer from Avignon, owned a forty-six-loom workshop in Lyons. Thus from the beginning the two factors of work and capital were present, a partnership that later on was to cause a great deal of trouble in the silk industry.

Just as in Tours, the industry in Lyons developed very slowly, despite the eloquent exaggeration of many contemporaries and several historians. As he went through Lyons in 1546, the Venetian ambassador Cavalli did not even note the beginnings of a precious fabric industry. The 1575 census records 224 masters specialized in velvet, taffeta, spinning, and dyeing, which supposes about 500 weavers. This weak industry was still unable to cope with the Italian competition that it was trying to imitate.

The sixteenth century, as it came more and more under the influence of Italian taste, saw the birth and blossoming of several other silk industry centers. Avignon, endowed with a solid and ancient tradition, had a production of remarkable quality. This city, outside of the kingdom because it depended directly on the Holy See, remained for a long time to come the most important silk center. Its velvets, which were its specialty, were as well known as those of Genoa. Around 1550 the brotherhood of velvet and silk workers codified its regulations. In 1553, for the arrival of Cardinal Farnese, the velvet manufacturers formed a company of three hundred fifty members all dressed in yellow velvet.

In fact, at that time all of southern France showed an increasing interest in the weaving of silk. Nimes, where this industry had existed since at least 1498, increased the number of its looms around the middle of the century and at the same time established the weaving of silk stockings. Henri II was especially interested to see this branch of the trade flourish.[19] Orange, Carpentras, Aix-en-Provence, and Toulouse also established silk manufacturing and solicited subsidies and privileges from the royal authorities. Closer to Lyons, Villefranche-sur-Rhône and

especially Saint-Chamond dedicated themselves to the manufacturing of silk fabrics. The latter soon became famous for the throwing of silk, which it alone handled for the Lyons manufacture. Near the end of the century, in 1585, Saint-Chamond, Saint-Etienne, and Lyons joined to elaborate "the regulations of the master fabric makers of the city of Lyons and other neighboring localities."[20]

To the north, Rouen, Orléans, and Paris continued to develop the manufacturing of silk fabrics. The community of Rouen received its permit in April 1543, and the Paris fabric makers improved their production techniques to such an extent that around 1585 they created a new fabric, "toque," which is a sort of gauze.

If we are to believe Cavalli, Tours enjoyed a rather favorable economic situation around the middle of the century, despite the strong grievances it presented in 1576 at the States General Assembly of Blois. In 1577 Cavalli noticed the high quality of Tours's silks, claiming that they were as good as those of Naples, Lucca, or Venice, and, best of all, less expensive.

Henri IV's accession to the throne in 1589 marked the beginning of a new era by the scope of the general reorganization programs in a kingdom more and more unified and politically structured. From then on one can detect the beginning of a nationalistic feeling, although still very faint, which was soon to rule all decisions.[21] Almost a century later, Colbert would be its most eloquent spokesman.

The silk industry, which was establishing itself throughout most of the kingdom where the consumption of precious fabrics was reaching new heights, was unfortunately weakened, if not ruined, as it was in many places, by the religious wars, genuine civil wars.[22] For example, at the very end of the century, Tours had hardly more than two hundred masters, not counting journeymen or apprentices, and they could no longer buy the raw silks essential to production. Annual consumption fell from the one thousand bales before the wars to under one hundred. In Lyons the industry numbered no more than a hundred masters with some eighteen hundred looms.

The Italian imports were triumphant because of the persistent infatuation of the rich with luxury.

Taffetas came from Lucca, Racconigi, and Milan; velvets, from Genoa, Avignon, Reggio, and Milan; damasks, from Florence; satins, from Genoa as well as Bruges; and silk *camelots*, from Lucca. At the end of the century France had spent more than seven million gold crowns on silk imports, although the kingdom was on the brink of ruin.[23] In order to avoid disaster, the immediate reaction was to close the borders. In January 1599 entrance into the kingdom was forbidden to all silk, gold, or silver fabrics. This prohibition was lifted the next year after it became clear that French production was insufficient to satisfy the kingdom's own demands.

Henri IV's first goal was self-sufficiency in regard to the raw material, which meant that France had to produce its own silk fiber. In this matter, the country had a lucid thinker and a visionary in Barthélemy de Laffemas, whose proposed reforms were at first rebuffed because of their scope and innovation. Until then, sericulture had existed only in the south, in particular in Provence and Languedoc,[24] and on a very small scale. Laffemas proposed to enlarge and develop this activity. He ordered the planting of nearly ten million mulberry trees in Venaissin, in Provence, and in the provinces south of Lyons. In 1596 the breeding of silkworms was successfully undertaken as far north as the Lyons region. The raw silks produced were so beautiful and of such good quality that they were preferred to those of Sicily.

At the same time, Laffemas with the help of Olivier de Serres, a prominent agronomist,[25] undertook an essential educational and scientific work. Olivier de Serres's fundamental study, *La Cueillette de la soye par la nourriture des vers qui la font*, appeared in 1599. This treatise was soon followed by a publication by Laffemas himself, *Propriétés des mûriers en leurs bois, fruits et racines*, which gave precise instructions for the production of the best sustenance for silkworms. In 1602 J. B. Le Tellier, a Tours silk merchant, published his *Bref Discours concernant la manière de nourrir les vers à soie*, illustrated with the famous engravings of the Flemish painter Stradan.[26] The next year he published his *Mémoires et instructions pour l'établissement des mûriers et l'art de faire la soie*. Many other treatises concerned the same subject, attesting to the intense and ever-growing interest in this aspect of the kingdom's economy.

In his work *Plaisir de la noblesse et autres qui ont des héritages des champs, sur la preuve certaine et profit des étoffes de soie qui se font à Paris*, Laffemas invited the wealthy landowning class to engage in sericultural undertakings. Henri IV himself set the example. In 1602 sixty miles of mulberry trees were planted in the Tuileries, the grounds of Fontainebleau, and other royal residences.[27] Silkworms were distributed; cocooneries, spinning, and silk-throwing mills were established. In 1603 the commerce assembly, recently created by the king at Laffemas's initiative, drew up a three-year contract, for twelve thousand pounds a year, with Le Tellier and Nicolas Chevalier from Tours; the purpose was to improve the establishment of mulberry planting in France. Numerous other similar initiatives were encouraged by the king throughout the country, especially in Rouen and Normandy.

Besides the effort to produce domestically the best raw material, a similar effort was made to manufacture excellent fabrics. Italian silks were still the best, and competition with them was encouraged by simply copying them. From this practice come the inextricable identification problems that face us today. However, the most important production centers, such as Lyons and Tours, continued to weave chiefly plain fabrics. This reluctance to innovate was due to several factors: the fear of investing, the undoubted shortage of funds, and finally the imperfection and inadequacy of the technical means. Another factor seems to have been the lack of judicial and technical regulation at the highest level. Surely the 1599 edict authorized and favored the manufacturing of silk cloth "in the manner of Milan, Genoa, Lucca, Florence, Venice, Naples, Bologna, Reggio, Modena, Chambéry, Avignon, Spain,"[28] but it did not regulate in any way its composition, as was the case for velvets and taffetas. Not until the coming to office of Colbert, under Louis XIV, would clear and precise production rules in general, and in regard to fabrics in particular, come into effect.

Meanwhile Tours showed its good will. The municipal body of the city deliberated in 1604 about introducing new designs and also decided to imitate foreign style. The width of Tours's fabrics was fixed in 1646. At that time plain cloth still constituted the bulk of the production with, however, the one innovation of *moiré*, for which the city held the monopoly. The moiré calender, in use after 1638, was even used for woolens, cotton, lisle thread, and camel's-hair cloth.

Lyons was slower to accept progress, forced to do so through a series of circumstances. First was the competition offered by the Customs of Vienne,[29] which had obtained several privileges and thus had succeeded in taking from Lyons the century-old exclusive monopoly that it had enjoyed on the trading of silk. New taxes further complicated the situation. Bills of exchange were depreciating, and finally, its fairs were losing more and more of their commercial impact. It was necessary to innovate to get out of the difficulty, especially because the ever-growing market for refined luxurious products continued to favor Italy. In 1610 an assembly asked for the manufacturing of "twenty types of work in gold, silver, and silk that are not made in Lyons." But, like Tours, and most likely for the same reasons, Lyons persisted in the manufacture of plain cloth whose quality and perfection earned different rewards from the consulate. The situation changed around 1604–1605 with the adoption of the continuous loom, perfected by a Milanese, Claude Dangon.[30] This loom, improved in Lyons, introduced the drawboy, a precious and indispensable auxiliary of the weaver. This new tool allowed Lyons to compete against Tours and Paris, especially for the making of beautiful *sortes*, or figured fabrics like those from Florence, Venice, Naples, Turkey,[31] and like printed cloth from India. The adoption of this new machine was slow, however, so that in 1619 the consulate authorized once again the manufacturing of "all kinds of mixed inexpensive fabrics," which gave the community a way out of its difficulties. The same year, new regulations made it more difficult to accede to the mastership and lengthened the "compagnonnage" from two to five years, upheld the creation of the masterpiece, and restricted each workshop to no more than twelve looms in active use.

The same regulations confirmed the structure of the profession and introduced a definitive distinction among masters. First, there were the masterworkers, who did not work their own material because they had no money to buy the raw material themselves; they hired themselves out to their colleagues or wholesale merchants foreign to the community.

Then there were the masterweavers who had sufficient funds to produce fabrics that they sold themselves. Finally, some merchants, who without belonging to the trade and without mastership letters, nevertheless had a sufficient fortune, bought fabrics and worked them. These three classes made up the silk producers of Lyons until well after the 1789 Revolution.

In 1661 Colbert came into office as Louis XIV's prime minister and right arm. Hated and despised by all the Sun King's courtiers, he played a decisive role in the French monarchy and in the kingdom's economy. He came from a rich family of drapers from Reims and thus was particularly sensitive to the textile arts and their problems. Although his own interest guided him more toward wool cloth than silks, he was the one who organized the silk trade and stimulated improvements in its quality, trying to come to terms with the old problem of France's dependency on foreign trade.[32]

In 1660, a year before Colbert's rise to power, Lyons's silk industry counted 841 masters with some 3,000 to 3,500 looms. The economic situation was relatively good. Earlier, in 1656, Octavio Mey had perfected the *lustering* of taffeta. In a letter to Colbert in 1665 the provost of Lyons's merchants (the equivalent of today's president of the chamber of commerce) wrote that the city's workers were able to equal any of the Italian silks except for Genoa's black velvets.[33] However, judging from his subsequent correspondence, the prime minister did not seem convinced. In fact, Colbert's ideas were entirely contrary to the structure of Lyons's industry, which was in real chaos from his point of view. In Lyons the manufacturing was carried out in many small workshops, each one headed by a master who made fabrics and often sold them himself. He was helped by his wife, his children, and sometimes one or two compagnons (journeymen). All these workshops were located on the first floor of houses and in garrets. No control was possible, which explained a production whose quality left much to be desired and was unable to meet foreign competition.

According to the general plan that Colbert had conceived for French industrial production, a method was essential in order to attain increasingly rigorous standards of perfection. Therefore he immediately grappled with Lyons's production.

In 1655 he started a correspondence with the merchants' provost in order to set up strict regulations and to expose the numerous defects that lowered the value of the merchandise. In November 1665 he asked for the creation of a fifty-member commission "charged with creating a plan" for reforms. The text drawn up by this commission addressed itself to all the details of the profession. Everything was regulated: the functioning of the community and its autonomous police force, the composition of the fabrics, their width, the number of warp threads, the number of reed teeth, the tension of the threads, the limitation of the number of mistakes, and the situation of masters, journeymen, and apprentices. Furthermore, Colbert made it obligatory to set the manufacturer's name on each roll with a lead seal: this had to be done in the inspector's office. Finally, the trade was forbidden to merchants who without holding mastership letters were employing workers. This last rule was very badly received. In effect, the merchants who were excluded were powerful people with considerable influence. They did everything in their power to save their privileges.

In view of the strong protest that the proposed reforms met in Lyons, Colbert sent the same proposal to Tours for study and discussion. There the master weavers' community was smaller and less powerful, and the statutes were drawn up with a few modifications and submitted for the king's confirmation on 3 March 1667. The people of Lyons followed Tours's example on 19 April, and on 1 May, royal approval was granted. Orléans received its regulations on 28 June, and Paris on 9 July. Marseilles received them in 1672, then Nimes in 1682. The statutes were adapted to the individual situation of each city.

In Lyons, however, the regulations, although partially accepted, continued to provoke strong protests. The clause excluding merchants without mastership letters was finally modified in their favor. All working merchants, as well as those who merely employed workers, were allowed to register as part of the community before 1 January 1665, in exchange for a fifteen-pound fee. After that date admission would require five years of apprenticeship and five years of compagnonnage.

These famous regulations recognized and confirmed the existence of the three classes: merchants who had workers but no workshop, master weavers who employed workers and had a workshop, and finally and most numerous, master workers who worked for others. But the latter had been slighted. They were forbidden to produce and sell on their own account. They could work for a new master weaver or merchant only if they produced an official note attesting that they were free of all debts toward their former employer. As soon as these humiliating measures were implemented, they gave rise to a violent uprising that lasted five days and five nights and had to be controlled by the militia.

Despite the imperfections of the new judicial regime, many silk manufacturers started up throughout France. They appeared in Reims, and Troyes in Champagne as early as 1665 and 1670, and in Toulouse in 1669. Even the city of Meaux had a royal manufactory in 1669, although it was short lived. In Nancy, capital of the dukedom of Lorraine, Duc Charles IV restored the trade in 1664, while in Paris and Tours production continued more or less successfully. Paris, capital of the kingdom, had two distinct weaving communities: the ribbon makers who could weave only fabrics less than a third of an *aune* in width (an aune equals about forty-five inches), and the gold cloth workers who wove all wider fabrics. The 1667 statutes enacted by Colbert applied only to the very important latter group.[34]

The purpose of the Colbert regulations was to create in each city a production restricted in its diversity but excellent in its quality. Thus Lyons became famous for its velvets and its glossy taffeta, Tours for its *pannes*, and Paris for its gold brocades.

The luxury of the court, maintained and encouraged by Louis XIV, gave rise to an unprecedented consumption of silk. The most important centers continued to be Lyons, Tours, and Paris. The servile dependence on Italian drawings and patterns continued for a while, until the arrival of innovative masters like Androuet du Cerceau, Daniel Marot, and Jean I. Bérain, who then imposed their own patterns, which were harmoniously suited to the French classical spirit.

Among the plethora of manufactories and workshops that Colbert's regime created or revived, the royal manufactory of Charlier in Saint-Maur-les-Fossés, near Paris, must be mentioned. This manufactory, one of the most remarkable undertakings of the seventeenth-century French textile industry, was probably created under Louis XIII, around 1634. Its production is mentioned in the accounts of the Royal Works Administration from 1666 on. Charlier's silks seem to have been mostly destined for the king and were the object of the most lavish praise. They appear many times among lists of royal gifts on the same level as tapestries or precious furniture.

One cannot examine Charlier's production, of which unfortunately nothing is left, but an idea of its importance can be seen from a description in *Le Mercure de France* of October 1678:

M. Charlier makes gold and silver fabrics, silk, gold cloth in the Persian style, and others in Italian style. He makes velvets, satins, damasks and all sorts of gold and silk cloth of the highest quality that one can buy directly in his Parisian shop, "At the Golden Hoop," rue de la Coutellerie, where he sells all of the above. This M. Charlier has the special talent for producing all kinds of fabrics. He makes admirable furnishing fabrics. In France, only he can do what he does. Each of his looms demand some fifteen thousand heddles to be assembled, which is an amazing sight.[35]

Other praises could be quoted, like that of Savary des Bruslons, manufactory inspector and author of a famous dictionary of commerce, whose father was a haberdasher in Paris. He expressed his admiration for a velvet made especially for Versailles:

Besides the ordinary cut velvet and the frisé *silk sometimes used in the flowered velvet, the frisé gold and silver were worked with so much craftsmanship that it provoked surprise and admiration. Each aune just out of the loom costs more than one thousand pounds, because a worker could do only an inch or eighteen lines per day. The pattern had been created by [Jean I.] Bérain, so well known for this kind of work. The small production of these velvets was used on a few portières (door curtains) for the private quarters at Versailles.*[36]

In 1686, on the occasion of the Siamese ambassador's visit to Paris and Versailles, Charlier's silks were among the wonders displayed for their admiration at the Manufacture Royale des Meubles de la Couronne. Charlier's gold and silver brocades, with French patterns, were among Louis XIV's presents to the king of Siam. To these must be added all the fabrics of breathtaking splendor that are

mentioned in the Royal Works Administration accounts. Unfortunately, this splendid manufactory disappeared during the Sun King's reign, as Charlier's successors were unable to keep up his high standards.

As mentioned, Colbert was more sensitive to the wool economy than to the silk, undoubtedly because wool cloth had an important and essential outlet, the army. For this reason, and hoping once more to free France from foreign dependency, on England in particular, in 1655 he invited Sir Josse Van Robais, Flemish in origin but settled in Holland, to come and establish himself in Abbeville, Picardie, in order to manufacture the best cloth in the world (figure 1). Van Robais, although a Protestant and bent on remaining one, enjoyed Colbert's privileges and favors, as well as his absolute protection. He arrived in Abbeville with thirty looms and fifty Dutch weavers and their families, all Protestants and natives of Middelburg.

Van Robais's privileges were considerable: total tax exemption, the right to dye and stiffen fabrics himself without going through a dyer's guild, total independence from any guild system,[37] and the authorization to hang his cloth even on Sunday. His manufactory was a royal one and depended solely on the intendant (controller) of Picardie who in turn answered only to Colbert and the king. Furthermore, Abbeville's drapers were forbidden to imitate his production.

Van Robais also enjoyed the privilege of importing, custom free, all his wools from Spain or elsewhere. Every three months he freighted a ship for Bilbao that brought back, on each trip, six hundred bales of Segovian wool, vastly superior to that of England. His production was so successful on the Parisian market that he was allowed to erect his own brewery. Last, but not least, the Picardie intendant received Colbert's order to ensure freedom of worship for Van Robais and all his workers.

Van Robais's first contract was for twenty years. Five years before the expiration date, he asked for another. At this time (ca. 1680) six thousand people were employed directly or indirectly by the manufactory. The work was broken down into thirty-two steps, among which dyeing was the most important. In fact, Van Robais's colors became so famous that certain drapers specified their products as "dyed with Van Robais's colors." The biggest secret was the black dye. It should be mentioned that at the time and since the Middle Ages, Picardie had been noted for its pastels. Abbeville's dyers had long ago acquired the reputation of being the best in the world. It was for them that Colbert enacted his famous 1669 regulations on the trading of dyes in France. (These statutes also contain a mine of technical information.) Van Robais could not have hoped for a better environment. With him in mind, Colbert for a while entertained the idea of importing Spanish Merino sheep to France, a project that was carried out only much later.[38] The Abbeville royal manufactory survived well into the eighteenth century, and its most handsome buildings still stand today. It was the precursor of modern textile mills, especially in regard to labor organization in that the workers no longer worked at home but came to the mill where their work was supervised.

If Josse Van Robais enjoyed the enormous privilege of freedom of worship in a Catholic and intolerant France, few others did. The repeal of the Edict of Nantes in 1685, a continuous state of war, and ever-increasing taxes all gave rise to a very grave crisis in the silk trade, in which many masters and workers were of the Protestant faith. This repeal, or Intolerance Edict, sent the workers of Tours and Lyons to England where, among other secrets, they took with them the technique of lustering. Others set up silk manufactories in Leyden and as far away as Berlin. Workers from Nimes set up looms in Lausanne, London, and Amsterdam. This exodus of capable and specialized workers, who often took with them substantial capital, dealt a severe blow to the kingdom's silk industry.[39]

However, in Lyons at the end of the seventeenth century, the situation had not yet become critical, in part because the city had kept its monopoly on the silk trade. In 1698 it numbered about four thousand looms, many of which were used to make inexpensive fabrics. Tours and Nimes were hit much harder. At the end of the century only the ribbon industry continued to flourish, with Paris as its most active center, followed by Lyons, Saint-Etienne, and Saint-Chamond.

During the difficult and troubled end of his rule, Colbert's industrial system received deadly blows. If his regulations were more or less enforced, it was not true of his production scheme: that is, the idea of the great industry bringing together all the workers under the same roof. Tours almost perished due to this excessive centralization. Lyons, where the manufacturing was still very fragmented, survived much better. The silk industry was one of the most sensitive of all the kingdom's activities. Colbert, having before him the immutable image of the Sun King, apparently did not realize this fragility—at least he was unable to conceive a structure other than this monolithic organization, strictly governed by the Cartesian spirit.

The end of Louis XIV's reign was as sad, even desperate, as the beginning and middle were brilliant. On this subject there are many contemporary testimonies.[40] The silk industry felt the negative effects of the general situation, and it was on the brink of ruin. In Lyons, work practically stopped. Consumption fell from an annual average of two thousand bales of silk to under six hundred, thus creating considerable unemployment. The consulate reacted with rigorous regulations; the number of looms was limited to a maximum of four per workshop, instead of twelve as established in 1639, and no foreign worker could be employed in the city for at least ten years. Finally, the struggle between merchants and master workers intensified.

Tours was not in any better shape. The number of looms per workshop was limited to forty in 1703! But in 1714 the community's procurator (attorney) owned fifty-one looms, while another master had sixty-seven. The situation improved considerably at the beginning of Louis XV's reign, one of the most flourishing periods for French silks. The mention of "figured fabrics" was increasingly frequent in the regulations. As early as 1702 they were also called *façonné*.

In 1737 Lyons received new regulations concerning the production of fabrics *à la grande tire*, *à la petite tire*, *à la marche*, and buttons.[41] The city's diversity of output was considerable: brocades (figure 2),[42] *persiennes*, druggets, *brocatelles*, *tabbies*, vénitiennes, florentines (floret), turquoises, valoises, damasin, satins brochés, ridged and checked taffeta, taffeta façonné and mottled, and more.[43] The new regulations were also concerned with the problem of design and pattern ownership, proposing sanctions

1 Furnishing fabric. Abbeville, seventeenth century. Linen and cotton. Lampas technique, double cloth. 26¹⁄₂ x 23¹⁄₄ (67.3 x 59.1). Musée Historique des Tissus, Lyons.

against designers who fraudulently transmitted designs, or against commissioners who obtained fabric samples before the completion of the work. This did not stop industrial pirating; according to Joubert de l' Hiberderie, several Parisian stores sold traced design intended for draftsmen.

The frequent censuses in the eighteenth century permit us to follow the economic evolution of La Grande Fabrique (the name given in Lyons to designate everything pertaining to the silk trade), for instance, the number of looms used for making façonné: in 1739, 4,874 out of 8,289 active looms; in 1752, 5,252 out of 9,404; and in 1769, 5,500 out of 11,000.

Several technicians were busy improving the mechanical aspects of the loom. In 1717 Gacon invented a machine that reduced to one the number of drawboys. In 1725 Reymond and Michel invented a mechanism that supposedly would eliminate all drawboys. These technical improvements were further pursued by Vaucanson,[44] a famous manufactory inspector.

Meanwhile Vaucanson was obliged to go to Lyons in order to get new statutes enacted because the master merchants considered themselves slighted by the 1737 regulations. The new bill, literally imposed by Vaucanson, was promulgated in June 1743, once again provoking strikes and riots. The manufactory inspector, besieged in his hotel, was forced to disavow the royal ordinance and to flee the town disguised as a Capuchin monk. He came back to Lyons in 1753, in charge of building the moiré calender in the English style, but his machine did not work well. In 1755 Badger brought back the marvelous cylinder process directly from England, another example of industrial pirating.

A few years before, another technical improvement had come from England—the flying shuttle, invented by an Englishman, John Kay.[45] At the time, however, the possibilities of this invention were not appreciated in France. Kay, because of his invention, which increased production speed and put many angry weavers out of work, was forced to exile himself to France where he died in poverty. The same fate awaited Thomas Highs, the inventor of the spinning jenny,[46] a machine able to load a number of spindles simultaneously.

Tours regained prosperity, but the amount of its façonné was proportionately less than in Lyons. The city had about two thousand looms in 1738, but the number decreased to sixteen hundred in 1774. Tours's main problem was the discrepancy between the old regulations and the new situation. In 1744 its production was still operating under the regulations enacted by Colbert in 1667. Its fabrics were little by little abandoned by the buyers. There were other reasons for this progressive disaffection, among them the competition produced by the printed cottons imported, in spite of their prohibition, by the East India Company.[47] Another reason was the high custom fees. Finally, the quality of the silks used, as well as the workmanship, was not of the highest caliber.

Despite successive attempts to strengthen the industry, the general situation did not improve.

2 Furnishing fabric. Ca. 1737–1740. Silk. Satin weave with supplementary patterning wefts (brocade). 25 x 37½ (63.5 x 95.25). Wadsworth Atheneum, Bequest of Mr. and Mrs. Drayton Hillyer, 1925.574.

Louis XV tried to provide incentives by allowing the import of Italian workers, and in 1739 he ordered fifteen hundred aunes for furnishing the sumptuous château of Choisy.[48]

Except for ribbon making, the trade was not faring any better in Paris. At the beginning of the eighteenth century the community comprised 735 weavers, among whom were 398 gold, silver, and silk fabric workers. The famous Saint-Maur-les Fossés manufactory which had already lost its brilliance, finally disappeared altogether around the middle of the century, after the death of Guillaume Charlier in 1757.

Nimes, on the other hand, made great strides, due mostly to Avignon's ruin by the 1722 plague.[49] The number of looms rose from 503 in 1735 to 2,200 in 1754. Its specialties were la petite tire (fabrics of narrow width) and mixed fabrics, that is, inexpensive productions. Nimes was at the time a serious competitor of Tours and Lyons.

The silk industry and sericulture flourished in all of southern France. Marseilles made reputable satins around 1730. Aix, Perpignan, Narbonne, and Lavaur were the sites of some more or less successful attempts, some of them bearing the title of royal manufactory.

In 1755 the city of Puy-en-Velay, in the center of France,[50] opened a royal manufactory endowed with considerable privileges, founded by the commerce intendant, de Gournay himself. In doing so, he intended to teach a lesson to the people of Lyons, whose guilds had never yielded to his demands. But his badly managed manufactory was on the brink of ruin by 1772.

The eighteenth century saw a real infatuation for silk fabrics. Manufactories sprang up in the most unexpected places and as far afield as the smallest Alsatian towns. At the time the French kingdom bore a lovely nickname: "satin country." Orders poured in from all over Europe: Portugal, Spain, Prussia, Poland, and Russia. Lyons received the biggest share of all this, and enjoyed its golden age just before the Revolution. More than two hundred kinds of fabrics were manufactured there for furnishings (figures 3–7), clothing (figures 8–10), and church ornaments (figures 11 and 12). The best designers were in Lyons, and the taste of its manufacturers was at its highest level.

3 Furnishing fabric. Lyons, ca. 1760. Silk. Compound weave, two loom widths. 41 1/4 x 103 (104.8 x 261.6). Wadsworth Atheneum, Costume and Textile Purchase Fund, 1982.48.

5 Furnishing fabric. Lyons, ca. 1750. Silk. Satin weave with supplementary patterning wefts, tied in a twill weave, 10½ x 9½ (26.6 x 23.13). Museum of Art, Rhode Island School of Design.

4 Furnishing fabric: "Asia" from "The Four Continents of the World." Lyons, mid–eighteenth century. Silk. Lampas technique, foundation weave: two complementary weaves, a) 3/1 twill, b) plain weave; supplementary patterning warp and weft. 26⅞ x 21¼ (68.5 x 54). Wadsworth Atheneum, Florence Paull Berger Fund, 1982.9.

7 Furnishing fabric. Lyons, Louis XV period. Silk, warp and weft, single faced, compound weaves. The foundation weave is a 7/1 satin weave with a small weft float patterned design. The small pattern is represented by a reverse drop repeat. The surface design of the textile is executed by supplementary discontinuous localized pattern weft floats. 21 1/2 x 41 3/4 (54.6 x 106). Wadsworth Atheneum, Costume and Textile Purchase Fund, 1984.43.

6 Furnishing fabric. Lyons, ca. 1730–1740. Silk. Plain weave, supplementary patterning wefts, tied in a twill weave. 21 1/4 x 40 1/4 (54 x 102.2). Wadsworth Atheneum, Costume and Textile Purchase Fund, 1984.44.

8 Dress Fabric. Lyons, 1770–1780. Silk. Foundation weave: plain weave; alternating stripes of two extra warp patterned weaves. 34 x 21½ (86.36 x 54.6). Wadsworth Atheneum, Florence Paull Berger Fund, 1983.737.

9 Dress fabric. Lyons, 1760s. Silk and four different metal threads. Single-face compound weave with supplementary patterning wefts. 38⅜ x 21 (97.9 x 53.3). Wadsworth Atheneum, Florence Paull Berger Fund, 1983.735.

10 Dress fabric. Lyons, Louis XVI period. Silk and metal threads, single faced compound weave, foundation weave of off-white plain weave. Added to this are supplementary continuous silver metallic weft threads held in place by every fifth warp on top of every other weft. The pink warp-wise stripe in the foundation weave serves as the basis for the entire design of this material. The flowers are woven into the foundation weave by a discontinuous extra weft patterning silk. The vine shape is a gold metallic wrapped silk chenille yarn that is a localized discontinuous extra weft pattern. Two selvages. 16¼ x 21 (41.27 x 53.3). Wadsworth Atheneum, Costume and Textile Purchase Fund, 1984.45.

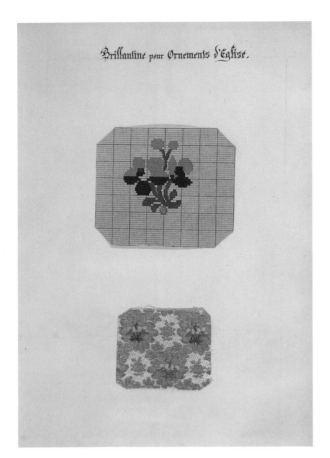

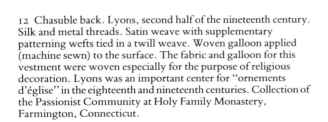

11 Plate from *Théorie*. Lyons, not dated (late nineteenth century). This plate illustrates a pattern especially designed for ecclesiastical textiles. Museum of Art, Rhode Island School of Design, Gift of the French Merci Train.

12 Chasuble back. Lyons, second half of the nineteenth century. Silk and metal threads. Satin weave with supplementary patterning wefts tied in a twill weave. Woven galloon applied (machine sewn) to the surface. The fabric and galloon for this vestment were woven especially for the purpose of religious decoration. Lyons was an important center for "ornements d'église" in the eighteenth and nineteenth centuries. Collection of the Passionist Community at Holy Family Monastery, Farmington, Connecticut.

Unfortunately, this ostentatious prosperity masked great poverty. The increasingly powerful merchants were dictating the regulations and thus reducing the workers to their mercy. Money became scarce; wars brought on miseries; the court was in mourning; fashion was capricious—all these factors resulted in the merchants' cutting down orders or having the workers work at half wages. Furthermore, the workers did not have the right to emigrate. Thanks to the warehouse and customs monopoly, Lyons's merchants had total control of the market which they manipulated as they pleased. They carried out speculations among competitors and rivals whom they often ruined. When business returned to normal, they concealed the abundance of the demand for silk in order to pay the lowest possible wages and increase further their wealth. This industry was then in the hands of some four hundred capitalists.

In Lyons, in 1777, of 11,356 looms, 4,924 worked à la tire. According to Roland de la Platière, manufactory inspector before the Revolution, in 1783 there were 18,000 looms of which some 12,000 specialized in figured fabrics. The 1788 census, the last one under the monarchy, mentioned 14,777 looms, most of which were weaving unicolored fabrics and gauzes. At this time France lived under the influence of British fashion.[51] Once more La Grande Fabrique went through a difficult time and would soon suffer total disaster.

During the second half of the eighteenth century, Tours, still in a precarious situation, had nevertheless a semblance of prosperity. In 1765 some seventeen hundred looms were specializing in about twenty kinds of fabrics, all $5/12$ of an aune in width, that is, $1/12$ less than in Lyons. Most of these fabrics were in no more than one, two, or three colors. The patterns were the work of a few excellent designers such as Louis Durand and Trichard, about whom very little is known. In the hope of pulling out of its stagnation, Tours, still operating in the spirit of Colbert, turned toward large-scale industry. In 1776 62 masters had 975 looms and in 1782, 46 masters had 1,150 looms. Eleven of these masters owned 640 of the looms.

Nimes, on the other hand, enjoyed a sustained growth. From 2,200 looms in 1754, it numbered 3,027 in 1784, equipped for all kinds of cloth. At that

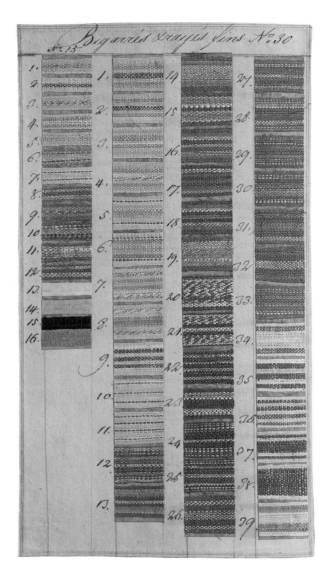

13 Sample book of trimmings. Ca. 1800. Design Library, New York.

time one of its most eloquent manufacturers was the famous Paulet, the author of the best treatise on silk weaving of the eighteenth century (*L'Art du fabriquant d'étoffes de soie*, Paris, 1773–1778), which gives us a glimpse of the industry's level of sophistication. The situation in Nimes deteriorated soon afterward, however, due to finance minister Jacques Necker's strict regulations and the loss of the Spanish market.

Saint-Chamond and Saint-Etienne also prospered in the field of trimmings (figure 13), thanks to the adoption of the Zurich loom which made it possible to weave several pieces at once. These two cities came into their golden age in the nineteenth century and the first part of the twentieth.

Among the other French cities, Paris was known for its gauze, Aix-en-Provence for its *Genoa velvets*, while Florentine or English taffetas woven in Avignon were preferred to those of Lyons. Montpellier and Ganges specialized in silk hosiery which they exported especially to Spain. As for northern France, Picardie, and Flanders, wool cloth was their primary industrial activity.

Just as it overthrew an entire social order, so the French Revolution overthrew the economic order, dragging the whole country into an unimaginable industrial and commercial catastrophe. Luxury industries, such as silk, were the hardest hit. In Lyons and elsewhere, the Revolution was motivated by the workers' desire for revenge against the merchants' oligarchy. Centuries of social hatred were at the source of some of the terrible days of 1793. The number of active looms fell to between 2,000 and 3,000, from the 14,777 that had been in operation in 1788.[52]

With the Directoire, stability and luxury returned, thus producing work in Lyons. In 1801 there were 8,500 looms, and 9,490 in 1802; more than three-quarters of those were making unicolored taffeta. This simple production brought back La Grande Fabrique. The noble fabrics were limited and solely destined for the Spanish colonies, Russia, and Germany.[53]

The guild system, often called into question during the Ancien Régime, disappeared in 1791, thus providing absolute freedom of work and allowing women into the trade. But workers found themselves so disoriented by the total lack of regulations that the old hierarchy was restored in 1806. Previously, in 1804, Napoleon had instituted the conciliation board (Conseil des Prud'hommes), operating throughout France and charged with settling differences between labor and management.[54]

Beyond the judicial structures and new regulations that he imposed, Napoleon also played a personal role in the silk renaissance. He went to battle against transparent, low-necked, and clinging dresses as well as against exotic fabrics. Every man and woman who had any official position in the

French republic (later the empire, composed of Germany, Italy, the kingdoms of The Two Sicilies, and Spain) had to dress in silks from Lyons and change their attire as often as possible. Anyone appearing at court had to have a set of clothes made from Lyon's fabrics. The first consul, later the emperor, set the example and imposed it on the dignitaries as well as on his brothers and sisters who all had inherited either a kingdom or a dukedom. This silk consumption was visible even on the walls

14 Camille Pernon. Wall hanging for Saint-Cloud. Ca. 1804–1805. Silk and silver threads. Ground of blue damask weave, supplementary patterning wefts in silver. Dimensions of the repeat, 21 1/4 x 16 3/4 (54 x 42.5). Mobilier National, Paris.

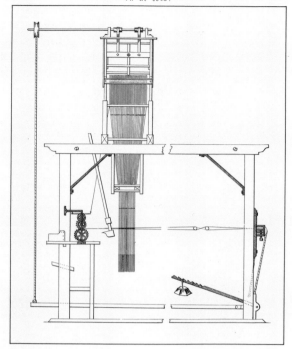

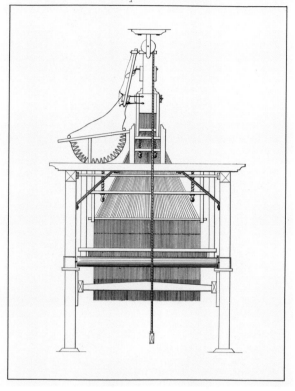

MÉTIER A LA JACQUARD
vu de côté.

MÉTIER A LA JACQUARD
vu par devant.

15 Plate from *Théorie*. Jacquard loom, side view. Lyons, not dated (late nineteenth century). Museum of Art, Rhode Island School of Design.

16 Jacquard loom, front view, from *Théorie*.

of palaces: first the Tuileries, Saint-Cloud (figure 14), Meudon, the Louvre, the Elysée Palace, Malmaison, Villiers, Monceaux, Versailles and the Trianons, Saint-Germain-en-Laye, Rambouillet, Compiègne, and Fontainebleau. Later on it was visible in the conquered capitals: Turin, Laeken in Brussels, Amsterdam, Utrecht, Rome, Antwerp, the Pitti Palace in Florence, and palaces confiscated from the church, like the one in Strasbourg. The civil list included nine additional palaces in Tuscany, more than twenty castles, residences, and crown property. The enormous stimulus given to Lyons's silks during the empire was unprecedented. At the end of 1812 the civil list showed an expense of nearly twenty-one million francs of the period, in furnishings and hangings.[55]

The great master of this production was Camille Pernon (figure 14). After having retired to Genoa during the Revolution, he came back to Lyons and

held the monopoly on supplying the courts of Europe until 1807. At the 1802 Paris industrial exposition he won the gold medal. The next year he was invited to dine with Napoleon, who entrusted him once more with an important order.[56]

These rich and sumptuous fabrics were still executed on the old *looms à la tire* (draw looms), which were difficult and time consuming to handle, despite the modest improvements in efficiency brought about by Falcon around 1728, by Vaucanson and Genin around 1749, by Galantier and Blache around 1767, and finally by Phillipe de Lasalle. Jacquard[57] introduced at last the long-awaited and hoped-for improvement that eliminated the drawboys (figures 15 and 16). However, this discovery did not become efficient nor was it put into effect until 1820, after further improvements by Breton. This invention, one of the most important in the entire textile industry, was not well received in

Woven Textiles 37

17 Page from a sample book of ribbons. 1847. Design Library, New York.

Lyons. The workers, fearing loss of work, incited a riot and burned in public a model loom deposited in Lyons's Palais des Beaux-Arts. This loom was nevertheless accepted and increasingly adopted in every kind of production. Toward the middle of the nineteenth century, about one hundred thousand hand looms were active in Lyons in the districts of Croix-Rousse, Saint-Georges, and Saint-Irénée. The family workshop, as it had existed since the sixteenth and seventeenth centuries, remained active up to the twentieth century with its typical organization: the master helped by one or two compagnons and sometimes by his wife and children in subordinate tasks.

The emperor granted favors to no city but Lyons, despite numerous solicitations from Tours's manufacturers. In 1807 this city numbered no more than 9 houses equipped with 211 looms. The industry regressed also in Paris, which nevertheless kept, at least for a while longer, its gauze specialty.

18 Picture, designed by Gaspard Grégoire. Lyons, 1815–1830. Silk. Velvet weave (cut), painted warp. 15 x 10⅝ (38 x 27). Musée Historique des Tissus, Lyons.

19 Jacquard woven shawl, detail. Ca. 1855. Wool. Compound twill weave. 140½ x 64½ (356.7 x 163.8). Yale University Art Gallery, Gift of Mrs. Albert H. Atterbury.

The work of Gaspard Grégoire (figure 18), a famous velvet maker, was a unique and solitary achievement. Born in 1751 in Aix-en-Provence and dying in Paris in 1846, Grégoire devoted his research to a specific technique, the picture woven in velvet, better known by the name of "velours Grégoire."[58]

Saint-Etienne remained the most important ribbon center (figure 17), not only in France but in all of Europe, while Saint-Chamond specialized in a related field: string, braid, and piping. In 1832 this city had twenty two thousand looms.

In Nimes, where production has seriously fallen off during the Revolution, the silk industry picked up again, but it turned increasingly toward hosiery, gauzes, and crepes. During the nineteenth century the city of Ganges in the Cévennes succeeded Nimes, while hosiery became important in city of Troyes in Champagne. Avignon pursued a fairly important production with 1,778 looms in 1810. Meanwhile silk production in Marseilles and Aix had totally disappeared.

Mechanization spread considerably after the final improvement of the Jacquard loom (figure 19), and around 1820 fabric manufacturing turned decisively toward the inexpensive production of mixed fabrics and prints. Lyons led the way: in 1824 it had about ten thousand Jacquard looms, some forty-two thousand in 1832, and more than one hundred thousand in the middle of the century. This course of industrialization meant the neglect of the artistic quality of fabrics, and later a rise to the great social crises, so tragically renowned in history.

Notes

The bibliography for this essay starts on page 183.

1   The rare fibers actually identified were linen and hemp, but rarely wool. The weaves were derived from tabby bindings. The analysis and study of almost all of these elements from prehistoric digs, in addition to the textiles from Greco-Roman sites concentrated essentially in Draguignan in the south of France, were undertaken in Lyons at the Musée Historique des Tissus while the author was its curator. We also extend our gratitude for the collaboration of two scientists of unequaled competence who remain insufficiently recognized in France: Gabriel Vial and Mrs. Hélène Meyer.

2   The results of these excavations are in great part conserved at the Musée des Antiquités Nationales de Saint-Germain-en-Laye, near Paris. However, some provincial museums, like that in Châtillon-sur-Seine (Côte-d'Or), possess some spectacular documents.

3   With regard to the trade of relics and its relationship to oriental silk work, one is advised to consult the studies of Abbé Chartraire, for instance *Le Trésor de la cathédrale de Sens* (Paris, 1926, 1931). He carried out a special study of the riches of this cathedral. Its treasury is without doubt the most important in the West, having conserved a tremendous quantity of relics, many still wrapped in their original silks dating from the sixth through eighth centuries.

4   East-West relations were cemented with the marriage of Otto II, emperor of the Holy Roman Empire, and Princess Theophano, daughter of the basileus of Constantinople, Romanus II. An incident often related about this marriage serves to confirm the interest of Westerners in the precious silks of Byzantium. Negotiations for the marriage were assigned to Liutprand, bishop of Cremona, Italy, who very awkwardly found all the purple silks he had bought in Constantinople confiscated. These silks, a supreme symbol of royalty, were not intended to be sold nor had they been given as presents by the basileus. The bishop had simply acquired them through the black market!

5   To give an example from a much more ancient text in Saint Augustine's *City of God* of the fifth century there are several mentions of "bysso" or "byssus," which even the best translators have rendered as "fine linen." E.g., Saint Augustine, *The City of God against the Pagans* (Cambridge, Mass.: Harvard University Press), 1.11, pp. 58–59: "quam impii divitis in purpura et bysso," or "that of the wicked rich man, clothed in purple and fine linen." This passage is itself extracted from Luke 16.19, where "fine linen" is evoked in all translations. The term "fine linen" is very often found throughout the Bible, in both Old and New Testaments; more specifically, in Genesis (41.42) and Exodus (26; 27.9,16,18; 28.5,6,8,39, and so on). It would be interesting to study the original Hebrew text, as well as the original Greek text of the Old and New Testaments, and then their first translations, the Septuagint in Greek and the Vulgate in Latin. In fact, all the terms relating to "fine linen," "byssus," or even to "purple" ought to be compared. This research is of the greatest interest, and goes far beyond the scope of a simple note.

Notwithstanding, the term "byssus" requires some explanation. What is involved is an animal fiber from the pods of a bivalvular Mediterranean mollusk, which aid it in fixing itself in the sand or upon rocks. The pods, or beard, quite similar to those of mussels, for example, are as fine as the silk fiber that they so oddly resemble. The fibers can reach up to several meters in length and were used in Greco-Roman times for weaving sumptuous cloths. They are thus unrelated to fine linen which is woven from vegetable fibers. The Latin term "byssus" must be retained as such, since no modern language has supplied a suitable translation. This example, perhaps too detailed in this context, is simply intended to demonstrate the false meanings that translations of ancient texts transmit in the field of textiles. There are so many. A review of the texts by experts is badly needed and would certainly provide some great discoveries.

6   Many paintings record this custom of using materials or precious carpets around windows and balconies, especially for processions, royal or princely entrances, or for tournaments. These practices, originally Italian, spread throughout Europe where they endured through the seventeenth century.

7   Avignon, Montpellier, and Nimes are located in the ancient provinces of Provence and Languedoc. In the thirteenth century these regions were themselves distributed among the Provence kingdom, the Narbonne dukedom, and the Toulouse earldom, over which the lordship of the king was respected only in Narbonne and Toulouse. All these cities held important economic and cultural roles. After Avignon had become the papal seat in 1308, it developed into an extremely prosperous European financial center. The arts, and especially silk weaving, also experienced enormous growth.

8   The French textile tradition goes back to the late Middle Ages, when it involved primarily accessories, that is, notions, bourserie en lisse (see Marianne Carlano's essay for information about these purses), trimmings, and ribbons. The well-known *Livre des Métiers* (Book of Guilds) by Etienne Boileau, covering the years 1258 to 1268 while he was prévost des marchands, deals chiefly with these businesses and their guild regulations. Gold and silver brocade, silk cloth, and velvets, only a small part of which were woven in France, remained luxury goods obtained through importation at the celebrated trade fairs that constituted a basic framework of medieval European economic life. To take an example, the famous pourpoint or doublet of Charles de Blois, dating from the fourteenth century and conserved in the Musée Historique des Tissus in Lyons, is cut in Sicilian silk. French cloths, even those woven in Paris at that time, were thought of as neither elegant nor rich enough to serve as processional dress for a prince.

9   The city of Avignon became reknowned as the seat of the papacy during the papal sojourn that extended from 1309 to 1378. Previously the city was a vassal of the Toulouse earldom and the Provence kingdom, Provence having the status of kingdom since it appertained to the Kingdom of The Two Sicilies. Jeanne I, queen of Sicily, was thus able to sell the city to Pope Clement VI in 1348. In establishing themselves in Avignon, the popes also implanted their court and their taste for luxury. This was a time when many artists and poets, among whom Petrarch is the best known, chose Avignon as the place where they wished to live. Among the various crafts of art and luxury that flourished here, silk was the most important and remained so for several centuries.

10 On this subject, it is necessary only to scan fifteenth-century European paintings in order to realize the exceptional fashion-ableness of Italian silks. Flemish paintings first and foremost, then Italian, German, and Spanish paintings of that century, are rarely without silk costumes or hangings. Some of the very handsome floral patterns based on the pomegranate and the thistle were designed by the most stylish artists, such as Jacopo Bellini and Pisanello.

11 As early as the twelfth century Lyons was a sort of extremely powerful ecclesiastical principality that enjoyed broad autonomy. It was governed by its own archbishop, who was virtually a prince of the Holy Roman Empire. This status lasted until Lyons's annexation to the kingdom of France in 1312. Subsequently, the aristocracy asserted its control through the development of trade, banking and currency exchange, then industry. The full economic expansion of Lyons in the fifteenth century turned the city into a pivotal point for all of Europe. These circumstances revived its artistic and intellectual life, making it the equal of Paris at this period. Its financial, banking, and industrial capacity was exploited most of all by Louis XI. In the sixteenth century its flourishing press put the city on the same intellectual level as some of the greatest European capitals. The remains of such splendor are still found in old Lyons, where most of the structures date from the fifteenth century. It was in this context that silk was introduced.

During the Italian Wars, at the end of the fifteenth and the beginning of the sixteenth centuries, the city took on even greater importance. It became the permanent seat of the monarchy almost until the year 1526, after continual reloca-tions of the king and his court across the south. It is evident that the kings of France had a special need for their bankers, which explains why François I stayed in the city in 1536.

For a more complete history of Lyons, consult the excel-lent nineteenth-century histories, for instance, those by Klein-clauss and Steyert.

12 The entire textile production was divided among powerful trade guilds that directed life in the cities and protected the artists. The silk weavers' guilds of Venice and Florence were indeed very well known. See also note 37.

13 According to estimates from that time, some forty thousand pounds were in fact required.

14 With regard to the start of silk manufacture in Lyons, see Godard L'Ouvrier en soie (1899) and Pariset, Histoire de la soie (1862–1865) and Histoire de la fabrique lyonnaise (1901).

15 On the general history of silk in Tours, see Bosseboeuf, La Fabrique des soieries de Tours (1900).

16 Cf. Dom Lobineau, Histoire de Bretagne (1707), 2 vols., in folio.

17 The example of Château Gaillon, summer and secondary residence belonging to Cardinal d'Amboise, archbishop of Rouen, is typical of the introduction of Italian taste into France at the very beginning of the sixteenth century. This château was begun in 1502 in pure flamboyant Gothic style and fin-ished in 1510 in the Italian fashion. In fact, the cardinal, who was a powerful statesman and an ambassador to Italy, brought the sculptor Bertrand de Meynal from Genoa, and a little later, the talented Girolamo Pacchiarotti (Jérôme Pacherot). Moreover, he had previously had the huge fountain now located in the gardens of the Château de la Rochefoucauld in

Charentes transported as well from Genoa. Other works of art were included in these Italian orders, and it would seem evident that silks were among the most significant. The prob-lem was, and is to this very day, simply that no one ever took any note of them, although accounts still exist. Many other analogous cases can be cited, such as the royal châteaux Blois and Chambord, but Gaillon is really the first imposing French residence that depended on Italy to such an extent. Italian taste first invaded France by means of the wars. Art works were then ordered directly from Italy. Finally, the patrons moved the Italian artists into their own homes. The same process applies to silk, a negotiable article that is infinitely more supple and easy to manipulate than a marble fountain from Genoa.

On Gaillon, see Elisabeth Chirol, Château Gaillon (Rouen and Paris, 1952, 1960); R. Weiss, "The Castle of Gaillon in 1509–10," Journal of the Warburg and Courtauld Institutes 16 (1953): 1–12. The latter study mentions château accounts recorded in 1510 by Jacopo Probo d'Atri, another Italian.

18 During the Middle Ages and the Ancien Régime orphans were taken in by some religious communities, or by the Aumône Générale, a charitable institution. In order to earn their keep, these children were then placed under a tutor such as Etienne Turquet, who put them into private homes generally from age six. In Lyons, orphan labor in the silk business often was a source of considerable gain. Public charity was remarkably well organized there, even as early as the Middle Ages, and was not always as sordid as one would assume from the exist-ence of child labor in the name of charity.

19 Dutil, "L'Industrie de la soie à Nîmes jusqu'en 1789" (1908).

20 Rondot, Les Soies (1885).

21 As time went on, there was a gradual centralization of the French kingdom, due to the royal and secular determination of the monarchies of the Capetians, the Valois, and the Bourbons. The monarchy sought to impose itself as the sole legitimate authority, and to this end it surrounded itself in great pomp. This show of magnificence called upon contri-butions from every branch of art at home and abroad, provided they were of the highest quality. The outcome of this unflinching determination culminated with the reign of Louis XIV. Silk work, the element most basic to ornamentation and pomp, was intimately related to all of this monarchistic "illustriousness."

22 These complex wars had catastrophic consequences through-out France. They extended over four reigns: François II (1559–1560), Charles IX (1560–1574), Henri III (1574–1589), and the first years of the reign of Henri IV (1589–1610). They paralyzed the country for almost forty years and completely obliterated the progress made by François I and Henri II. The origin of these internal tensions, as much social as religious, can be reduced to Calvinists against Catholics. The wars were an attempt of several ancient and powerful noble dynasties to reconquer the positions and the might they had been forced to abandon under previous reigns, which worsened the already weak position of the crown. Sides were taken: thus, the House of Lorraine identified itself with the cause of Catholicism, while the Bourbons allied themselves with the Protestants. At first Protestantism took hold primarily among the middle-class urban bourgeoisie. The aristocracy was affected only toward the middle and during the second half of the sixteenth century. The bourgeoisie, just like the aristocratic class after-

ward, exploited the crisis in an attempt to regain their former liberties. However, very quickly they came to realize that the enfeeblement of royalty brought about by these civil wars was also to its detriment, for it reinforced the old feudal nobility. The crisis was resolved with the ascendancy of the first Bourbon king, Henri IV, a Protestant who finally converted to Catholicism, declaring: "Paris is surely worth a mass!" During the Reformation many silk craftsmen, like many other artists, were won over to the new religion. Lyons became almost entirely Protestant. For this reason the repeal of the Edict of Nantes, or the Edict of Tolerance, in 1685 caused a general exodus of silk workers from all French centers.

23 While France knew only strife during the entire second half of the sixteenth century, both Italy and Flanders recovered the political stability needed for economic development. Their silk trade and production greatly benefited. Italian silks continued to all of Europe, including France, throughout the sixteenth century. Genoa and Venice were the capitals of two powerful republics. Milan, also the capital of a very strong dukedom, was favored by the support of the Hapsburgs. Avignon was integrated into the Pontifical States, which also protected Tuscany with its dependency, Lucca. The kingdoms of Naples and Flanders (with cities like Bruges), both booming centers of silk production, belonged to the all-powerful House of Hapsburgs. Thus at the end of the sixteenth century France was entirely dependent for luxury goods upon imports. This situation motivated the serious initiative toward self-sufficiency during the reign of Henri IV.

24 Provence and Languedoc silkworm breeding would not have existed, let alone survived, had it not been for the demand of Avignon for raw silk.

25 Olivier de Serres (1539–1619) lived in the province of Vivarais, on the right bank of the Rhone between Lyons and Avignon. He transformed his land into a virtual model farm, experimenting with various agricultural methods that were revolutionary for the period. He imported and grew madder, hop, maize, and especially mulberries. Henri IV called him to Paris in order to intensify the mulberry culture, which is essential to silkworm breeding. To this end, he published two studies, *La Cueillette de la soye par la nourriture des vers qui la font* (1599) and *La Seconde Richesse du mûrier blanc* (1603). He was an adamant Protestant, like his colleague Barthélemy de Laffemas (1545–1611). Laffemas, on the other hand, was an economist. His interests extended to trade, industry, and especially to the development of the market for luxury goods, which led him to concentrate on mulberry plantations.

26 Some of these engravings, of particular interest in regard to the silkworm breeding and silk weaving, are reproduced in Tuchscherer and Vial, *Le Musée Historique des Tissus de Lyon* (1977): p. 5, selecting the silkworm grain and the formation of the cocoon; p. 11, spinning; p. 17, feeding the silkworm; p. 24, spreading cocoons over screens and the emergence of the silkworm.

27 The art of gardens in France was just beginning to develop at this time. The plants used were all local, which explains the great utilization of the mulberry. Cabbage, some lettuce, and medicinal plants were also then part of the ornamental vocabulary of gardens. This art was later refined, under the reigns of Louis XIII and especially Louis XIV, with the importation to

France of new varieties. The influence of floral design on the art of silk was considerable, though unstudied to date.

28 The date of this edict gives an idea, however vague and incomplete, of the origin of the enormous volume of imported silks at the beginning of the seventeenth century. It should be noted that Chambéry and Avignon, both modern French cities today, were foreign at that time. Chambéry was the capital of the dukedom of Savoie, attached to France only in 1860. Attempts to imitate silk imports continued for many years. Tours underwent the same trend from 1604 on. This edict is merely one example among many that attest to silk as one of the first preoccupations of the kingdom. It would be both interesting and very useful to have all of the edicts and royal decrees relating to this industry compiled and published. This documentation would greatly facilitate historical, economic, and even technical research.

29 Present-day Vienne is a minor city located about twenty miles south of Lyons on the Rhone. In past centuries, however, it held a significant role due to its location within the limits of the kingdom, just as did Lyons. Under the Roman Empire it was more important than Lyons. Its archbishop was primate of the Gauls, a title that later returned to Lyons's archbishop. From the fifteenth century on the customs offices of Vienne and Lyons were in constant competition.

30 On Dangon, his influence, and his role in the silk industry of Lyons, see Hennezel, *Claude Dangon* (1926).

31 Until the end of the sixteenth century Italy remained almost the only supplier of silk. However, a new interest in oriental trade arose, probably due to the influence of Venice or to that of the first East Indies companies created by Portugal and Spain at the end of the sixteenth century. At the beginning of the seventeenth century there was a timid intrusion of Orientalism in the taste and then the art of France. This "exoticism" became very popular from the middle of that century up into the twentieth century. Literature abounds on the subject, yet the art of silk, despite its importance, is hardly treated in depth.

32 On Colbert and his tremendous contribution, it is interesting to consult the voluminous catalogue of the exhibition, *Colbert, 1619–1683*, that was presented at the Hôtel de la Monnaie in Paris, 4 October–30 November 1983. This publication, despite articles and methods that are inconsistent, is nevertheless basic to understanding the general role and personality of Colbert during the reign of Louis XIV.

33 In the seventeenth and eighteenth centuries Genoa continued to manufacture sumptuous velvets of multiple aspects, that is, with different colored piles, which doubtless were difficult to imitate, except perhaps for the Charlier mill. These velvets, of bright and iridescent colors, exorbitant in price were known as Genoa velvets ("velours de Gênes"), and sometimes as garden velvets ("velours jardinière") because of their floral designs. France, and Lyons specifically, did not succeed in copying them perfectly until the eighteenth century. With regard to black velvets, Genoa had possessed both their secret and monopoly since the Middle Ages. Their quality was derived especially from the beauty and uniformity of the dyeing which, furthermore, did not attack the fiber. This is surprising because the base of black dye was often a ferrous or ferric salt that in oxidizing ate the cloth.

34 The silk regulations are published in Clément, *Jean-Baptiste Colbert* (1861–1882).

35 Clouzot, *Le Métier de la soie en France, 1466–1815* (n.d.), p. 63.

36 Ibid., p. 64. Verlet, *Versailles* (1961) gives a general look at the silks produced for the Palace of Versailles in the time of Louis XIV. The references to silk, taken from Guiffrey, *Comptes des bâtiments du roi* (1881–1901), are distributed throughout the text, in relation to each room and building studied. To its great credit Verlet's study, the best synthesis yet on the subject, places the orders for silk work on an equal footing with other furnishings, decorations, and art objects.

37 The system of guilds in Europe, under the Ancien Régime and in fact from the Middle Ages, guarded the strict separation of trades. Each trade had its guilds, perfectly organized, within the cities. At times some of the very strong guilds wielded almost absolute power over the towns and over competition as well. The result was positive in the high-level quality of production that was maintained for a long time. It was negative, though, in the guilds' exclusivity and protection of acquired privileges which impeded development in every way. Consequently, the guilds and the monarchy became intimately associated.

In the case of Van Robais, normally he would had to have had his material treated by the dyers in the city, all the more so because the dyers of Abbeville constituted a famous guild. The privilege of the royal manufactory exempted him, however, allowing him to take charge of his own dyeing.

Another typical way that the guilds operated is seen in the manufacture of eighteenth-century Parisian furniture. As a case in point, a commode might have been started by a joiner who would build only its substructure. Its inlaid work would then be passed on to a cabinetmaker from a different trade guild. Its bronze work would be manufactured by both a founder and an engraver-gilder, representing two additional guilds. The marble top would have been made by a marble craftsman. And if the piece required paint, lacquer, or varnish, a painter-varnisher, some of whom were quite well known in Paris, would have to be contracted. All of these guilds worked separately. However, the direction and coordination of the whole job were often overseen by a cabinetmaker or by the wares merchant. The same division of labor applied to silk work: production of the fiber, throwing and spinning, dyeing, designing, cartooning, looming or assembly of the loom, weaving, etc.

38 During the reign of Louis XVI the Bergerie Royale de Rambouillet was created.

39 There have been many studies on the emigration of Huguenot Protestants from France, as well as on their industrial, commercial, and banking ventures abroad. The following essay on silk alone gives ample evidence of their undertakings, which also benefited the spread of French art in this field to other countries.

40 The writings of Fenélon exemplify this, for instance, some passages of his *Télémaque* (1699); as well as Vauban's *Dîme royale*.

41 Technical questions about the various looms brought about their reconstruction in Lyons during the nineteenth century. Some of these models, remarkably restored by M. Goux, former professor at the Ecole de Tissage in Lyons, were exhibited in the Musée Historique des Tissus while the author was curator from 1973 to 1982. Other similar models have been conserved at the Conservatoire National des Arts et Métiers in Paris.

Note that large draw-loom materials are about a half-aune (i.e., two feet). Materials produced on the small draw loom are chiefly ribbons. Treadle and *button looms* designate two different principles of warp action and selection: the treadle activates the warp by the pedals alone, while the button principle is close to that of the draw loom. Cf. Paulet, *L'Art du fabriquant d'étoffes de soie* (1773–1778).

42 This term, frequently seen in all texts from the sixteenth through the nineteenth centuries, is ill considered today due to its lack of precision. It mainly designated rich cloths, woven from silk and from gold and silver threads.

43 All of these terms, related to specific materials, are analyzed and explained in the excellent and irreplaceable study by Bezon, *Dictionnaire général des tissus anciens et modernes* (1856–1867).

44 Jacques de Vaucanson (1701–1782), French inventor and scholar, Inspecteur des Arts et Manufactures, played an important role in several technical areas: clock making, automata, and especially the silk loom. Named inspector of silk factories in 1741 by Cardinal de Fleury, the tutor and then prime minister of Louis XV, he revised the regulations and designed perfected looms, machines to empty cocoons, as well as other textile mechanisms. The Vaucanson loom, comprising a programmed cylinder, is one of the direct ancestors of the Jacquard loom. All of these inventions aroused the resentment of the Lyons "canuts" (silk weavers). Vaucanson accumulated automata (one of which was his famous walking, drinking, and urinating duck) and machines that were destined to become the first collection of the Conservatoire National des Arts et Métiers. In 1746 he also became a member of the Académie des Sciences of Paris.

45 John Kay (1704–1764), English engineer and machine inventor, was born in Lancashire. The son of a wool manufacturer, he assumed responsibility for his father's factory from a very early age. He solved many of the technical problems involved in weaving by his own inventions, one example of which was the flying shuttle. On 26 May 1733 he obtained a patent for the invention named "New Engine or Machine for Opening and Dressing Wool," which included his flying shuttle. For a description of how it works, see the *Encyclopedia Britannica*, 11th edition, s.v. "Arkwright, Sir Richard," "Cotton Manufacture," and "Weaving." The few hand looms existing in Lyons today still operate on this principle.

46 According to English tradition, the invention of the mull jenny (or spinning jenny) is attributed to Samuel Crompton (1753–1827). This interpretation comes from the simple fact that Thomas Highs was too discreet to defend or exploit his invention. Cf. Rodier, *The Romance of French Weaving* (1931), p. 291.

47 Abundant literature can be found on printed cottons in France, both imported and made domestically. The first studies on this subject were undertaken by H. Clouzot and H. R. d'Allemagne in the first half of this century. (See the essay by Jacqueline Jacqué in this volume.)

48 Choisy-le-Roi was one of many royal residences in the vicinity

of Paris. Louis XV acquired it in 1739 from the Duc de la Vallière and sumptuously transformed it. Today almost nothing remains of this masterpiece of eighteenth-century French taste. This example of the acquisition of silk works demonstrates once again the impact and the stimulating role of royal homes in the country's economy and art.

For more information, see Georges Poisson, "Choisy-le-Roi: Les Résidences royales," in the exhibition catalogue *Hommage aux Gabriel* (Paris: Hôtel de Rohan-Archives Nationales, 1982), pp. 242ff.; Christopher Tadgell, *Ange-Jacques Gabriel* (London: A. Zwemmer, 1978), pp. 151ff.

49 This sadly notorious plague started in Marseilles in 1720 and spread to several cities in the south of France. It affected not only the economy but also art and literature. The plague of Marseilles was as famous as that of Venice in 1575–1577 or that of London in 1665.

50 In the eighteenth and nineteenth cenuries Puy-en-Velay was most famed for its laces, a tradition that continues to this day, as seen in the recent creation of the Conservatoire de la Dentelle (lace school) in Puy. This institution, affiliated with the Mobilier National de Paris, publishes an interesting review.

51 The influence of English styles on French fashion prior to the Revolution had a detrimental effect on silk. Cf. Boucher, *Histoire du costume* (1965), pp. 296ff.

52 Lyons played a role in the history of the French Revolution that is too considerable to describe here. The city was the seat of the counterrevolution as early as May 1793; it revolted against the Montagne Convention like Bordeaux, Marseilles, and others, and was occupied by Kellermann's army. The city surrendered on 9 October 1793 and was then declared "Lyon—Ville Morte" (Lyons—condemned city). The repercussions of this revolt were catastrophic for its entire industry.

53 The diary mentioned in note 11 in the following essay gives a continuous account of the biggest foreign orders recorded by Camille Pernon, a Lyons company, throughout the revolutionary period. These orders came especially from Spain and Russia.

54 The Conseil des Prud'hommes of Lyons also guaranteed protection of the models; it was the ancestor of modern jurisdiction over the protection of industrial property. In this capacity it accumulated an entire store of extremely precious silk samples, all identified and dated. In fact, this exceptional depot contains material from pre-revolutionary Lyons up to 1914, including several hundred collections in all. It is now part of the Musée Historiques des Tissus in Lyons, due to the initiative of the author while curator there. It constitutes an inexhaustible source of information, although little known to researchers.

55 The catalogue *Soiries Empire* (Paris: Mobilier National, 1980) describes this colossal effort.

56 Cf. Poidebard and Chatel, *Camille Pernon* (1912).

57 On Jacquard, see Lapierre, "La Vie et l'oeuvre de J.-M. Jacquard" (1925). Also noteworthy is the research undertaken for several years by Rita Adrosko of the Smithsonian Institution, Washington, D.C. See Adrosko, Rita J., "The Invention of the Jacquard Mechanism," in *Bulletin de Liaison du Centre International d'Etude des Textiles Anciens*, no. 55–56, Lyons,

1984, pp. 89–117. For a general, nontechnical overview, see Cayez, *Métiers Jacquard* (1978).

58 See Algoud, *Gaspard Grégoire et ses velours d'art* (1908). This is the only work that deals with the subject in general. The Musée Historique des Tissus has in its possession a sizable and valuable collection of Grégoire velvets. It may also be noted that Tassinari & Chatel, a Lyons firm, has the complete design for the cloth from which these velvets originated. This design, measuring approximately 20 by 20 feet (about 6 by 6 meters) gives an idea of the extreme complexity of the technical research involved. It is not surprising that since the death of Grégoire in 1846, almost no technical expert has addressed this problem. Every thread ("poil") was programmed in these designs. The French expression "au poil près" (to the last detail) has thus been adopted to mean anything that is extremely exacting.

The Art of Silk ❖ Jean-Michel Tuchscherer

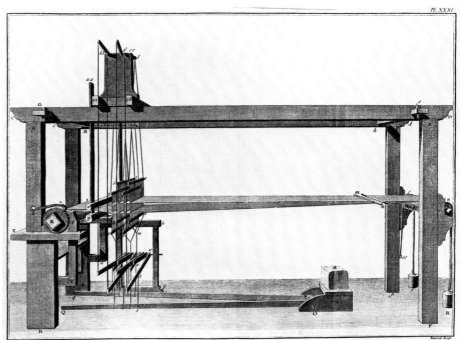

Pl. XXXI

Soierie, Vue Perspective du Métier pour fabriquer les Étoffes unies Comme Taffetas, Satin et Serge, la Chaine ouverte au premier Coup du Taffetas.

20 Plate 31 from Diderot's *Encyclopédie:* side view of a draw loom for weaving silk taffeta, satin, and serge weaves. Private collection.

In comparing the history of silk to that of other textile fibers, one immediately notices the interest that it always created in the realm of power, temporal as well as spiritual. In France the silk trade would never have taken on such importance without the constant support of royalty, which considered the fabric to be one of its most beautiful assets. The successive statutes that distributed privileges and business facilities had a common objective: to improve quality. During the Ancien Régime, only the wealthy could buy silk, which was sold at prices that we can't imagine today. At the end of the Middle Ages only Italy, Sicily, southern Spain, and the East consistently produced high-quality silk. Without skilled and competent workers it was difficult if not impossible for France to produce or copy these silks.

Two centuries would go by before France could satisfy the royal needs and was able to produce silks worthy of the most beautiful residences or of the most sumptuous attire. From the first establishment in Lyons in 1466 to the middle of the seventeenth century, when the court's needs were finally met, the central power constantly had to stimulate, legislate, and subsidize in its effort to free France from foreign dependency. The statutes show a concern for the quality of the raw material, its importation into the kingdom, its domestic manufacture, the composition of its threads, colors, and most importantly its dyes, the weaving and fabrication techniques, and of course all the commercial, judicial, and corporative questions.

French silks became an artistic craft at the very beginning of the seventeenth century, especially after the perfection of the draw loom around 1604–1606 by a technical master of Milanese origin, Claude Dangon, which made it possible to copy, then to improve upon, the imported figured fabrics.[1] While this development was undoubtedly as important as Jacquard's invention two centuries later, we know very little about it, although it most likely involved the organizing of the different colored wefts. Thanks to this technical progress, French silks became independent of Italy and began to develop their own style.

With the intention of improving the quality of manpower, as well as of stimulating the creative spirit, a school for future silk workers was established in Lyons, "the most convenient site" in France. On a proposal from the merchants' provost and municipal magistrates, the direction of the school was entrusted in 1600 to Dangon, who was considered the best worker and the most capable person to undertake and direct the manufacturing of fabrics "in the Turkish, Indian, Italian styles" or in styles from anywhere else for that matter.

This educational innovation did not have immediate results for French manufacture if one judges from the important wardrobe inventories of certain powerful individuals in the kingdom, for instance Mazarin, whose taste for luxury was without equal. At his death in 1661, the very precise inventory of the cardinal's wardrobe made by Colbert, then his steward, did not mention a single garment made with French fabrics.

During this period, however, the first artist interested in silk designs appeared. Around 1660 Paul Androuet du Cerceau published *Bouquets propres pour les étoffes de Tours*, the first collection of French textile designs.[2] The style was still very much influenced by Italy, and the flowers looked much like the ones drawn by botanists of the time. *Dessins nouveaux pour étoffes de brocart à fond d'or ou d'argent*, another of Androuet du Cerceau's publications, showed greater originality. The new *loom à la tire* (figure 20) most likely helped to translate these beautiful designs into fabric, undoubtedly answering an increasing demand for precious cloth. This demand, which had always been strong, was kept alive by the typical French taste for an ever-changing clothing style, the French "finding it boring to wear the same attire for any length of time."[3] In fact, these early designs were destined exclusively for clothing.

As a result of the governmental reorganization undertaken by Colbert, his own role as administrator of the royal works, and finally the importance given to the construction and especially the decoration of Versailles, the manufacturing of silk furnishings grew very important. It became a substantial part of the absolute monarchy's official art. The royal palaces that Louis XIV had built or redecorated (the Louvre and the Tuileries, Saint-Germain-en-Laye, Vincennes, Fontainebleau), in addition to those that the kingdom's dignitaries or the king's mistresses had built for themselves, were showcases where French art, was put on display for the prestige of France and the pleasure of Europe.

Charles Le Brun,[4] the theorist of painting and decorative arts, as well as Colbert's right arm in this domain, created a genuine school whose talented artists are commonly admired. Although he was not directly involved with the creation of fabrics, they were not unfamiliar to Le Brun, then director of the Manufacture Royale des Meubles de la Couronne (royal furnishings manufactory). Despite the considerable bulk of the orders, systematically registered in the invaluable accounts of the Royal Works Administration since 1666, very few names of artists working in silk are known to us. However, certain descriptions give an idea of the sumptuousness of the fabrics, and it is justifiable to think that they must have been made by true artists. Daniel Marot[5] was most likely among them, since he was a gifted decorator, several of whose engraved designs for silk furnishings have come down to us. His style is open, sober, and majestic. His patterns are composed of bouquets of flowers and stylized foliage always organized in symmetrical composition and with many large repeats. His work is animated by a new spirit, which was not yet present in that of Paul Androuet du Cerceau. He was totally free of Italian influence. With him was born a typically French classical style in the decoration of fabrics. Certain *brocatelles* from the Musée Historique des Tissus from the second half of the seventeenth century show a spiritual relationship with some of Marot's drawings. Their colors are limited to two or three, usually greens, reds, and golds.[6]

As mentioned in the preceding essay, the most beautiful and sumptuous silks of the period were woven in Charlier's royal manufactory in Saint-Maur-les-Fossés,[7] and were intended for royal consumption. The royal accounts mention a white *damask* embroidered in gold with the royal monogram to be used in Versailles's Grande Galerie, at the cost of fifteen hundred pounds an *aune*; a cloth embroidered with gold and silver *frisé*, darkened with a crimson floral cornucopia with a blue satin scallop; a velvet for Versailles's Cabinet des Curiosités; a blue and crimson brocade with a silver and gold embroidered *persienne* for 440 pounds; a crimson brocade embroidered with gold, silver, and multicolored silk for one of the Trianons; a gold and silver brocade for Versailles's Salle du Trône and the adjacent chamber; a gold Parisian brocade figured with gold

and silver lyres marked with the royal monogram in gold frisé outlined in brown silk. The list is endless.

The manufactory, narrowly tied to that of crown furnishings, surely employed the same artists as did Le Brun. However, to date only Jean I. Bérain's[8] collaboration with Les Gobelins, and his decors and costumes for the Académie Royale de Musique, give a precise idea about his style. It is almost certain that Bérain was the creator of a magnificent brown and gold cut and uncut velvet that now belongs to the Musée des Arts Décoratifs, Paris (figure 21). Another fragment is in the textile museum of Lyons. The technical and artistic quality of this fabric is such that a relationship can be established with certain entries in the royal accounts concerning Charlier's fabrics. Bérain's spirit is evident in the repetition of the grotesque, in the animals crouched on architectural fragments, and especially in the typical use of the baldachin. The pattern is of course symmetrical, on a golden yellow satin. This sumptuous fabric gives us a glimpse of the magnificence of the silks during Louis XIV's reign. Unfortunately, they are virtually unknown to us, although we know that they were very much admired at the time.[9]

Another fabric of no less magnificence deserves mention. It has been used as a model in the recent restoration of the king's bedroom in Versailles, that is, the room overlooking the marble court where Louis XIV settled in 1701 and where he died in 1715. This fabric, which is kept in the collections of the Mobilier National in Paris, is of an unequaled splendor. A majestic design, symmetrical and radiating, with only one repeat per panel, stands out on a crimson background. The design itself is brocaded with gold and silver threads of different nuances and tensions. The technical aspect of the production, within the limited means available at the beginning of the eighteenth century, defies the imagination. Again the designer remains anonymous. What strikes the connoisseur's eye, in the last two fabrics mentioned, is the absolute mastery of the technique, which is in perfect harmony with the design and the colors.

Among the profusion of decorators who were working in Paris as well as in the provinces, particularly in Lyons, it is difficult to distinguish the artistic personalities involved with silk. But it is even more difficult if not impossible to identify those who were

21 Furnishing fabric. Probably after Jean I. Bérain. Late seventeenth century. Silk. Voided cut and uncut velvet. 250 x 230 (100 x 84). Musée des Arts Décoratifs, Paris.

responsible for making a certain style fashionable. Besides a sober, classical, and somewhat austere style in composition, pattern, and colors, the end of the seventeenth century and the beginning of the eighteenth century saw two tendencies come into being that have always intrigued textile art historians, mostly because no specific artistic personality has ever been identified with either trend. On the one hand are the so-called lace-pattern silks ("décor à la dentelle"), which used lace motifs as an ornament and which were enormously popular at the time, especially in clothing (figure 22). On the other hand is a baroque tendency, evidenced in "bizarre silks"

("soieries bizarres") (figures 23–25 and figure 28). These included fabrics of a rare sumptuousness which show a skillful mixing of gold and silver with bright or mute colors, in keeping with the chromatic scale of the period. These two trends existed in Lyons, perhaps also in Paris and elsewhere, but it is impossible to determine their impact or their creators.[10] However, it was in realistic design imitating nature that the French designers excelled, especially those from Lyons.

Research is revealing the evolution of silk design at the beginning of the eighteenth century—a time when silk design in Lyons was at the threshold of a

22 Chasuble back. Lace-patterned fabric made ca. 1720. Silk. So-called *lampas liseré*, weft patterned with supplementary patterning wefts. 47½ x 27½ max. (120.6 x 69.85 max.). Wadsworth Atheneum, Florence Paull Berger Fund, 1983.32.

23 Furnishing fabric. Ca. 1705. Silk. Damask weave. 38³/8 x 21 (97.53 x 53.3). Wadsworth Atheneum, Florence Paull Berger Fund, 1983.734.

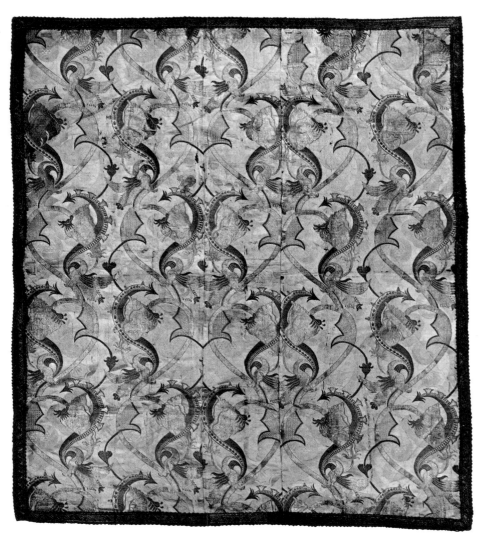

24 Furnishing fabric. Ca. 1710. Silk. Damask weave with supplementary patterning wefts of silk and metal. 60¹/₂ x 50³/₄ (153.67 x 128.9). Wadsworth Atheneum, Florence Paull Berger Fund, 1982.58.

26 Fragment. Ca. 1750. Silk. Plain weave, with supplementary wefts of silk and metal. 36 x 19 max. (91.44 x 48.26 max.). Wadsworth Atheneum, Gift of Mrs. June R. Bingham, 1968.64.

25 Furnishing fabric. Ca. 1700. Silk. Foundation weave: damasklike combining satin and plain weaves, with supplementary patterning wefts. 47¼ x 22¼ (120 x 56.5). Wadsworth Atheneum, Florence Paull Berger Fund, 1982.56.

brilliant breakthrough that would dominate textile art throughout Europe. It was also the period when technique and art, design and color, achieved a most harmonious perfection.

At the beginning of the eighteenth century, the major preoccupation of Lyons designers was to translate as well as possible their original graphic motifs into cloth. To accomplish this, they had to possess a sophisticated technical knowledge. At that time it was unthinkable for a silk designer to ignore the technique available. The problem of shadowing is a case in point. Jacques-Charles Dutillieu[11] and Joubert de l'Hiberderie,[12] contemporary observers and Lyons designers whose opinion is especially valid, noted that the first efforts made in that direction were accomplished by a certain Lyons designer named Courtois (died in Lyons in 1750). "In 1730 [he] wanted to break with the tradition of depicting unicolored images in fabric, . . . resulting in a flat print whose only grace came from its delicate outline. Courtois, an inventive genius, conceived of

a complete shading; that is to say, he applied a light color, then one shade darker, and so forth up to the darkest, and this began to give a certain relief to the woven images."[13] Joubert de l'Hiberderie confirmed this innovation, while insisting, however, on the "poor quality of Courtois's drawing ability."[14] Joubert attributed more talent to designers such as Deschamps, Monlong, and Pierre Ringuet.

At the beginning of the eighteenth century, the most influential individual in Lyons silk designing was Jean Revel (figure 31).[15] Many great artists followed his example. Joubert de l'Hiberderie, to whom we will refer frequently, devoted an entire chapter to him.[16] Jean Revel's father, Gabriel, was also a talented artist. He had worked for Charles Le Brun in Versailles, after which he established himself in Lyons, where Jean acquired his basic skills as a designer.

Abbé Pernetti described in great detail Revel's innovation in blending colors, which was based entirely on his sophisticated technical knowledge:

He has brought the manufacturing design of this city to the highest level of perfection. It is to him that we owe the technique "des points rentrés" to produce color. This tech-

nique consists in mixing silks whose colors are so sharply different that they look dry and hard next to each other. He did this by superimposing a dot of brown color onto a dot of lighter color and a dot of the lighter color onto a dot of the brown: the junction point thus becomes softer in tone with the blending of these two colors, thus removing the unnatural harshness of the hue. From this ingenious blending, unknown before him, came the harmony and the pleasing visual effects in fabrics, which often superseded the brilliancy of the color. Also, he was the one who found the secret of placing shades all on one side, thus producing genuine paintings on these fabrics. No one else had ever designed in this style with such grace. His composition was noble and bold, his shades of colors, perfect; he is still a model for the best designers: they regard him as their Raphael (figures 26 and 27). [17]

This invention of point rentré, also called "berclé," occurred around 1730. Legend also credits Revel with the invention of *mise en carte* (*charting*) (figures 29 and 30). In any case, thanks to him, according to Joubert, "design was considered a distinguished art, noble as well as profitable."

In his treatise devoted to the silk designer, Joubert tried to codify all the intricacies of this art. In Lyons, like everywhere else, the importance of silk designing had been quickly recognized, and the designer became highly respected (figures 32 and 33). The beauty and richness of a design were all the more appreciated at the beginning of the eighteenth century when technical research was very limited. The 1744 regulations confirmed this importance by stipulating that "it was forbidden directly or indirectly or in any ways or means possible, to lift or copy a design from old or recent fabrics." [18] Pirating or copying by foreign countries greatly preoccupied the authorities. In 1755 the commerce intendant de Trudaine, warned the merchants' provost, Flachard de Saint-Bonnet, that Boucharlat, a native of Lyons and director of the Naples royal silk manufactory, [19] was in constant communication with individuals from Lyons, who were conveying to him the new designs as soon as they were produced.

27 Fragment. Ca. 1708. Silk. Plain weave, with supplementary patterning wefts of silk and metal tied in a twill weave. 45 1/2 x 11 3/4 (115.57 x 29.84). Wadsworth Atheneum, Gift of the Hartford Art Society, 1934.44.

As the indispensable role played by the designer was universally recognized, it made necessary serious and elaborate design training. Until 1756 no official school existed as such. The designer's craft was more a condition, a talent, than a profession. Formal studies were long and costly, and therefore could be undertaken only by wealthy young men.

In 1756 Abbé de Lacroix-Laval established a free royal school of design, a project begun in 1751. Before then a boy who intended to choose design as a career had to study with a private tutor, usually the town's official painter, who taught the young candidate the basic principles of his craft. Thus Daniel Sarrabat was the first master of Philippe de Lasalle and Donat Nonnotte. Further instruction was taken with a flower painter, because floral motifs had always been considered the core of silk design. In Lyons around the middle of the eighteenth century, the most reputable flower painter was Douet, J. B. Monnoyer's former student.[20] Sometimes the student finished his education in Paris, at the free school of design founded by Jean-Jacques Bachelier, or in the atelier of a painter-cartoonist from Les Gobelins. As early as the end of the seventeenth century, flower motifs played a considerable role in tapestry, and the Gobelins manufactory was in constant communication with Lyons's silk industry, or La Grande Fabrique.

Technical training was always learned on the job in a silk manufactory where the designer spent a certain amount of time. In the eighteenth century a silk manufactory of any importance employed at least one designer among its directorial staff. Thanks to this daily contact with the trade, the designer was thoroughly initiated into the art of fabric making. Joubert de l'Hiberderie's deepest desire was that designers also be gifted technicians, and indeed several designers, among them the most talented, were responsible for technical improvements.

In order to keep abreast of the trade, a sort of continuing education existed, which entailed an annual trip to Paris to renew the designer's taste and knowledge, and mostly to keep him informed of the latest fashion trends. The trip to Paris was considered so essential, somewhat like a trip to Rome for painters and architects, that it was included in all the designers' contracts, and the expenses were paid by the employer. Joubert gives a detailed guide for this sojourn, including even the location of lodgings in Paris.

These preoccupations, aimed solely at the perfection of the craft, bore fruit in the eighteenth century. Shortly before the Revolution, Abbé Bertholon reminded the people of Lyons of the importance of design: "Never forget, O Lyons, that it is your designers who are responsible for the prosperity of your manufactories."[21]

In the eighteenth century Philippe de Lasalle was the shining light of all these sustained efforts, and he brought glory to La Grande Fabrique. He was not only a designer of European renown but also an extraordinary technician and an ingenious inventor who contributed in many ways to the improvement of the loom. Born near Lyons, he went there when he was very young after his father's death to learn the basics of painting in Daniel Sarrabat's atelier. Exhibiting a great deal of talent, he attended the public school that Bachelier had just founded in Paris. Then he studied with François Boucher, painter to the king and his mistress, the Marquise de Pompadour. While in Paris, Charryé, a designer manufacturer from Lyons, became aware of the youth's talent for ornamentation. After several attempts he succeeded in persuading de Lasalle to establish himself in Lyons, where he became first Charryé's associate, then his son-in-law.

De Lasalle gave the full measure of his talent and his art during his collaboration with Camille Pernon.[22] Pernon's manufactory, one of Lyons's greatest, was the supplier to the French court as well as to many other royal and imperial European houses, including Russia, Spain, and Lorraine. The new market was very favorable to the development of this great talent. With the assistance of his eminent designer, Pernon produced, until the Revolution, the most sumptuous silks ever to come from Lyons's looms. Among these remarkable silks was the hanging destined for Queen Marie Antoinette's bedroom in Versailles, and subsequently displayed at Fontainebleau during the Empire.[23]

The Russian orders, placed by the Saint Petersburg chancellery and intended for Catherine the Great's palaces, were surely the most numerous: the famous peacock and pheasant hanging destined for the summer residence of the czarina at Tsarskoe Selo (now Pushkin); the flower baskets and doves

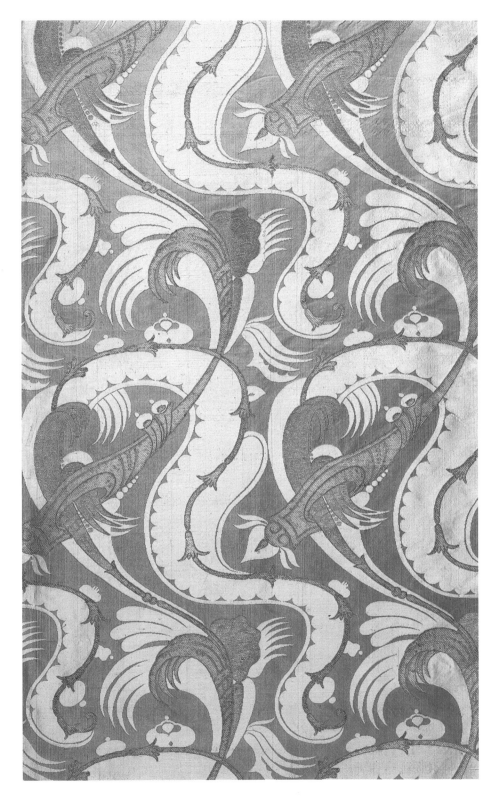

28 Panel or table cover. 1700–
1710. Silk. Damask weave
with supplementary pat-
terning wefts of silk and
metal. L: 96 (243.8); W.: 44¹/2
(113). Museum of Fine Arts,
Boston, Textile Income
Purchase Fund, 1977.179.

29 Jean Revel. Mise en carte. Lyons, 1733. Gouache on paper. 22 x 17³/4 (56 x 45.1). Musée Historique des Tissus, Lyons.

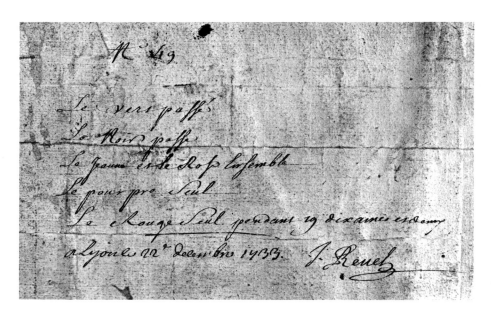

30 Reverse side of figure 29, showing Revel's signature.

hanging for the same palace (figure 34); hangings commemorating Tchesmé's victory and the conquest of Crimea; and many others. The importance of Pernon's supplying the Saint Petersburg court was of such magnitude that it inevitably provoked envy. In fact, eighteenth-century gossip had it that Pernon had handsomely bribed Grimm and d'Alembert, "intimate friends of the Semiramis of the North," in order to be presented to Catherine the Great.[24]

This jealous gossiping did not prevent de Lasalle from giving his all to silks. The hangings created in Pernon's manufactory, almost exclusively lampas, are the eloquent testimony of a profound knowledge of the art and its techniques. The material, the decors, and the colors were treated with a new richness and a great dexterity, which skillfully contrasted the background with the overall design of the decor. De Lasalle knew bindings better than anyone and he used them with great competence in order to obtain a visual contrasting between mat and shiny or an optical division of a background: for example, the use of a fine *cannetillé* in the partridge hanging harmoniously underlines the decor. Elsewhere he used chenille to obtain a velvety relief or in-depth effect. All this accompanied a powerful design, free of petty details, as well as a perfect understanding of color (figure 35).[25]

De Lasalle's fabrics deserve to be studied in depth. The numerous inventions and technical improvements that earned him a series of distinctions also merit attention. Some of his inventions were recorded in a report presented to the Académie des Sciences in 1775, which he himself had published in Lyons in 1802. He died on 23 February 1805.

Philippe de Lasalle's art is without a doubt the best ever produced in eighteenth-century Lyons. However, other artists had an important influence on silk design, (figure 36), especially Jean Pillement, whose style, called by his name, was evident for a good part of the eighteenth century, well beyond the realm of silk decoration. Pillement (1728–1808) was born and died in Lyons. Although trained in design, he is not usually considered a silk decorator. After having been a designer in the Gobelins tapestry manufactory in Paris, he traveled throughout Europe from Portugal to Saint Petersburg as a painter and a decorator. He was a prolific artist in-

volved in all facets of art. An original decorator, his influence in the field of silk design was transmitted through his numerous published engravings. His charming floral stylizations with flowers shaped as parasols (figure 37) and his chinoiseries became known through his publications. His ornament played an important part in establishing the originality of the Louis XV style and in its expansion throughout Europe. Among the collections that he engraved are the sequence of six pieces published in London in 1755, *A New Book of Chinese Ornaments Invented and Engraved by Pillement*, his *Collection of Different Flowers in the Chinese Style Suited for Silk Fabrics and Indian Print Manufactures* (London, 1760), his *Fleurs persannes*, and finally his many notebooks on a diversity of subjects. Undoubtedly influenced by his Lyonese origins, in 1763 he proposed to the Marquis de Marigny to direct a manufactory of "painted silk in the Indian style." But the project did not materialize. Although Pillement's unique style lasted until the beginning of the nineteenth century, it belongs exclusively to the period of rococo and Louis XV, while Philippe de Lasalle's work clearly marks the transition between the two periods Louis XV and Louis XVI (figure 39).[25]

The free royal school of design, founded in Lyons in 1756, which seemed so logical and natural, met from the start very strong opposition from the designer manufacturers. They objected that the training, quite long as it was, now devoted too much time in teaching students to draw from the round, than from the model. In effect, only half of the ten years of training was reserved for floral study and charting. At the heart of this strong objection was a desire to prevent the vulgarization of the art of design: the manufacturers wanted a shorter and more specialized instruction, which would also include cultivating "a garden of many plants and flowers chosen for their beautiful shapes." This last wish materialized only in the revolutionary year VI (1799), with the foundation of the special flower schools, created by Abbé Rozier; to this was added Lyons's Le Jardin des Plantes, the botanical garden that was the beginning of the Parc de la Tête d'Or. In 1756 the faculty was composed of Jean-Jacques Frontin, professor of painting; Michel-Antoine Perrache, professor of sculpture; Pignon, professor in floral design and ornament; and de Gournay, who

31 Chalice veil or furnishing fabric. Design attributed to Jean Revel, ca. 1730–1740. Silk. Taffeta with supplementary patterning wefts of silk and metal (trimming: woven silk). 22 x 21 1/2 (56 x 54.6). Musée Historique des Tissus, Lyons.

taught geometry.[27] In 1762 Donat Nonnotte directed the painting class. A similar initiative was taken in Tours in 1756: Antoine Rougeot, silk painter and designer, gave free lessons in design. He became the director of the Ecole Académique in Tours, officially created in 1781.

The foundation of the Ecole de Dessin in Lyons did not yield any results before the end of the eighteenth century, when it produced its most brilliant student, Jean-François Bony (1754–1825). Bony, who inaugurated the new antique revival style, became one of the undisputed masters of Empire silk design. However, before becoming the master of this new classicism he collaborated for a while with Philippe de Lasalle in the Pernon manufactory, where he practiced the flowery and supple Louis XVI style. He was probably responsible for the sketch of the sumptuous brocade (grand broché) ordered for Marie Antoinette's bedroom in Versailles and delivered on 27 April 1788.[28] He disappeared during the Revolution, to reappear after the storm as Bissardon and Cousin's associate and as professor of the floral class at the Ecole de Dessin. An important part of his work was also devoted to embroidery design, as discussed by Marianne Carlano in her essay. In this regard, special mention must be made of the white satin hanging embroidered with flowers and birds, which was ordered in December 1811 for a drawing room of Empress Marie Louise's apartment in Versailles. In this magnificent work, never installed, Bony's style is light, graceful, and of impeccable design, thus succeeding in giving to the empire style a more feminine and less austere appearance. It shows a total mastery of the art of floral design.[29] Bony is thought to have killed himself in 1825, after being ruined by one of his collaborators.

Antoine Berjon (1754–1802) and Pierre-Toussaint Déchazelle (1752–1835) were Bony's contemporaries and contributed, as he did, by marking the transition between the Ancien Régime's style and that of the empire.[30] Berjon, who had an unstable and violent temper, succeeded Bony as professor of the floral design class. He also contributed drawings to Bony's manufactory. Despite the considerable amount of his work in painting, drawing, and engraving that has come down to us, no silks can be attributed to him with certainty.

The same can be said of Déchazelle, although he played an important part in La Grande Fabrique, notably when the industry was reorganized after the Revolution. He is thought to have been one of the key figures in Lyons silk designing at the beginning of the nineteenth century. His flowers in the Dutch style were very much appreciated.

Among those artists spanning the eighteenth and nineteenth centuries, a special place is reserved for Jean-Démosthène Dugourc (1749–1825),[31] whose delicate and precise designs produced remarkable works (figure 38). The major part of his work has been preserved, although it is not well known. Dugourc was not a silk designer in the strict sense of the word, and he also came from a different milieu. His designs were only part of a larger activity, as was also the case of Thomas Germain, the famous Parisian goldsmith, and the architects Charles Percier and Pierre Fontaine.[32]

Jean-Démosthène Dugourc was born in Versailles and educated in Paris. His father was chamberlain of the Duc d'Orléans's household. He received a polished education and very early devoted himself to drawing, geometry, and architecture. At the age of fifteen he had the good fortune to go to Rome with the Comte de Cani, who had been appointed special ambassador. This initial contact with Italy was a turning point in his future because it roused his interest in antiquity—a taste reinforced by his marriage to an older sister of François Bélanger, director of "menus plaisirs" and first architect of the Comte d'Artois, the future Charles X. Bélanger was, with Claude-Nicolas Ledoux, one of the most ardent instigators of neoclassicism in eighteenth-century French art.

In his autobiography Dugourc mentioned his propensity for the new style: "During the nine or ten years that preceded the Revolution, [I] was the first to use the Arabesque and Etruscan genres, not only in architectural decorations but also for hangings and furniture, and since that time, in Lyons, all of Pernon's designs, as well as the bronzes and jewels presented at court have been created and supervised by [me]."

Most of the silk hangings woven by Pernon from Dugourc's designs can still be found in Spain, in the palaces of the Escorial, Aranjuez, the Prado, or in La Casita del Labrador near Madrid. These remarkably

32 Panel. First half of the eighteenth century. Silk and metal. Silk satin weave with supplementary warp, and silk and metal supplementary weft. 65 x 21 (165.1 x 53.3). Wadsworth Atheneum, Florence Paull Berger Fund, 1970.44.

preserved works were the result of Dugourc's collaboration with the Spanish court between 1800 and 1814, when he was "first architect of the king of Spain and prince of peace." It was in Spain that he accomplished the bulk of his work.

The Revolution, which caused so much misery, also interrupted, at least for a while, French silk production, and most of Lyons's manufacturing. In the meantime fashions changed. For men, the cloth coat replaced the silk one. For women, if at the end of Louis XVI's reign they had favored unicolored silks, veils, and linen batistes, they now dressed in Indian muslins, *satin-stitched* cottons, and printed calicos.

The situation had greatly deteriorated when Napoleon, as first consul, took an interest in the silk economy and in Lyons. When he became emperor, at Lyons's request he displayed an ever-growing taste for luxury, which he sometimes imposed by decree and which reached its zenith after his coronation and the establishment of the ostentatious imperial court.

This political emphasis on luxury allowed La Grande Fabrique, the emperor's favored industry, to regain its former strength. Napoleon showed his interest by his frequent visits to Lyons. Camille Pernon had the favor of the new regime, but from 1860 on the rest of the silk manufactories benefited from the imperial largesse. This generosity was

33 Fragment. Second half of the eighteenth century. Silk. Plain weave, warp chiné à la branche. 16³/₄ x 25¹/₂ (42.6 x 64.7). Musée Historique des Tissus, Lyons.

renewed several times, which gave Lyons a new vitality (figure 43). Tours's manufacturing was also helped, but to a lesser degree.

The nineteenth-century silk industry, technilogically well advanced by the inventions of Jacquard (1752–1834)[33] and endowed with a solid artistic tradition, enjoyed a sustained prosperity. Most of Lyons's designers continued to be educated at the Ecole de Dessin transformed into the Ecole des Beaux-Arts in 1807. The designer was an important figure whose function had the status of a profession and who was greatly appreciated in the manufactory that employed him. His personality gave its silk fabrics their style and their taste. However, his role and his relationship with the silk manufacturer was about to change.

Around 1830 the practice of independent design appeared for the first time, and the designer became above all a tradesman and an industrialist. He no longer set the fashion, but on the contrary had to submit to it. He was now required to display versatility above talent. At the same period, fashion increased the seasonal changing rhythm, requiring an infinite diversity of fabrics. At all levels of production, imagination was bound to an increasing demand for versatility that smothered real talents because depth and originality were no longer important. This unrelenting demand gave rise to

overproduction and, unfortunately, mediocrity.

The workers' strikes and revolts of 1831 and 1834, the American panic of 1837, and the 1848 revolution hampered the output of silk, and were even more detrimental to creativity. The social and political crises that transformed society also transformed production. Luxury items, which had been for centuries Lyons's prerogative, were increasingly abandoned in favor of mass-market goods.

Another storm gathered on the horizon. At the beginning of the Second Empire (figures 40–42), *façonné* was no longer in fashion, and Alsatian cottons came into favor, a trend that lasted fifteen years. According to Edouard Aynard, one of Lyons's most eminent personalities of the period, the cause of the public change of heart was the lack of decorative imagination and the bad taste displayed by the designers. This lack of originality and creative ability undermined Lyons's production for most of the nineteenth century. It was said that "contemporary industrial art is still the donkey carrying the relics of the past," which meant that designers conformed too closely to old schemes and at times, simply copied them. Some decorated fabrics were no more than pictures on silk, which were difficult to use in fashion and even unappealing. "Woman, with her keen intuition of what looks good, quickly became aware of these errors of judgment and called

34

35

36

34 Philippe de Lasalle. Wall panel. Lyons, ca. 1775. Silk. Satin weave, with patterning wefts tied in a twill weave. 75 x 21 (190.5 x 53.3). Wadsworth Atheneum, Costume and Textile Purchase Fund and J. Herbert Callister Fund, 1983.29.

35 Philippe de Lasalle. Wall panel. Lyons, ca. 1785. Silk, brocaded. 103 x 26¾ (261.6 x 67.9). Musuem of Fine Arts, Boston, Seth K. Sweetser Fund 1, 1984.221.

36 Panel. Design attributed to Jean–Baptiste Le Prince (1734–1781). Lyons, ca. 1750. Silk. Plain compound satin, brocaded. 77½ x 21½ (196.8 x 54.6). Wadsworth Atheneum, Healy Fund, 1943.131.

upon the costumier and the seamstress to redress them. These new craftsmen created for the silk dress a suitable decoration that the designer was no longer able to give it. Braids, *passementeries*, laces, ribbons, and ingenious manipulations of the fabrics replaced the light arabesque and all the floral designs that the designer no longer knew how to do."[34]

This analysis sums up the story of fashion and silk design in Lyons during most of the nineteenth century. The situation was first recognized at the London Great Exhibition in 1851, the first event of this kind where Lyons silks were evidently represented, and again at the Exposition Universelle in Paris in 1855. Simon Saint-Jean, painter and silk designer, gave a disillusioned report of the London exhibition. This negative appraisal had the effect of provoking a collective awareness which gave rise on the one hand to the reshaping of the curriculum of the Ecole des Beaux-Arts, and on the other to the creation of an educational industrial art museum, which is now the Musée Historique des Tissus.

In the nineteenth century Lyons silk design no longer possessed the artistic strength that it had during the preceding century. However, production increased, and designers had never been more numerous. They formed a school in the real sense of the word, the Lyons School of Floral Painters, with its own personality and characteristics. Many talented artists deserve to be mentioned: Simon Saint-Jean (1808–1860), Augustin Thierrat (1789–1870), Jean-Marie Regnier (1815–1886), Joanny Maisiat (1824–1910), Jean-Pierre Laÿs (1825–1887), Pierre-

Adrien Chabal-Dussurgey (1819–1902), Jacques Martin (1844–1919), Adolphe-Louis Castex-Dégrange (1840–1918), and François Vernay (1821–1896). They all wore two hats: silk designers and painters.

The independent designers who first appeared in 1830 became almost the sole suppliers for Lyons's silk designs during the nineteenth century. Those designers still employed by manufacturers no longer played a creative role but simply refined designs bought elsewhere. Around the middle of the century a large number of ateliers established themselves in Paris, the center of fashion. These less specialized ateliers found in the capital were easy and important outlets: Alsatian manufacturers of printed fabrics, wallpaper makers, Lyons's manufacturers of course,

and finally, the various crafts newly created or renewed, which all together formed what is now called haute couture or high fashion. When the latter became definitely established, Lyonese manufacturers all placed agents, if not their headquarters, in the capital. During the second half of the nineteenth century, and even more so in the twentieth, fashion and silk design were created, at least in spirit, exclusively in Paris. Certainly, design workshops continued to exist in Lyons because the production's complexity demanded skilled hands. However, pure creativity had left Lyons, and the city contented itself with the realization of others' ideas. This new role meant the neglect of the technological growth, which in turn gave an increasingly important place to printed fabrics to the detriment of façonné.

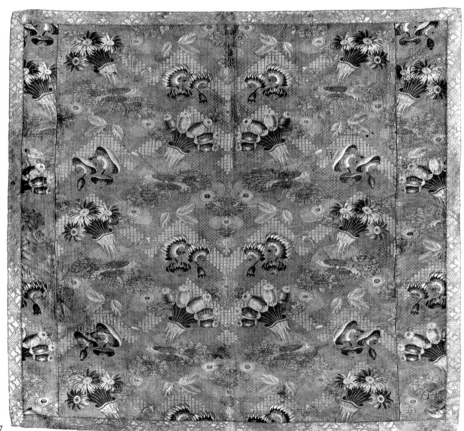

37

37 Furnishing fabric. Ca. 1750. Silk and metal. Foundation weave: plain weave weft-wise rib, supplementary patterning wefts. 27¼ x 26¾ (69.21 x 67.9). Wadsworth Atheneum, Florence Paull Berger Fund, 1982.11.

38 Jean-Démosthène Dugourc. Wall panel. Lyons, Camille Pernon & Cie., ca. 1775. Silk. Satin weave, brocaded, some embroidery. 93 x 18 (236.2 x 45.7). Museum of Art, Rhode Island School of Design, Mary B. Jackson Fund.

39 Dress. Ca. 1760. Silk. Plain weave with supplementary patterning wefts; laces not original. Wadsworth Atheneum, Purchased in honor of Florence Paull Berger, Curator Emeritus, on her ninety-fifth birthday, 1966.570.

39

38

40 Panel. Ca. 1860. Velours de Gênes. Silk warp, weft, pile. This panel, woven in the style of a particular type of velvet associated with Genoa, was made for Baron Pereire. Collection Tassinari & Chatel SARL.

41 Panel. 1866. Lampas broché. Silk warp, weft, and supplementary patterning wefts. This panel was woven for the bedroom of Empress Eugénie at the Tuileries. The design was inspired by the textiles of the late eighteenth century associated with the taste of Marie Antoinette. The heavy pattern of leaves which form the ogivals is, however, typical of the nineteenth century. Collection Tassinari & Chatel SARL.

42 Panel. 1866. Silk warp, weft, and supplementary patterning wefts. Another example of the plethora of revival styles popular during the Second Empire, this design is an interpretation of the textiles used to decorate the Chambre des reines at Fontainebleau, in the taste of the 1860s. Collection Tassinari & Chatel SARL.

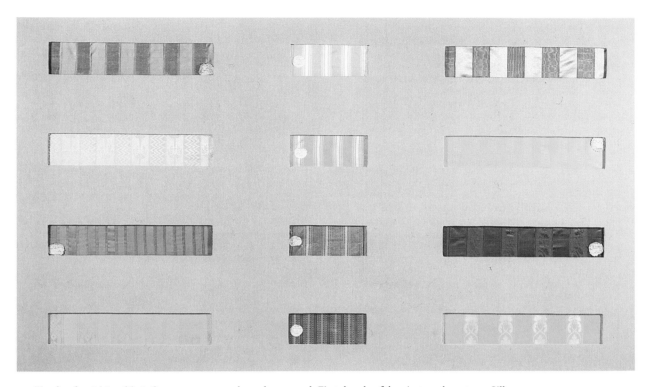

43 Twelve furnishing fabric fragments mounted on a large panel. First decade of the nineteenth century. Silk, woven.
Mobilier National, Paris.

Notes

The bibliography for this essay starts on page 183.

1 On Claude Dangon, see d'Hennezel, *Claude Dangon* (1926). Dangon perfected an earlier loom, once thought to have been created by Jean le Calabrais, upon which all ornamented silk work of former periods was made. Documentation relevant to this loom has yet to be discovered. Could it have comprised a control system for the arrangement of the weft forming the decoration? Many theories are plausible. D'Hennezel and others presume that it was Dangon who introduced the simple or silk reeler, which was an essential accessory until Jacquard's invention. For a more complete and detailed technical description, see Paulet's important work, *L'Art du fabriquant d'étoffes de soie* (1773–1778). This treatise, written in a manner similar to the *Encyclopédie* of Diderot and d'Alembert, and published under the auspices of the Académie des Sciences, is basic to a thorough understanding of traditional silk weaving techniques. However, a good general approach to all of these technical questions is offered in Gabriel Vial's study, "Silk Techniques," in Tuchscherer and Vial, *Le Musée Historique des Tissus de Lyon* (1977).

2 Paul Androuet du Cerceau was a decorator, though better known as a goldsmith and engraver, who lived in Paris toward the mid-seventeenth century. Although little is known of his life and work, it is said that he was the grandson of the famous French Renaissance architect, Jacques Androuet du Cerceau (1510–1584). Some of his engravings for cloth can be found in the library of the Musée Historique des Tissus in Lyons.

3 Michel, *Recherches* (1860), II: 285.

4 In 1663 Charles Le Brun, one of the greatest painters during the reign of Louis XIV, became director of the Manufacture Royale des Meubles de la Couronne located at Gobelins on the Faubourg Saint-Marcel in Paris. This factory, still operating today, is known by the name Les Gobelins. It now specializes exclusively in tapestry, whereas its role under Louis XIV was to create and manufacture all furniture and art objects needed in the royal palaces. As director, Le Brun brought to it a new and exceptional dimension, perfectly suited to the ambitions of Louis XIV, for which he was ennobled in 1662 and appointed Premier Peintre du roi in 1664. Painters, sculptors, goldsmiths, furniture makers, smelters, and tapestry makers all worked under his direction and very often according to his own drawings and sketches. Le Brun is especially known for his great decorative projects: the Galerie d'Apollon at the Louvre, the chapel and the Pavillon d'Aurore for Colbert in the Sceaux château, and at Versailles, the Galerie des Glaces, Salons de la Guerre et de la Paix, as well as the Escalier des Ambassadeurs; furthermore, he was responsible for the entire decoration of the sumptuous château at Marly where silk work held a notable place.

5 Daniel Marot, called "Le Vieux" (ca. 1663–1752), was draftsman, engraver, and architect, as had been his father Jean Marot (1619–ca. 1679). He left France following the repeal of the Edict of Nantes because he was Protestant and took refuge in Holland, where he became the first architect to William of Orange. The latter, having been crowned king of England under the name William III, entrusted him with the creation of the palace gardens at Hampton Court near London. In Holland, particularly in Amsterdam, Marot was kept very busy in the architectural trade. Yet he concerns the present study more for his collection of engravings printed in Amsterdam in 1712. This collection contains several sketches for silk in the Louis XIV style.

6 Until the end of the seventeenth century, the chromatic range of dyes was extremely limited.

Since the Middle Ages dyers had depended on the same colors and dyeing techniques used for centuries. The only means of obtaining variety in the shades of silk was by sheer artfulness in spinning and weaving, or by the use of gold and silver to add greater luxury. The problem of color in textiles, or dyeing, is closely linked to the perception of color in all the art of the period. Newton's optical discoveries, in particular his 1704 treatise, had a sizable impact on dye research and practices of the eighteenth century.

The scope of the present study is unfortunately not broad enough to treat this important subject. Great dye masters from the seventeenth century on, such as Jean Hellot (1685–1765), Charles François du Fay de Cisternay (1698–1739), Pierre-Joseph Macquer (1718–1784), Claude-Louis Berthollet (1748–1822), Jean-Antoine Claude Chaptal (1756–1832), and especially the renowned Michel-Eugène Chevreul (1786–1889), all contributed to silk work with the intention of adding to its beauty.

7 Aside from the publication by Jules Guiffrey of the accounts of the royal buildings under Louis XIV, from which we have gleaned a bit of information, no study whatsoever has been carried out on seventeenth-century silk, nor upon the Charlier mill in Saint-Maur-les-Fossés. Most textile documentation had obviously disappeared. It would be valuable to know more about the first great boom of French silk work. Not only did dress call upon this sumptuous material, but indeed the theater, opera, ballet, innumerable receptions, and many of the palaces already cited, such as Versailles, utilized silk fabric for everything—including the decoration of all sorts of rowboats and sailing craft traveling the Grand Canal for the pleasure of the courtiers. Iconographic, archival, and documentary research would surely uncover some unexpected secrets. For those interested, we should note that a little-explored source is the Minutier Central des Notaires at the National Archives in Paris.

8 On Bérain see Roger-Armand Weigert's excellent work, *Jean I. Bérain* (Paris, 1937). Unfortunately, his possible collaboration in the royal works at Saint-Maur-les-Fossés is not discussed.

9 No study identifying this silk piece exists at the present time. It does not, in any case, come from the king's bedroom at Versailles. According to Muriel Muntz de Raissac of the National Estates, it might reasonably have been a bed tester or carriage canopy. One of the rare examples of "royal class" dating from the end of the seventeenth century, it served as the model for a quite spectacular copy. It was rewoven by two Lyons companies, Prelle & Cie., and Tassinari & Chatel.

10 Thornton, *Baroque and Rococo Silks* (1965), offers the best approach to "lace-pattern silks" and "bizarre silks." At first glance, it would appear that lace decoration is originally more French and the "bizarre silks" more baroque and Italian in nature.

11 Jacques-Charles Dutillieu was an eighteenth-century silk

manufacturer in Lyons. He wrote a diary, actually memoirs, which gives details of the Lyons silk business of the day, as well as on his own trade. For a biography, refer to Bréghot du Lut, *Le Livre de raison de Jacques-Charles Dutillieu* (1886).

12 Nicolas Joubert de l'Hiberderie was a silk designer who owed his fame to the publication of an important treatise: *Le Dessinateur pour les fabriques d'étoffes d'or, d'argent et de soie* (Paris, 1765), in which he wrote about the best designers of his time, while providing a fairly complete review of the kinds of cloth produced in Lyons and in France, in the middle of the eighteenth century. At the end he gave a sort of guide to Paris to aid designers on their annual obligatory trips to the French capital. The real interest of the book, however, stems from its information on the training and knowledge required to become a designer. An unpublished doctoral thesis has dealt with this treatise: Weiderkehr, "Le Dessinateur pour les fabriques d'étoffes d'or, d'argent et de soie" (1981).

13 Bréghot du Lut, p. 23.

14 Ibid., p. 23; Joubert de l'Hiberderie, p. xi.

15 On Deschamps, Monlong, Ringuet, and Revel, consult the biographical notes in Audin and Vial, *Dictionnaire des artistes et ouvriers d'art du Lyonnais* (1918–1919).

16 Joubert de l'Hiberderie, p. xii, see also n. 12.

17 Pernetti, *Les Lyonnais dignes de mémoire* (1757).

18 Leroudier, *Les Dessinateurs de la fabrique lyonnaise au 18e siècle* (1908), p. 7.

19 The royal silk works of the Bourbons in Naples was located close to the Caserta palace. Famous for the quality of its production in the eighteenth century, this mill has remained in operation to the present day, although now as a private enterprise in San Leucio.

20 The relationship of Douet and Monnoyer derives chiefly from the association of La Grande Fabrique of Lyons with Les Gobelins, of which Jean-Baptiste Monnoyer (1636–1699) was one of the most famous tapestry cartoon artists. He distinguished himself mostly in the painting of "petit genre" (domestic flowers and fruits), for which he received much acclaim. His role in textiles was fundamental, not only at Les Gobelins, but particularly for his influence upon the art of silk. The opulent and majestic style of his flowers is repeated in some silk flower work at the beginning of the eighteenth century. This style is typified by the juxtaposition of bright and pure colors, deepened by a thorough knowledge of the fabric used. The vivacity of some of his tapestry borders is comparable to the floral designs of certain Lyonese silks from the early eighteenth century.

21 Bertholon, *Etude sur le commerce de Lyon* (1787).

22 On Pernon see Poidebard and Chatel, *Camille Pernon* (1912). His mill still exists in Lyons under the name Tassinari & Chatel. Even though it no longer holds many archives from the time of Philippe de Lasalle and Pernon, a very interesting collection of accounts, extending from the end of the eighteenth century through the greater part of the nineteenth, is still to be found there. All of the largest orders, some of which were for the most prestigious palaces of Europe, are recorded therein.

23 This hanging is now being rewoven by Prelle & Cie. and by Tassinari & Chatel of Lyons. Its history is related in Marie-Thérèse Schmitter and Félix Guicherd, *Philippe de Lasalle. Exposition de tentures* (Lyons: Imprimerie Vaucanson, 1939),

p. 33 and pl. XII.

24 Information furnished by the director of the Pedrovoretz (Peterhof) Palace near Leningrad, July 1981. The Russian textile collections, in the Hermitage and in other museums and palaces, are incredibly rich in every way. French silk is generously represented, as Russia was always one of the most important clients of Lyonese silk. All of the great Russian imperial palaces were hung with silk from Lyons in the eighteenth and nineteenth centuries. Unfortunately, very little is known of these collections in the West for lack of published material.

25 The Musée Historique des Tissus in Lyons possesses several original designs intended for some of the most beautiful hangings by Philippe de Lasalle, including the peacock and pheasant hanging for Catherine the Great. All of these items are of the utmost importance for any detailed technical study, yet none was consulted for recent restorations, since they were then still unknown.

26 The peacock and pheasant hanging ("tenture au paon et au faisan"), for example, is a typical piece documenting this transition. The flowing movement of the latticework holding flowers and grapes is still completely Louis XV. This same latticework, however, with its ribbons and baskets, and especially its outlining, its space rigorously arranged into medallions, is a precursor of the Louis XVI style. This sense of transition is also seen in the partridge hanging ("tenture aux perdrix"), originally made for Catherine the Great as well, but rewoven in a technically and coloristically different version for the Bourbon palace in Paris. Samples of these two pieces are owned by the Musée Historique des Tissus, Lyons. Philippe de Lasalle was finally won over to the new neoclassical style, as shown in the hanging now found in the queen's chambers at Fontainebleau. The use of pastoral and musical trophies, the presence of ancient ruins, and the organization of the surface are all typical Louis XVI elements. The color of this material, fresher and much less baroque than that of the partridge hanging, is also an indication of the new style.

27 For biographical information on these artists, not well known outside Lyons, refer to Audin and Vial.

28 The cartoon for this magnificent material was long ascribed to Philippe de Lasalle, of whom it does indeed show a direct influence. Its attribution of Jean-François Bony was confirmed however, by Marguerite Jallut, former curator of the Palace of Versailles. She has carried out numerous studies on the furnishing and decoration of the palace, much of it (including this subject) unpublished. This hanging was rewoven for Versailles immediately after World War II by Prelle & Cie. and Tassinari & Chatel of Lyons. See "Le Grand Broché de la Reine" (1967).

29 For a very detailed description of this hanging see the catalogue *Soieries Empire* (Paris: Mobilier National, 1980), and also *Silk from the Palaces of Napoleon* (New York: Fashion Institute of Technology, 1983), no. 36.

30 Audin and Vial's biographical dictionary contains information on these two artists. For the work of Berjon see Custodero, "Antoine Berjon" (1971–1972); a copy of this unpublished thesis is in the library of the Musée Historique des Tissus in Lyons.

31 The overall contribution to textiles of J.-D. Dugourc has never been studied, in spite of its excellent quality. He is the

only silk designer of the Ancien Régime whose original creations still remain in the palaces where they were initiated. Some of them are well conserved and provide a very good idea of French taste at the end of Louis XVI's reign as well as of the Directoire period. Several American museums own silk weavings in the Dugourc style, including the Museum of Art, Rhode Island School of Design, Providence, and the Museum of Fine Arts, Boston. The present-day Lyons company, Tassinari & Chatel, successor of Camille Pernon, has in its archives works of art by this artist: embroidered pieces, cartoons for textiles, gouaches and watercolors, and finally, a collection of almost two hundred drawings of many subjects (architecture, decorative arts, documentary drawings). For the latter collection see Hartmann, "Etude et catalogue raisonné" (1974–1976). A copy of this thesis, partly published, is in the library of the Musée Historique des Tissus, Lyons. Some of the present information is taken from it.

32 These two artist-architects, true dictators of taste under Napoleon, marvelously integrated silk furnishings into their architectural projects and redecoration of the royal palaces.

33 On Jacquard, a key figure of modern industry, consult Lapierre "La Vie et l'oeuvre de J.-M. Jacquard." See Adrosko, R., "Jacquard mechanism," 1984.

34 *Lyon en 1889* (1889), pp. 54ff.

Embroidery ❖ Marianne Carlano

44 Bayeux Embroidery, detail: "A house on fire." Normandy or England, 1066–1077. Wool embroidery; linen ground. Overall: 19½ in x 231 ft (49.53 cm x 70.40 m). Musée de la Reine Mathilde, Bayeux.

45 Bayeux Embroidery, detail, back side: "Harold is praying in front of William the Conqueror."

Introduction

Before beginning this history of embroidery from the Middle Ages (500–1500) through the Second Empire (1852–1870), it is necessary to define the term "embroidery." For the purpose of this study, embroidery is needlework done on a foundation fabric. It is created by using a needle of some sort, including the hook used in *tambour work*. Toward the middle of the nineteenth century technological advances enabled some kinds of embroidery to be produced by machine, and this kind of stitchery is no less valid than that made by hand.

Some sixteenth-century embroidery techniques are often called lace, as this was a period when various kinds of embroidery were worked free of the ground fabric. The steps that led to this new art form we call lace are included in this essay; the freed forms are discussed in the essay by Anne Kraatz.

It is the purpose of this essay to describe the nature of the embroideries as well as to attempt to answer the questions, Who made these works of art, and how and why were they created? The reader should understand that in many cases there are no certain answers to these questions due to the lack of extant documents or works of art. Furthermore, the embroideries that do exist are rarely signed.

Embroidery in France during the Middle Ages

During the Middle Ages splendid secular and religious celebrations required a number of lavishly embroidered textiles. We know about these items mostly from inventories and chronicles; very few have survived due to their fragile nature and due to the fact that these precious embroideries were often stolen and melted down for their gold and silver content.

The church, because of its great wealth, was able to command altar hangings, other paraments, and sumptuous vestments of the finest materials available, including various types of gold and silver threads[1] and precious stones that were set onto the surface of the textile. The gold and silver used for embroidery during the Middle Ages was of a superior quality; later on, these metals were mixed with others and their color is much different. But it was not only the church that produced such extravagant embroideries. The nobility decorated their homes with lavish embroidered furnishing fabrics, and they decorated their clothing with equally lavish ornamentation. Embroidered banners, made to hang in a palace or to be carried in a procession, were created for special events.

Although embroideries from the East had a corner on the market during the first centuries of the Middle Ages, Gregory of Tours (538–594) mentions that women of French nobility were making embroideries in the sixth century. The earliest extant embroideries made in France date from the seventh or eighth century. They are a group of decorative bands and gold rosettes on a silk tunic from Chelles (Seine-et-Marne). The embroidery is executed in *point de chainette*, in imitation of the cloisonné work of the period.[2] We do not know who made the Chelles embroideries, but references indicate that some women of the period were making embroideries, such as Berthe, the mother of Charlemagne (742–814).

In the eleventh century one of the most monumental embroideries of the Middle Ages, the Bayeux Embroidery, was made (figures 44 and 45). Its exact origin has been debated for centuries, some scholars claiming that it was made in England and others claiming that it was made in Normandy. The only extant wall hanging of this period, the Bayeux Embroidery, was probably made for Odo, bishop of Bayeux and half brother of William the Conquerer, between 1066 and 1077. It tells the story of the Battle of Hastings (1066) and is organized in episodic format so that an illiterate viewer could "read" the story. This masterwork is executed on a linen fabric in plied woolen threads of yellow, green, blue, and black. The inscriptions, faces, hands, and outlines are in *chain*, *stem*, and *split stitch*; the remaining embroidered surface is executed in *couched work*. Whether or not this wall hanging was made in France, as it certainly could have been, its presence in Normandy since medieval times has made it a part of the history of the needlework arts of France.

During the thirteenth century embroidery in France reached a level of sophistication in composition and technique that merited the title *peinture à l'aiguille* (needle painting). Indeed, the quality of the surface of these textiles was more spectacular than that of paintings of the day. Not many of these fine needle paintings are extant, for the reasons mentioned above and because many of these items were deliberately destroyed by their owners, who, caught up in the antiluxury teachings of powerful religious fanatics of the time, cast their most prized belongings, including precious embroideries, into street fires in an effort to purge themselves of the sin of vanity.

The most sought-after type of embroidery during the thirteenth century was known by a variety of different names including *opus anglicanum*, which it is still called today. These embroideries were created with a minimal repertory of stitches, including *underside couching*, split stitch, *point fendu*, *satin stitch*, and couching. England was the center of production for these exquisite textiles, and they were sought after by many foreigners, including the French. Church inventories indicate just how desirable these embroideries were. For example, the inventory of the Treasury of Saint Seige, of 1295, lists 113 items of opus anglicanum.[3] The chroniclers of the day also mention the interest of the papacy in obtaining these embroideries. Matthew of Paris in his *Historia Major* tells of the greed of Innocent IV (ruled 1243–1254):

About the same time [1246] my Lord Pope, having noticed the ecclesiastical ornaments of certain English priests, such as choral copes and miters, were embroidered in gold thread after a most desirable fashion, asked whence came this work? From England, they told him. Then exclaimed the Pope, "England is for us surely a garden of delights, truly an inexhaustible well; and from there where so many things abound, many may be exhorted." Thereupon the same Lord Pope, allured by the desire of the eye, sent letters, blessed and sealed, to well nigh all the Abbots of the Cistercian order established in England, desiring that they should be sent to him without delay, these embroideries of gold which he preferred above all others, and with which he wished to decorate his chasubles and choral copes, as if these acquisitions would cost him nothing. This command of my Lord Pope did not displease the London merchants who traded in these embroideries and sold them at their own price.[4]

Pope John XXII (ruled 1316–1334) received gifts of opus anglicanum including three embroidered copes from Queen Isabella, Walter Reynolds, archbishop of Canterbury, and John Hotham, bishop of Ely.[5]

But opus anglicanum was also made on the Continent. We know that there were organized guilds of professional embroiderers in Paris from the late thirteenth century. The statutes of 1292 tell us that there were two hundred embroiderers in Paris at the time, that they began their apprenticeship at eight years of age, did not work at night or on holidays, and that there were both male and female workers.[6] These embroiderers were relatively well paid and held in high regard by society, for they produced masterworks of the finest quality with the best grade of gold available. Their clients were the nobility and the church.

There is a small group of extant thirteenth-century embroideries that were probably made in France, although they have been published both as English and as French.[7] The cope in the chapel of St. John, in the basilica of Saint-Maximin, in the Var region of southern France, is one such embroidered garment. It was a bequest to the monastery of the predicant friars, Saint-Maximin, by Saint Louis of Anjou, the bishop of Toulouse. Other French embroidered textiles from this period include the cope of Montieramey in the cathedral treasury at Troyes, originally from the old abbey of Montieramey.[8] An orphrey from the chasuble of Manasses is in the collection of the Musée de Cluny, and an embroidered antependium is at the Musée Paul Dupuy, Toulouse. Thirteenth-century French embroideries are represented in Swedish collections as well. Two of the best-known French vestments were probably brought to Sweden around 1270 when Uppsala Cathedral was founded: the cope at the cathedral of Uppsala and the chasuble at the cathedral of Skara. The attribution of the embroidered cope at Uppsala to France is based on the fact that although opus anglicanum techniques are utilized, the style is closely related to French painting and the iconography includes French saints.[9]

Embroidery reached its peak both in terms of technique and in terms of drawing style in the fourteenth century. The quality of these embroideries aroused a greater demand from the patrons, and in turn more were produced. From the embroidery statutes of 1316 we know that there were 260 members of the embroiderers' guild of Paris and that there were just as many male as female members.

The guild continued to produce works for the

nobility and for the church, but they were not the only people creating fine embroideries.[10] As in previous centuries women embellished domestic textiles with their needlework, but the activities of all classes of women is better documented in the fourteenth century. Literary references as well as inventory listings offer a clearer idea of the kinds of embroidery produced at this time. Young girls made rugs, squares (*lacis*?) decorated with seed pearls, and embroidered tablecloths and towels for their trousseaus. They also made *chaperons*, *corsages*, and decorated sleeves of linen, silk satin, or *cendal*, in silver and gold thread. Like the young Aelis in the novel *L'Escoufle*, they also made small purses called aumôinières. Another group of women who created embroideries were those living in convents. The poet and writer Christine de Pisan (1363?–1431) wrote a poem after a visit to her daughter, who was living in an aristocratic convent, she remarked that the women there were making small purses ("boursettes"), decorated with birds of gold and silk, as well as belts of fine ornamentation.[11]

Many aristocratic women had embroiderers as members of their household staff. Madame de Courcy had eighteen horses in her stable, two tailors, and eight embroiderers at her hôtel in 1396.[12] This indicates that, because of the lavish ornamentation, it took much more time to embroider than to sew a garment or household furnishing fabric. While this may not seem incredible to us now, it should be noted that the costume of the fourteenth century was extremely elaborate. Johan Huizinga suggests that this excessive ornateness of clothing, especially of the period 1350–1480, signifies a decadence in art in which harmony and measure were replaced by lavish decoration and horror vacui compositions, and a time in which the true meaning of art and beauty was lost in a sensuality and greed that were perhaps best manifested in the dress of the time.[13] Much attention and time were spent on the decoration of sleeves. The sleeve was considered the most impressive aspect of male and female dress, since, being highly visible, it functioned as an overt symbol of one's wealth. It took as long as six months for an embroiderer to embellish a pair of sleeves because of the elaborate decorative schemes that were popular. For example, a sleeve belonging to the young Duc Charles d'Orléans (1391–1465) had the first verse of a

poem, "Madame, je suis tant joyeux," with the musical notations embroidered on it. The staves and the bar lines were of gold thread, and each note was of four pearls sewn en carré.[14] The inventory of household furnishings of Charles V (1337–1380) includes a number of different kinds of embroideries. The largest category of items is religious objects such as embroidered miters, chasubles, altar hangings, and other paraments. Five coverlets are mentioned, all described as being white and quilted. This is one of the earliest references in a French source to the embroidery technique of quilting.[15] Coverlets were made in France; for example, Marguerite de Lery made four thick coverlets for the king and duke of fine green and red velvet which were embroidered.[16]

Servants employed by noble households tried to impress their mistress or master by writing flattering verse that expounded on the virtues of the servants. References to embroidery are often found in these works, for instance: "je entends par coeur le petit poinct, le grand et celuy de Hongroie, en carreaux et tapisserie."[17]

The first half of the fourteenth century was the last glorious time for ecclesiastical embroideries, for during the second half of the century the decorative scheme of vestments became less excessive, due in part to the rich velvet fabrics then in vogue. Embroidery, instead of ornamenting the entire surface of copes, chasubles, and hangings was now confined chiefly to border areas such as the orphrey bands of ecclesiastical vestments. Although stunning liturgical embroidered works were still being created in France, the influence of opus anglicanum was waning.

The miter from the church of Sixt in the Haute-Savoie region of France is an outstanding example of the uniquely French approach to embroidery design during the first half of the fourteenth century (figures 46–48). The needlework is executed on a silk foundation with gold and silk polychrome threads. On one side of the body of the miter is the Annunciation to the Virgin; on the other side is the Coronation of the Virgin; Saints Peter and Paul are represented on the lappets. The *cartoon* for this work has been attributed to the workshop of Jean Pucelle, and dated to about 1340.[18] The sense of delicacy and refinement of the drawing and the influence of both Sienese and English figure styles are particularly

46 Miter: Coronation of the Virgin. First half of the fourteenth century. Gold and silk embroidery; silk ground. 11⁷/₈ x 11⁷/₈ (30 x 30). Eglise de Sixt, Haute-Savoie.

reminiscent of Pucelle's oeuvre. Certainly an elegant embroidery of this quality could have been designed only by a most skilled master.

How do we explain the presence of a miter of high artistic merit in a church of secondary importance? The miter was originally in the monastery of Sixt, which was a prosperous institution at the time of Abbé Hudric de Villars (served 1315–1343). The abbot was from a noble family and a friend of the counts of the dauphine; it was under his influence that such splendid objects, such as this miter, were made for Sixt. [19]

Another fine miter, which may be from the workshop of a Parisian miniaturist active prior to Jean Pucelle, is at the Musée d'Evreux, in Normandy. This miter, which belonged to Archbishop Jean de Marigny, is embroidered with polychrome silk threads in split stitch and gold couched threads on a green silk foundation. [20] In needle painting, the split stitch was particularly useful in the blending of colors, that is, in rendering the embroidered surface more painterly.

Secular needlework from the Middle Ages is less plentiful than that made for the church but there are several small aumônières in public and private collections of Europe and the United States. The cathedral treasury at Troyes houses three such embroideries. [21] Aumônières, or aumôsnières as they were spelled in contemporary documents, [22] had the same function as did pockets later; small purses, they were suspended from a cord wrapped about the waist and contained precious goods. Originally they were used to carry alms, but by the fourteenth century they were filled with gems, money, books of hours, and religious artifacts. Adapted from the Arabs, they were first referred to as "bourses sarrasinoises" or "sarrasinoises." There was a trade guild in Paris set up to make copies of the Asian bags, and statutes governing their manufacture exist from 1266–1299. Many literary references to these purses exist in which they are described as being made of both fancy silks and plain cloth, and one man boasts of owning many different kinds. [23]

The aumônière said to have belonged to Thibault IV (1201–1253) is made of canvas, and is embroidered with couched gold threads, silk polychrome threads in *raised work*, split stitch, and *appliqué* in green velvet (figure 49). The composition and

47 Detail of figure 46: lappets with Saints Peter and Paul.

48 Detail of figure 46: Angel (from the Annunciation to the Virgin).

sophistication of the design assures that this piece was created in the fourteenth century and therefore could not have belonged to the count and chansonnier Thibault IV.

The iconographic scheme of the embroidered aumônière is divided into two sections. The composition of the upper area consists of, on the right-hand side, a woman dressed in a long gown, with a cruciform at the neck, leaning against a mound, and in a gesture very typical of that found on fourteenth-century ivories, usually construed as symbolizing death. To her right a winged figure, in keeping with the pictorial traditions of the fourteenth century, probably a love goddess, leans toward her and gestures in her direction. The foreground is filled with a running vine pattern. An oak branch spreads over the background. In the center of the lower section is embroidered a heart on a table, with the blades of a saw going through it. At either side of the table a seated woman holds a handle of the saw. From above, the arm of a third woman emerges from a cloudlike form with an ax in her hand, which is pointed toward the woman to our right. In the foreground is a berry pattern; the background is filled with oak branches.

While the source for this iconography is possibly a poem or chanson of the Middle Ages, it might also be a unique interpretation of a contemporary attitude toward love that may not necessarily have been codified in the literature of the day. It is impossible to be entirely certain about the meaning of the story told here, as we see only two episodes. Although at first glance there seems to be a similarity between these scenes and those of an ivory casket in the collection of the Metropolitan Museum of Art that has vignettes from the story of the Châtelaine of Vergi carved on its faces, no substantial evidence points to a relationship between this story and the scenes depicted on the aumônière.[24]

Another aumônière from the treasury of the cathedral at Troyes is said to have belonged to Henri, count of Champagne (figure 50).[25] Of the same techniques and approximate date as the above, this work has a less enigmatic theme. The upper area of the purse shows a man with a cape, vest, and long gown placed against a ground of vine and leaf motifs. The composition of the lower area consists of a man, to the right, holding a spear that is pointed

at the head of an animal. To the left of this animal a woman is seated on a throne decorated with animal motifs. She holds a round object in her left hand. The ground is filled with a leaf and vine motif. This scene represents a chevalier defending the honor of his lady; the man pictured in the upper area may be the chevalier for whom the aumônière was made.

During the fourteenth century a unique French embroidery style emerged. The compositions and drawings utilized by the needleworkers were often created by the leading miniaturists of the day or by artists working in media other than embroidery. The stature of the embroiderer continued to rise, as can be noted by the number of people employed by the Paris guild, the references to the embroiderers' art in literature, and by the fact that their splendid handwork continued to satisfy the craving for art and beauty of both the nobility and the church.

In 1420, with the fall of Paris to Henry V of England, artistic centers began to develop in the Touraine, at Lille, Arras, and Dijon. The courts of Berry and Burgundy sponsored some of the most extravagant embroidery works of all time; most were designed by Flemish or Italian artists working at the courts, or by a collaborative effort between the two groups of artists.

Incredible technical achievements were made at this time, the most important of which was the *or nué* or shaded gold stitch that originated in the Netherlands. Couching the gold thread with polychrome silk threads produces a greater contrast between light and shade, which gives, in the silk threads, an iridescent shimmering effect. Embroidery of the fifteenth century reflected the new interest in painting, and it was the court painters who supplied the designs for major needlework commissions. The subject matter for the embroideries was no different from that of painting. For example, Jean, Duc de Berry (ruled 1401–1416), ordered several embroideries of the representation of the head of Veronica[26] in the manner of small panel paintings.

An orphrey from a chasuble in the collection of the Saint Louis Art Museum suggests this new situation (figure 51). A representation of the Crucifixion with Saint John and the Virgin, this embroidery is done with polychrome silk and silver and gold threads on a linen foundation. The elegant court style of this masterwork is apparent in the delicate

49 Aumônière. Fourteenth century. Couched gold threads, silk raised work, split stitch, and appliqué; canvas ground. 14½ x 12½ max. (37 x 32 max.). Cathedral Treasury, Troyes.

50 Aumônière. Fourteenth century. Couched gold threads, silk raised work, split stitch, and appliqué; canvas ground. 14½ x 12½ max. (37 x 32 max.). Cathedral Treasury, Troyes.

drawing and in the prominence of the line, the supple quality of the drapery, and the sweet sentimentality of the figures. Specific characteristics of this embroidery are related to the oeuvre of Jean Malouel (d. 1415), especially his *Pietà* tondo in the Louvre.[27] A clue to the way embroideries were produced is revealed by the inverted "N" of the inscription INRI above Christ's head. Although the composition of this work was provided by a master of the day, the embroiderer was probably illiterate and thus did not notice his or her error.

The Saint Martin roundels are some of the best-known embroideries of the fifteenth century (figure 52). These textiles, which as a group tell the story of the life of Saint Martin of Tours, total thirty in number and are divided among various institutions.[28] The gold threads are laid on the linen foundation and couched with polychrome silks. The figural areas are done in split stitch, with locks of hair usually in chain stitch, and borders of garments usually in cross stitch. The primacy of painting is again evident in the fact that the embroidery stitches follow the lines of the drawing, in the way that pen or brush strokes would be executed. These roundels, which date from about 1420 to about 1440,[29] are in the Franco-Flemish style with a strong tie to the school at Dijon.[30]

Such splendid objects could have been ordered only by an extremely wealthy person for an extremely important purpose. Philip the Good or any of the illustrious members of the Burgundian court had the means to request such a project. Perhaps the commission was for a church dedicated to Saint Martin, or for Pope Martin V (ruled 1417–1431). While it is impossible to be certain about the commission, it is likely that the roundels, each one representing one episode from the life of Saint Martin and thus each needing to lie flat and to be clearly readable, were part of a liturgical hanging, such as an altar frontal.[31]

But not only the court of Burgundy sponsored such elaborate embroideries. In 1462 King René d'Anjou gave a magnificent set of paraments to the cathedral at Angers. They were embroidered by Pierre de Villant, René's court painter and embroiderer, who was from Avignon.[32] Charles VII was also a great patron of embroidery, and many of the

51 Orphrey from a chasuble: the Crucifixion. Ca. 1450. Couched silver and gold threads, herringbone pattern for the cross, checkerboard background, satin stitch and split stitch for the figures; linen ground. 40½ x 23 11/16 (105.4 x 60). Saint Louis Art Museum.

most important needleworkers of the day were at his court in Bourges.

Tapestries were much desired during the fifteenth century, so much so that the embroidery technique was used to create large needlework pictures in imitation of woven tapestries. Also at this time the term *tapisserie* begins to appear in inventories describing embroideries. Many of these large works were produced in convents, and many hands worked on one composition, resulting in less than professional craftsmanship.

52 Embroidered roundel: The Bishop of Cologne Hears Angels Singing as the Soul of Martin Goes to Paradise. Franco-Flemish. Ca. 1420–1440. Silk and silver-gilt foil, split, chain, cross stitches, and couching; canvas ground. 6³/₄ x 6³/₈ (17 x 16.3). Walters Art Gallery, Baltimore.

Embroidery in France during the Sixteenth Century

Embroideries of the fifteenth century were strongly influenced by the Flemish artists so popular at the court of Burgundy and also by Italian art in general. The Italian influence was stronger still in the sixteenth century. While unique paintings or drawings had often been the source for embroidery designs in the previous century, the perfection of the printing process changed this situation in the Renaissance. Embroiderers relied primarily on prints for their ideas, circulated throughout Europe, and on pattern books, first published in Germany and Italy during the first half of the century. This new system accounts for the fact that it is often difficult to identify securely the provenance of a specific embroidery of this time, since the same prints and pattern books were available in Italy, France, and most of the Continent, and, generally speaking, the same stitches and fabrics were used.

Technically, the beginning of the sixteenth century was a time when *cutwork* and *reticella* needlework developed into lace (figure 53). The sumptuous or nué shading was gradually replaced by raised work, that is, by designs in relief, by all-silk compositions, and, at the end of the century, by all-wool or wool and silk embroideries. Among the reasons for these changes was the fact that the increase in demand for secular works prompted embroiderers to seek less time-consuming methods. Also, the kinds of works commissioned were much larger, generally speaking, than those of the previous century. Pragmatically speaking, these materials were less costly than silk. It was fashionable during this time to cover walls with large hangings and to own elaborate sets of bed hangings that consisted of many panels of fabrics such as valances, curtains, coverlets, canopies, and wall coverings.

The subject matter of the embroideries was still chiefly religious, but mythological subjects begin to appear due to the influence of the neoplatonic thought of the Italian Renaissance as well as the general influence of humanism. There was also a purely decorative style that consisted of interlaced band or strapwork; these types of designs were often executed in appliqué. However, by far the most important French decorative genre of the sixteenth century is the School of Fontainebleau style.

François I (ruled 1515–1547) called Rosso Fiorentino and Primaticcio from Italy to be in charge of the decorations at the Château of Fontainebleau. The style that emerged there can be characterized as a unique interpretation of classical forms with a refined vocabulary of floral and antique-type ornamentation, and it is epitomized by the art work in the Galerie de François I at the château. Textiles of this school are rare, and they are mostly true peintures à l'aiguille in that they are essentially pictures designed by the most important painters at Fontainebleau quite literally translated into silk and metal. The best known of these extant pieces is an embroidered corporal box with a scene of *The Descent from the Cross*, in the collection of the Musée de Cluny. Previously attributed to Primaticcio, the design for this masterwork has most recently been ascribed to perhaps Jean Cousin or L. Penni.[33] While the specific provenance of this embroidery is not known, the

53 Cushion cover. French or Italian. Sixteenth century. Reticella, cutwork with embroidery; linen. Open at one side. Tassels, hand braided; linen. 14³/4 x 18¹/4 (37.46 x 46). Private collection.

fine draftsmanship and execution indicate that it was probably commissioned for a most important church or for a private chapel of an illustrious noble.

A group of raised work pictures including the *Penitent Magdalene* in the collection of the Metropolitan Museum of Art, *Adam and Eve* in the Musée de Cluny, an unnamed design in the Cooper-Hewitt Museum, and a panel at Compiègne may have been produced in France, though the Cluny piece is after a print by the Flemish artist J. Sadeler, after Martin de Vos.[34]

Sixteenth-century needlework pieces were often created to complement an overall decorative scheme. Embroidered panels were set into furniture (such as *La Chasse du cerf* and *Le Combat de l'ours* in the Musée Historique des Tissus, dating to the reign of Henri III and illustrating scenes from the life of his father, Henri II) and were applied to large panels of velvet or other woven fabrics that were made into bed hangings, banners, or other ceremonial

GENESE XLIX.

Ses douze enfans Ifraël fit venir,
Pour leur donner fa benediccion
Auant mourir : & leur tems à venir
Leur reuela, par fa prediccion.

G 4

54 Bernard Salomon. Plate 12, from *Quadrins historique de la Bible* by Jean de Tournes (Lyons, 1560). Woodcut.

55 Embroidered picture: Jacob and His Children. 1566. Silk, wool, and metal, long and short stitches, double running backstitch, couching, split stitch; silk ground. 37⅞ x 65 (96 x 165.1). Collection Michael Hall, Jr., Esq.

textiles. For example, an imperial bed dating to the time of François I is described as having embroidered decorations with designs based on Raphael compositions.[35] A large embroidered scene of *The Rape of the Sabines* (figure 56) is in the collection of the Museum of the Palazzo Venezia, Rome. Executed on a linen foundation with silk and metal threads in the or nué technique, this piece was once applied to a large red velvet fabric that served as the backpiece ("dossier") of a baldachin. It dates to the last quarter of the sixteenth century, to the period of Henri II.[36]

An unpublished masterwork in the School of Fontainebleau style is in the collection of Michael Hall, Jr. (figure 55). The superb composition is done with silk, wool and metal threads, in *long and short*, split, *double running backstitch*, and couching stitches, on a silk foundation. The fantastic grotesque motifs, which are clearly the focal point of this embroidery, may have been adapted from the oeuvre of Jacques Androuet du Cerceau (1510–1584), and the garlands of fruit, the braids, and the twisted designs seem to

be lifted from the ornamentation at Fontainebleau. There is also a close relation between this embroidery and the tapestries designed for the Galerie de François I at Fontainebleau.[37] However, the source for the composition of the central medallion is a work by the Lyonese artist Bernard Salomon. Lyons was at this time an artistic center and home to many designers and embroiderers. Salomon's prints were utilized by the enamel painters of Limoges, by majolica workers, for tapestries as well as embroideries, and for furniture. The Salomon woodcut for this medallion is taken from the *Quadrins historiques de la Bible*, first published in Lyons in 1553, illustrating a scene from the Old Testament, Genesis 49. 1–2, "And Jacob called unto his sons, and said, Gather yourselves together, that I may tell you that which shall befall you in the last days. Gather yourselves together, and hear, ye sons of Jacob; and hearken unto Israel your father" (figure 54). This panel is dated 1566 in two places, and partially visible inscriptions appear in the cartouches.[38] Perhaps this embroidery was part of a series that decorated an entire room or perhaps it was created as a unique panel. Its relatively good condition may be attributed to the fact that this piece, like many other embroideries that required a great amount of time to complete, never fulfilled its original purpose. In this case, it might have been made to hang above a doorway at Fontainebleau, where from 1566 on, the court was not in residence.[39]

This panel was undoubtedly produced in a professional workshop, the precise location of which remains a mystery. The grotesque style that dominates it was popular throughout France, and Salomon's prints were widely available. We do know that in the recent past it belonged to the Count and Countess de Castellan, of Paris.[40]

Three embroidered valances of the same period, with grotesque decorations, are in the collection of the Musée Historique des Tissus (two) and the Metropolitan Museum of Art (figure 57). The Metropolitan panel illustrates the following scenes from Ovid: the Rape of Europa, the Metamorphosis of Actaeon, Jove Appearing to Semele, Pyramus and the Death of Thisbe, and the Legend of Salmacis. These scenes are also based on prints by Salomon,[41] but the background of these three pieces is not covered with embroidery as is Mr. Hall's panel.[42]

56 Embroidered picture: The Rape of the Sabines. Sixteenth century. Silk and metal, long and short stitches, double running backstitch, couching, split stitch; linen ground. 71 x 60 (178 x 152.4). Museo del Palazzo di Venezia, Rome.

57 Valance, detail, panel with scenes from Ovid: Pyramus and the Death of Thisbe, detail. 1560–1570. Silk. Primarily split and stem stitches; silk satin-weave ground. Overall: 14³/4 x 78 (37.46 x 195). Metropolitan Museum of Art, Rogers Fund, 1956.27.

A southern Mediterranean influence can be seen in two large embroidered hangings now at the Musée de la Renaissance, Château d'Ecouen, outside of Paris. Each panel has at its center a roundel with a scene from the life of Saint Catherine, *The Mystic Marriage of Saint Catherine* (figure 58), based on a print after Primaticcio, and *The Angels Lifting the Body of Saint Catherine*, based on a print by the Flemish engraver Cornelius Cort, dated 1575.[43] But the splendor and spirit of these embroideries come from the fanciful fruit, floral and animal decorations that fill the horror vacui composition. It is these motifs that offer clues to the function and provenance of the textiles.

The layout of the pattern indicates that *calques* were used to mark the decorative units. The symmetrical composition was accomplished by flipping over the pattern pieces; in places where the same image appears twice, such as the bound bouquets in the upper right and lower left areas of the *Mystic Marriage*, the same calque was used in each location.

Executed on a heavy linen canvas foundation, the embroidery is done entirely in brightly colored silks with a few areas embroidered over with metal. The stitches utilized are split stitch and stem stitch, but, as is the case with most large-scale pieces of the period, most of the ground is filled with long satin stitches in order to lessen the physical weight of the hanging and to economize on the expensive silk threads. The ubiquitous religious symbols of these embroideries, the grapes and wheat of the Eucharist, the varieties of lilies referring to the Virgin, and the ripened fruit, a symbol of the church as the seeds are united in one body, all surrounding a scene from the life of Saint Catherine of Alexandria—in female hagiography second in importance only to the Virgin—point to the probability that these hangings were destined for the walls of a convent dedicated to this saint. It is, therefore, not unlikely that the panels were made by members of that religious community. This theory is entirely plausible also in terms of the overall quality of the decorative style of the drawings,

58 Wall hanging: The Mystic Marriage of Saint Catherine. Based on a print by Giorgio Ghisi, after a painting by Primaticcio, ca. 1560. After 1560. Silk, split stitch, long and short stitches, satin stitch, and metal; linen ground. 194⁷/₈ x 157¹/₂ (495 x 400). Musée de la Renaissance, Château d'Ecouen.

which is not nearly so elegant as related compositions of Paris and Lyons. In fact, these hangings are most closely linked stylistically to a series of large hangings illustrating scenes from the life of Saint Teresa now in a convent in the Midi.[44]

In 1553 Catherine de'Medici (1519–1589), daughter of Lorenzo II de'Medici, was married to the dauphin who became Henri II in 1547 (ruled until 1559). Her influence in the field of embroidery was great: she was responsible for introducing a variety of domestic needlework techniques to the women of France, including those related to costume, some of which fall under the category of lace. The legendary comment that she worked at her embroidery every evening after dinner is substantiated somewhat by the vast quantities of textiles listed in the inventory made at the time of her death.

When Catherine arrived in Paris she brought her personal embroiderer, Federico Vinciolo, with her. Besides Vinciolo's well-known pattern book of 1587, his expertise in the field of embroidery awarded him the exclusive right to manufacture the large starched ruffs that Catherine made fashionable in Paris. Moreover, his most important contribution was in educating the French in specific Italian openwork, cutwork, and darning techniques. Items of these kinds became prevalent in the late sixteenth century and are listed in household inventories. At the time of her death Catherine de'Medici left many examples of *carrez de gaze*, a term referring to the type of *buratto* work pictured in the frontispiece to *Les Singuliers et Nouveaux Pourtraicts* (figure 59).[45] Other embroideries mentioned in Catherine's inventory include quilted coverlets[46] and pieces of *point de Hongroie*, lacis, and *canvaswork*.[47]

In fact, the last decades of the sixteenth century saw the increase in the number of works in both *gros* and *petit point*, most of which were worked with all-wool or wool and silk threads. (However, Claude de France, wife of François I, created her famed canvaswork embroideries in the first half of the century. Reknowned as these works were, they seem to have been isolated examples rather than representative of general habits of needleworkers.) This phenomenon was prevalent in France, Flanders, Scotland, and England. The French upbringing of Mary, Queen of Scots, included schooling in

dressmaking and embroidery. When she returned to Scotland she still imported starched ruffs and embroideries from France and was probably responsible for introducing petit and gros point *tent stitch* canvaswork to her native country.[48]

Characteristic of this genre of needlework is the heavy, relatively open-weave foundation fabric and the predominant use of the tent stitch. The overall appearance of these works is that of a verdure tapestry, with the shallow rendering of space, borders done in the style of tapestry weavings, and the surface texture of a woven textile, giving the impression from a distance that these textiles were, in fact, products of the loom. In many contemporary inventories these pieces were referred to as tapisseries, a word that was synonomous with needlework compositions, usually tent stitch pieces on canvas

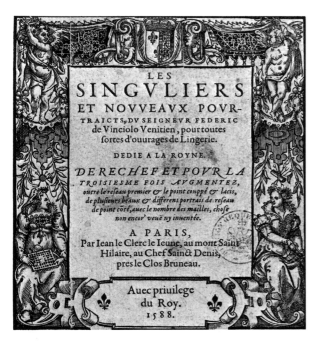

59 Frontispiece from *Les Singuliers et Nouveaux Pourtraicts* by Federico Vinciolo (Paris: Jean le Clerc, 1588).

60 Embroidered picture: Calvary, with legend: *Parce Domine Parce Populo Tuo Quem Redemisti Pretioso Sanguine Tuo Nec in Eternu[m] Iras Caris Nobis. O Bone Jesus Esto Nobis Jesus* 1594. Below, heads of adversaries of Christ: Pilate, Herod, Judas, Caie, Anne. 1594. Silk and gold threads, tent, split, long and short stitches, and couching; linen ground. 23 x 18 (58.4 x 45.7). Metropolitan Museum of Art, Gift of Irwin Untermeyer, 1964.

61 Follower of Jean Clouet. François I. The embroidered surface ornamentation on the king's garment is typical of the lavish costumes worn at his court. Louvre, Paris.

ground. The subject of the canvaswork embroidery is usually mythological or religious (figure 60). Although many of the extant pieces are of a professional quality, others were made at home by ladies and their attendants, though a household embroiderer was often employed to supply the patterns. The relatively large number of extant canvaswork suggests that these items decorated the home.

But embroideries of the period were not made exclusively by women. The Paris guild was still going strong with an equal number of men and women employed, both of whom had the same rights and the same salary—an amazingly progressive situation by today's standards![49] There were semiprofessional workshops in Paris such as that of La Trinité, which was founded by Henri II to provide apprenticeships for poor children. These youngsters made tapestries, *passementeries*, and embroideries,[50] but very little is known about the specific works produced there.

Furnishing fabrics and small squares used for domestic decorations were not the only items to receive elaborate attention by the needleworker. Fashions in France during the Renaissance followed the Italian style and were characteristically full of surface ornamentation (figure 61). As was the custom in the Middle Ages, sleeves were still the main vehicle for embroidery, though coats, dresses, and bodices were all worked with painstaking attention to detail and often incorporated pearls and precious gems in their designs.

If the sixteenth century was a time when the stylistic and technical influence of Italy was the strongest, from the School of Fontainebleau to Catherine de'Medici and Federico Vinciolo, the greatest innovation throughout Europe was the way in which artists worked, due to the circulation of prints. More important, the pattern book led the way to the democratization of embroidery, since a wide spectrum of designs became available to a greater number of women and young girls.

The Seventeenth Century

Another Medici queen, Maria de'Medici, who married Henri IV in 1600, employed many embroiderers, such as Nicolas de Vaudray, Jean Boiteaux, Jean Michel, Louis Bucherot, and Nicolas Desforges. Pierre Dupont, founder of the Savonnerie factory, who designed needlework in addition to doing carpet weaving and illumination, may have been responsible for the design of an embroidered coffer now in the collection of the Louvre (figure 63).

Maria de'Medici was more fond of other lesser-known embroiderers whom she employed. The queen liked embroideries in the oriental style and employed a group of women from the East to create this type of work. These young women were known at court as "les filles greques" but only two, Adrienne Théodorant and Marguerite Thamary, were actually from Greece. Of the others, Anne Ossache, whose name appears often in contemporary documents, was Turkish of Polish origin; three unnamed women were from Turkey. The painter François Benard supplied some of the designs that were worked by these women.[51]

In 1606 Henri IV increased the number of court

62 Israel Silvestre (1621–1691). Le Nôtre's design for the garden at Vaux-le-Vicomte, in the "en broderie" style, detail. Engraving.

embroiderers from 160 to 360, granting some of them apartments in the Louvre.[52] Of these artists perhaps none was as well respected as Pierre Vallet, whose pattern book of 1608, *Jardin du roi très chrétien Henri IV*, which contained mostly floral designs, was immensely popular. In 1650 it was reprinted,

63 Coffer with the monogram of Maria de'Medici. First quarter of the seventeenth century. Silk and gold threads, tent stitch; canvas ground. 17 x 23 ½ x 10 (43 x 60 x 25). Louvre, Paris.

with additional designs by Vallet and Jehan Robin, herboriste du Roy, who organized the first Jardin des Plantes in France. The relationship between gardens and embroideries was close at this time, as many people visited gardens for inspiration for their needlework compositions. Beyond this fact is the similarity of terminology; a certain garden style was called *en broderies* because of its curvilinear rinceaux that looked as if they were embroidered on the earth. The gardens by Le Nôtre at Vaux-le-Vicomte (figure 62) and those at Versailles come to mind, as well as those at smaller chateaus such as Meudon, Saint-Cloud, and Champs-sur-Marne.

Pattern books and gardens were not the only sources for botanical designs. Prints by major French artists such as Jean-Baptiste Monnoyer (1635–1699) were organized in books to serve the decorative arts. Monnoyer's *Livres de plusieurs vases de fleurs faicts d'après le naturel*, *Livres de plusieurs paniers des fleurs*, and *Livres de plusieurs corbeilles des fleurs* were all influential in embroidery designs of the late seventeenth and early eighteenth centuries. M. Jacques's

Nouveau livre de fleurs is another collection that was utilized by needleworkers. Jean le Pautre made several compilations of garden designs, most notably *Les Plaisirs de l'isle enchantée* (Paris, 1673), and a plate from this book is the source for an embroidery in the Metropolitan Museum of Art. Some of the drawings by Georges Baussonet, an artist from Reims, were specifically marked "pour la broderie" and are among the most delightful of all French designs.[53] In seventeenth-century France embroidery design was at last in the hands of French artists, with Charles Le Brun, Jean Bérain, and Daniel Marot responsible for some of the great masterworks of the century.

The Baroque Style and Louis XIV

The splendor of the baroque style as set by the court is epitomized in the large furnishing fragment now in the collection of the Wadsworth Atheneum (figure 64). No longer concerned with scientific renderings of perspective and anatomy, the new exuberant floral style was flat and full of the energy that characterized the spirit of Versailles. The strapwork that frame the composition are representative of the oeuvre of Daniel Marot. This piece is part of a large decorative hanging and may have been part of a set of bed hangings or any of the vast variety of wall ornamentations so typical of the era.

Louis XIV's building campaign set the vogue for large-scale embroidered panels to embellish the walls of the new palaces, especially Versailles. Hangings were changed often, with the season or at the whim of the owner, and they were transported from hôtel to château and back again. Four large panels from the Hôtel Sully, Paris, now in the Musée de Cluny, are perhaps the greatest extant civil furnishing fabrics from the first half of the seventeenth century, and they indicate that Henri IV was himself a strong patron of embroidery. Originally seven panels, the wool, silk, and metal pieces from the Hôtel Sully were based on drawings by Gaignières and, like the Ecouen pieces, are designed in a tapestrylike format with a border on all sides.

Women continued to be practitioners and patrons of the needlework arts. Madame de Rambouillet, who had an enormous influence on the language and taste of the time, was also a sophisticated interior designer as can be seen from the three inventories from the Hôtel de Rambouillet. Chairs were covered with point de Hongrie and tapisserie à l'aiguille, the latter in a floral design on a brown ground. A set of bed hangings is described as black silk satin ground with floral embroidery in polychrome silks.

But it was for Versailles that the most sumptuous textiles were commissioned. Indeed, the embroideries associated with the court are praised as the most beautiful of all time, but this glorious era ended with the close of the reign of Louis XIV. Embroidered textiles of all kinds were displayed throughout the palace from the throne room to the private chambers of the members of the royal family. The Sun King commissioned incredible state embroideries, such as the well-known bed hangings by Delobel. Less known are the items ordered for the Cabinet du Dauphin. The room, decorated by the famous furniture maker Boullé, was a showcase for upholstery fabrics. Four armchairs and six folding chairs were covered with embroidered pictures in *point satiné* with gold and silver, representing the Elements, the Seasons, and other subjects. Other chairs had fabric embellished with point satiné in blue and silver "in the manner of porcelain." In the room was a three-piece hanging made of *tapisserie de petit point*, with gold and silver, representing fables and scenes from Ovid's *Metamorphoses*. Another hanging of *tapisserie de broderie*, of gold and silk, was made of eight pieces. Each piece contained nine octagons; some displayed the arms of Navarre and others displayed stories from the Old Testament.[54]

The high demand for civil embroideries resulted in a flowering of semiprofessional workshops that served both royalty and the church. The daughters of the school of Saint Joseph de la Providence in Paris produced more works than any other atelier. Girls from noble but impoverished families were sent to the school for religious education, "to sew and to make linens, shirts and tablecloths," and to perform other domestic duties. In 1681 Madame de Montespan became director of the community, but in 1691 she announced that she was leaving the court because of the king's preference for their mutual friend Madame de Scarron. Shortly thereafter, in 1693, Madame de Montespan established herself at Saint

64 Large fragment, detail. Ca. 1710. Silk, metal, and chenille embroidery; silk satin-weave ground. 43 x 150 (109 x 381). Wadsworth Atheneum, Costume and Textile Purchase Fund, 1983.7.

65 Allegory of Spring and Air. Design attributed to Charles Le Brun. Late seventeenth century. Wool and silk; linen ground. 140 x 77 (355.6 x 195.6). Minneapolis Institute of Arts, Gift of the Lowry Estate, 15.210.

Joseph's. The embroidery workshop made many items for the church, such as a complete set of paraments in couched and raised work of metal threads with flowers in *point d'Espagne* for the Jesuits at the Collégiale Royale de la Flèche, and for Versailles, some of these covered with pearls. The pieces manufactured there enjoyed widespread recognition as masterworks and were considered by some to be

of a more outstanding quality than those made at the royal workshop.[55]

The Manufacture Royale des Meubles de la Couronne, also called Les Gobelins, was established by Colbert in 1667, and Charles Le Brun was named director. Although Les Gobelins is perhaps best known for the tapestries produced there, many of the same artists who designed tapestries designed embroideries as well. The importance of needlework at the time was manifested by the fact that under Le Brun, a director of embroidery, Philbert Balland, was appointed. There was apparently a pleasant working relationship between Saint Joseph's and Les Gobelins, as there was an exchange of personnel on both the private and professional levels. Philbert Balland married a retiree from Saint Joseph's, and Marthe Le Roy, who was director at Saint Joseph's, employed some of the artists who worked for the crown. Items for Versailles were designed by François de Troy le père and made at Saint Joseph's.[56]

The parallel relationship of tapestry and embroidery designs produced during this time is best illustrated by hangings in the collections of the Metropolitan Museum of Art, Versailles, and the Minneapolis Institute of Arts (figure 65). An *Allegory of Spring and Air* is a panel designed in the same way as a tapestry of the period, with trompe-l'oeil borders and with a composition full of trophies, flowers, and the architectural element of the molded straight bar or bandwork so typical of Le Brun's taste. In fact, an unfinished drawing for this work in the collection of the Louvre indicates that Le Brun made at least the preliminary plans for this monumental piece.[57] The theme reflects one of the favorite subjects at the court; as we have already seen with regard to items in the Cabinet du Dauphin at Versailles, upholstery panels depicting the Seasons and the Elements were prominent. Here both a Season and an Element are simultaneously the subject, with obvious symbols of both filling the composition. The flowers, watering cans, and astrological signs of Taurus, Aries, and Gemini allude to Spring; a zephyr accompanies Spring in the central area; and the oboe, recorder, bagpipe, all wind instruments dependent on air, are incorporated into the central floral grouping. The technique used here, a canvaswork type, was the method usually employed with these large tapestrylike hangings. Indeed, to the nonspecialist these textiles appear woven, which is characteristic of canvaswork.

Another center for needlework was the religious community of Saint Cyr in Noisy, set up in imitation of the community of Saint Joseph in Paris. The works produced at Saint Cyr were not so professionally rendered as those of Saint Joseph's. Nonetheless, Saint Cyr was patronized by the crown and employed a staff of embroiderers including Lhermot and Lhermot fils, De Reynes, Simon Fayet, Christolphle and Michel Gasse, François LaRoche, and Alexandre Lallemant. The court provided pensions for retirees who were relatively well paid denoting their respected status in society. Certain artists who worked at Saint Cyr were specialized; for instance, Fayet was paid for his figures for embroidery while Balland was paid for landscape designs.[58]

Men were involved in embroidery not only in a professional capacity. The Marquis de Vernins spent several years in bed engrossed in his canvaswork stitchery.[59] Powerful religious authorities such as Mazarin and Richelieu decorated their abbeys with Parisian embroideries, and their wardrobes were even more elaborate than those at court. Mazarin's inventory, dated 1653, lists linens and chapel decorations, most of which were of fancy silks without any surface ornamentation. However, one chasuble is described as having both front and back embroidered in "point royal" (definition unknown to editors) of gold and silver threads with a floral and foliage pattern. These embroideries were executed on Chinese taffeta.[60]

The church in general actively commissioned embroideries as it had for centuries, to decorate cathedrals and other buildings and for use in processions. Many antependia, or altar frontals, of the late seventeenth century, symbols of the sacrament of the Eucharist, received special attention from the designers and embroiderers and were particularly stunning (figure 68). Covered with glass beads, the surface of this antependium catches the light, mesmerizing the viewer. Months of tedious stitching were required to create this masterwork.[61]

Methods of working were still basically the same as they had been with many embroidery compositions based on printed sources. A hood from a cope (figure 66) in the Saint Louis Art Museum depicts a

66 Hood of a cope: The Agony in the Garden. Eighteenth century. Silk, satin stitch, double running backstitch, couching; silk satin-weave ground. Border of silk, metal threads, and chenille. 22 x 21 (56 x 53.3). Saint Louis Art Museum, Gift of Mrs. William A. McDonnell.

67 Game sack. Seventeenth century. Silk and metal threads; silk velvet-weave ground. Diam. 9 (23). Collection of Maurice Deramaux.

68 Antependium, detail. Late seventeenth or early eighteenth
century. Glass beads, wool, silk, parchment wrapped with silk;
linen ground. 35 x 71 (89 x 180). Collection of Daniel and
Josiane Fruman.

scene from the Passion of Christ, *The Agony in the Garden*. The design is possibly an interpretation of a print by an unknown artist from a book entitled *Abrégé de la vie et passion de Jésus Christ*, published in Paris in 1663.[62]

It has been stated over and over again in publications that the church received from wealthy parish members many of the rich fabrics that decorated the nave, choir, side chapels, altar, and other areas. But specific references are rare. In her will of 3 June 1628 Anne Molé, a noblewoman from Brittany, made lengthy notations about the destination and utilization of her belongings. To the church of Notre Dame de Liesse she left six hundred livres for a chasuble; to her church, Saint Jean, she left six hundred livres to help them make a tapisserie; to the poor of the Hôtel Dieu de Paris she left six hundred livres to buy sheets and coverlets. But, most telling of all, she left to the church of Saint Croix de la Bretonneyre her set of bed hangings of green velvet, which consisted of three valances, the bedcover, and the baldachin of green velvet; three large curtains and two *bonnes graces* of green damask, all edged with passamenteries of green silk, to make a parament for the altar. She specified that her insignia and that of her husband be embroidered together somewhere on the sacred cloth.[63] Thus, private citizens continued to contribute needlework to the church, even after death.

Sumptuary laws have always tended to make fashionable that which they prohibit, and this was the case during the reign of Louis XIV. Although only the elite few could wear gold and silver embroideries, the plethora of extant waistcoats and jackets using these materials indicate that these items were owned by a broader section of society. The Sun King established a court style of dress that kept the embroiderers busy. The three-piece suit for men consisting of the "gilet" or waistcoat, jacket, and breeches was covered with opulent needlework. In 1664 Louis XIV created the "justaucorps à brevet" covered with gold and silver embroidery, which only a select number of gentlemen were allowed to wear.[64] The excessively elaborate dress of the male at the court of Louis XIV was often satirized by Molière. In *L'Ecole des maris*, which was first performed in 1661, Sganarelle bemoans the ribbons, ruffles, and laces he must wear in order to impress the ladies. Joking about the edicts made to limit luxury in dress Sganarelle says to himself, "Je voudrais bien qu'on fît de la coquetterie, comme de la guipure et de la broderie."[65] Men also had embroidered accessories such as special bags associated with the sport and ritual of the hunt that was so much a part of the life of a nobleman. A game sack (figure 67) is typical of the genre. Almost always made of cut velvet and decorated with gold or silver embroidery in relief, the game sack was used to hold monies and small playing pieces such as dice, which were used in the card and die games popular at the time. Game sacks, which were kept in the studies of illustrious men, were made primarily in France but were exported throughout Europe.[66]

Women's dress was less a showcase of stitchery, as their garments were usually made of patterned silk with lace as the primary vehicle of surface ornamentation. A few items were decorated with needlework, such as the bodice (figure 69) and *camisole*. Embroidered camisoles were ordered from Provence. As early as 1606 embroidered tops from the south of France were considered desirable lingerie pieces to own. Orders were sent especially to Toulon, in maritime Provence, for items made in the delicate *boutis* technique.[67]

An unusual petticoat of pink silk satin embroidered in a quilting stitch, with images of the Sun King depicted throughout, is in the museum of Château-Gombert, just outside of Marseilles, further indication of Provence's position as a quilting center in the seventeenth century.

Women also had a variety of bags and purses. Marriage purses and lovers' purses were embroidered with cupids, mottoes, and the ubiquitous heart motif. Other types of purses were made for giving as gifts. As was the case with men's bags and purses, France was the main producer of these items but they were the rage throughout Europe.[68]

Embroidery during the Eighteenth Century

The Régence (1715–1723), that transitional period between Louis XIV and Louis XV is characterized by fanciful types of ornamentation that point in the direction of the rococo. Some of the most wonderful ecclesiastical vestments of all time were created

69 Ant. Masson, after Petrus Mignard. *Marie de Lorraine, Duchesse de Guise, Princesse de Joinville*. 1684. Engraving. Wadsworth Atheneum, Gift of Forsyth Wickes, 1960.321.

clear picture of how embroideries were made and the kinds of stitches that were most popular at the time. Monsieur Rivet also worked for the court, producing silk needlework portraits after paintings.[71] The Lyonese artist Philippe de Lasalle (1723–1805) designed both silk weavings and embroideries. Lyons at this time was a major textile center; in 1778 an astonishing six thousand embroiderers lived there.[72]

In Paris the embroiderers' guild was as busy as ever. More and more people were embroidering as a leisure activity, and for young women being talented with a needle was synonymous with being well educated. In Lyons, fine embroideries were produced in the workshops, such as the reknowned vestments made for the coronation of Emperor Karl VII Albrecht (1697–1745).

Pattern books were still a major means of transmitting embroidery patterns to the masses, and several books produced in France indicate that these publications were now of a more specific nature. There were books of patterns for waistcoats and other articles of dress, such as patterns published by the embroidery firm Saint Ruf, in the Cooper-Hewitt Museum (gift of the Misses Hewitt, 1920), or

during the regency of Philippe d'Orléans, such as a stunning example from the Fruman collection (figure 71).[69]

The large-scale somber-toned embroideries of the Louis XIV style were replaced by small-scale, delicately rendered, more subtle designs that were confined, in general, to borders. However, the needlework of the eighteenth century is considered to be the more aesthetically pleasing, as it was executed by a new professional class of designers whose heightened sense of composition was aided by a wide range of needlework techniques, which helped to achieve masterful results.

Among the embroiderers who worked for Louis XV none is as well known as Charles Germain de Saint-Aubin, his official designer and embroiderer. His *L'Art du brodeur*,[70] published in 1770, offers a

70 Man's cap. 1700–1750. Straw embroidery; silk ground. H.: 6 (15.2). Museum of Fine Arts, Boston, Gift of Philip Lehman in memory of his wife, Carrie.

71 Chasuble. Régence period (1715–1723). Silk, metal threads, and paillettes, in satin stitch, couching, raised work; linen ground. 42 1/2 x 28 1/3 max. (108 x 72 max.). Collection of Daniel and Josiane Fruman.

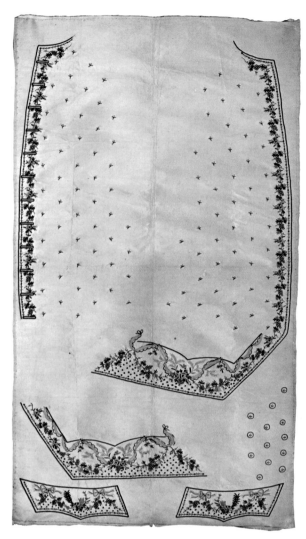

72 Uncut waistcoat. Eighteenth century. Silk, tambour work; silk ground. 41 x 22 (103 x 56). Collection of Maurice Deramaux.

those at the Musée de la Mode et du Costume and the Metropolitan Museum of Art.[73] A newly available item was the predrawn and sometimes partially embroidered canvaswork panel that was purchased by less ambitious individuals.

The vocabulary of stitches most frequently employed in eighteenth-century embroideries is described in *L'Art du brodeur*. According to Saint-Aubin, couching was, "generally speaking," the most popular stitch.[74] *Guipure*, that heavy thick stitch that Sganarelle could not bear to wear, was in 1770, mostly used for the decoration of horse

trappings! *Gaufrure*, a stitch with a wafflelike appearance, embroidery with *paillettes*, and embroidery with glass beads and with an array of strange materials such as fur, chenille, and straw (figure 70) were also popular. Although Saint-Aubin believed that needlework on canvas was inferior to other kinds and was taken up by religious communities because it was easy to do, his prejudice is unfounded if one considers the hangings produced at Saint Joseph's. He also relegated chain stitch and tambour work to a lesser category because these kinds of embroideries were made mostly by ladies in their spare time.[75] One need only to examine the many articles of clothing (figure 72), the hangings (figure 73), and other extant material to realize the prejudice of his statement.

Marseilles embroidery is a type of all-white needlework in which layers of fabric are stuffed and embroidered. The ground is covered with little *knots*. This type of stitchery, which probably did originate around Marseilles, was practiced in northern Europe as well as in France. The boutis technique is not mentioned in Saint-Aubin, or perhaps he considered it a subgroup of Marseilles embroidery. Often done with all-white fabric but also executed in other colors (figure 75), boutis work was indigenous to maritime Provence and Arles. Made of cotton fabric and stitched with cotton threads, boutis was such a tedious process that the work was usually confined to articles of children's clothing such as christening dresses and caps or other small personal items such as the coverlet pictured in figure 74. It was also used to decorate women's skirt hems and camisoles.[76]

Large quilted coverlets of printed and painted fabrics which were very popular in France are listed in many household inventories. These items entered ports at Marseilles, Bordeaux, and elsewhere, and were then quilted. Many of the quilted (piqúe) coverlets were handled by the merchants in Provence, such as the Wadsworth Atheneum's stunning example (figure 74), which was marketed by the Orange company, Party & Cie.[77]

Another typical eighteenth-century type of needlework, done with all-white fabric and thread, was referred to as *whitework*. Often called lace because of the sheerness of the ground fabric and because of the fact that it was used primarily for

73 Wall hanging or bed cover. Eighteenth century. Silk and metal threads, tambour work, couching, raised work; silk satin-weave ground. 68 x 58 (172.7 x 147.3). Wadsworth Atheneum, Gift of Misses Amy Ogden and Emma Avery Welcher, 1973.135.

74 Coverlet. Party & Cie., merchants of Orange. Ca. 1755. Chinese export silk, painted, quilted, for the French market. 119⅝ x 118 (304 x 300). Wadsworth Atheneum, Costume and Textile Purchase Fund, 1982.50.

75 Coverlet. Provence, first half of the eighteenth century. Cotton thread, cord, and fabric, boutis work. 46⁷/₈ x 29¹/₂ (118.9 x 75). Wadsworth Atheneum, Costume and Textile Purchase Fund, 1982.49.

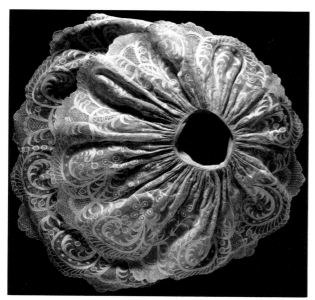

76 One of a pair of engageantes. Eighteenth century. Cotton, so-called Dresden type of whitework; linen ground. Diam. 17³/₄ (45). Collection of Maurice Deramaux.

lappets, *engageantes* (figure 76), and other intimate accessories, it is actually a combination of *deflected element* and embroidery techniques. Whitework, which was manufactured in Saint Quentin, Nancy, and elsewhere in the Lorraine, was made popular by Marie Antoinette.

Embroidery *en rapport* was used extensively for civil uniforms and court presentation costume (figure 77). Based on chivalric orders of the Middle Ages, organizations such as the Order of Saint-Michel, founded in 1469, the Order of Saint-Lazare et de Notre Dame du Mont Carmel, founded in 1291, and the Order of the Saint-Esprit, established in 1578 by Henri III, were much like today's Rotary or Lions service organizations. The Order of the Saint-Esprit was one of the most distinguished of these confraternities, and the king was its grand maître.[78]

Coronation dress was the most lavish of all civil vesture. Although the style of these costumes had been set in 1179 by Louis VII, they became particularly lavish from about 1750 onward. The purpose of these robes, capes, and other regal items was to raise to the highest level of splendor both the occasion and the individual wearing the clothing. It is no accident that these items bear a strong resemblance to liturgical vestments, as the sovereigns of the period thought of themselves as secular dieties. This phenomenon became most pronounced during the reign of Napoleon I.

77 Cloak of the Order of the Saint-Esprit. 1750–1777. Embroidery en rapport, paillettes, canetillé, gold and silver threads; silk woven ground. Musée de la Mode et du Costume de la Ville de Paris, Gift of Baron Edmond de Rothschild.

From Napoleon I to Napoleon III

The simple geometric forms and designs in the antique style that emerged in the 1750s were established throughout Europe by the late 1770s. For embroidery this decorative style was a disaster since the sparseness of ornamentation meant less employment for needleworkers. The decline in the membership of embroidery guilds began to reverse itself after Napoleon became first consul in 1799 and emperor in 1804, as he was responsible for the grandiose commissions of hangings and other decorative fabrics for his palaces. The empire style promoted by Napoleon and Josephine and their architects was a combination of neoclassical designs coupled with Napoleonic symbols such as bees, laurel wreaths, initial N's, and égyptiennerie. An embroidered panel in the collection of the Saint Louis Art Museum (figure 78) is a splendid example of the new dimension that embroidery design assumed during the reign of Napoleon. Probably designed by J. -D. Dugourc (1749–1825) for the palace at Saint-Cloud, the gouache preparatory drawing for this panel is in the collection of Tassinari & Chatel, Lyons (figure 79).[79] According to information passed down orally in the company, the gouache design represents only part of a larger decorative scheme. The decor may have been consecrated to the glory of the imperial family: Malmaison recalls Napoleon; the port, the king of Holland; Vesuvius, the king of Naples.[80] Two panels of the same overall composition but depicting the goddesses Athena and Demeter, in the Metropolitan Museum of Art, would seem to corroborate this idea.[81]

Napoleon refurbished not only his palaces but his entourage as well. Official costumes were full of raised embroidery motifs en rapport as well as in other techniques. The engraver Chaillot created a collection of embroideries for military uniforms, scabbards, uniforms for administrators of military hospitals, and a model for uniforms of the Officiers de Santé with designs that are still associated with the medical profession today. The most sumptuous fabrics were those created for the coronation ceremonies of Napoleon and Josephine and later Marie Louise, as can be seen in this engraving of the emperor, after François Gérard (figure 80).

78 Embroidered panel: Mars. Design attributed to J.-D. Dugourc. Ca. 1800–1810. Satin stitch, appliqué, tambour work, chenille, painted; silk ground. 99 x 35 (251.4 x 88.9). Saint Louis Art Museum.

Josephine wore a muslin gown with gold embroidery. The original sketch and fabric sample for her ensemble are pictured here (figures 81 and 82). The peculiar style of the time for women to wear lightweight sheer open-weave fabrics of this type with heavy gold embroidery illustrates the fact that looking fashionable came before comfort and common sense.

Marie Louise, whom Napoleon married in 1810, may not have been the fashion innovator that Josephine was, but she was a skilled painter and needleworker. Besides the influence of Napoleon's court two other great changes affected the fate of embroidery design of the first half of the nineteenth century. First, in the first two decades of the century needlework became, as it is still today, chiefly a female occupation. Second, the industrialization of the textile arts and specifically the perfection of embroidery machines toward 1835 resulted in the disappearance of the master embroiderer. Together these two circumstances produced inferior designs,

which ultimately led to the crafts revival movement and to art nouveau.

Women were trained from childhood to make embroidered samplers of the alphabet, mottoes, and landscapes. Early in the century pattern books were again utilized as the primary source for needlework information. These books were made for young girls and contained a series of exercises and designs as well as technical diagrams (figure 83). Girls learned a more limited repertory of stitches than had their ancestors. They began by practicing gros point on canvas, then proceeded to satin stitch, gros and petit point combined on canvas, work with gold and silver threads, and work with chenille.[82] Items they decorated included muslin dresses, upholstery, and a variety of linen fabrics. The sampler in the Philadelphia Museum of Art is a well-executed example of a pictorial sampler (figure 84). Less formal compositions are more common, such as the counted stitch and *darning stitch* sampler pictured here (figure 85).

79 Project for a wall hanging for the palace at Saint-Cloud. Design attributed to J.-D. Dugourc. Nineteenth century. Gouache on paper. 17½ x 14 (44 x 35.5). Collection of Tassinari & Chatel, Lyons.

80 Auguste-Gaspard-Louis Desnoyers, after Gérard. Napoleon Le Grand. Steel Engraving, ca. 1805. Wadsworth Atheneum, Bequest of Albert R. Hatheway, 1939.397.

81 J.-F. Bony. Sketch for the coronation dress of Josephine. 1804. Gouache on paper. 11 ½ x 10 ¼ (28.8 x 25.9). Musée Historique des Tissus, Lyons.

82 J.-F. Bony. Embroidery sample for the coronation dress of Josephine. 1804. Metal, silk, paillettes; silk ground. 21 ¼ x 15 ¾ (54.6 x 40). Musée Historique des Tissus, Lyons.

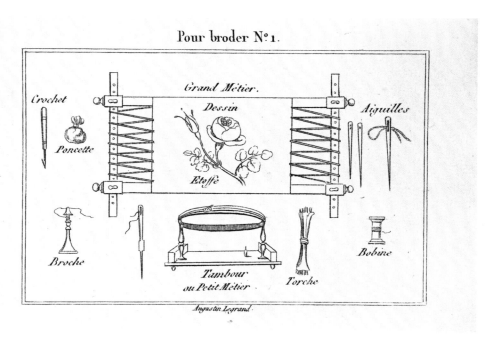

83 Page from *Petit Nécessaire des jeunes demoiselles*, "Pour broder No. 1," by Augustin Legrand (Paris, 1819).

84 Sampler, "A L'amitié Filiale." Mid–nineteenth century. Silk and wool, tent and cross stitches; canvas ground. 18 x 22 (45.7 x 56). Philadelphia Museum of Art, Given by Pet Incorporated.

85 Sampler. Mid–nineteenth century. Silk, linen, and wool embroidery, counted stitch and darning stitch; linen ground. 23½ x 22⅞ (59.7 x 57.9). Collection of Maurice Deramaux.

86 Louis Lafitte. Sketch of an embroidery design for the uniform of the Grand Ecuyer. Undated.
Watercolor on paper.

The empire style was still in vogue during the restoration monarchy (1815–1830). However, in 1820 Louis XVIII issued an official declaration stating a change in the dress of royal administrators and other persons employed at court. Article 5 of this document stated that "the embroideries will be in gold, with a standard design for all the ranks and it will be framed by a *baguette* pattern (figure 87), the highest ranking officials will wear embroideries on the collar, the cuffs, the pockets, and the borders of the suit. The embroidery on the pockets will be decorated with three fleurs de lys."[83]

Once this decree was made it created the need for new embroidery designs. Louis Lafitte (1770–1828), who was appointed designer to the king during the restoration, made a series of engravings of embroidery designs for court garments. Figure 86 shows one of his color sketches of a pattern for the uniform of the Grand Ecuyer (Master of the Horse).

There were not many embroidery machines in France until the Second Empire, but machine-made items were imported from Switzerland and England.[84] Some machine-embroidered textiles of a superior quality both technically and artistically were manufactured in Paris under Napoleon III. The chain stitch cushion cover by J. d'Antoines Broderies (figures 88 and 89) is made of high-grade silk with a simple revival design; the reverse side indicates the path of the machine and the level of mechanical virtuosity of which these machines were capable.

87 François le Villain (active early nineteenth century). Embroidery design for a court uniform. 1820.

89 Detail of reverse side of figure 88.

88 Cushion cover, with label: "J. d'Antoines Broderies, 64, rue des petits champs, Paris. Silk, machine embroidery; silk satin-weave ground. Undated. 24 x 22 (60 x 55). Musée des Arts Décoratifs, Paris.

90 A. Coudev. Proposal for a set of vestments: Adam and Eve in the Garden of Paradise. 1844. From *Exposition de l'industrie française* (Paris, 1844), not paginated.

The third quarter of the century was not a period of grandeur for the art of embroidery. At the numerous industrial arts exhibitions textiles with embroidered ornamentation tended to look like very close duplicates rather than interpretations of Byzantine, Gothic, or Renaissance fabrics. A proposal for a set of vestments for the archbishop of Paris by A. Coudev (figure 90) depicts the sort of theme popular with the Paris guild, *Adam and Eve in the Garden of Paradise*. The border areas of the cope and hood are covered with motifs adapted from Gothic architecture. Although it is not known whether or not these vestments were ever made, two of the most prominent members of the Paris guild, Hubert-Menage and André Kreichgau'er, were involved with similar projects.[85] Church embroidery of midcentury was executed in high and low relief with metal threads and with the technical virtuosity associated with the Middle Ages, reflecting the concerns of the artist-craftsman movement.

Fashions of the Second Empire were extravagant and lavishly embellished, but, with the exception of men's uniforms and other ceremonial costumes, the

91 Marie Louise of Austria. Table covering, detail. Ca. 1830–1840. Silk, double running backstitch, chain stitch, knots, appliqué; wool ground. 78³/4 x 59 (200 x 150). Museo Glauco–Lombardi, Parma.

92 Woman's jacket, detail of right front. Pont l'Abbé, Brittany,
late nineteenth century. Silk, chain stitch, satin stitch; wool
ground. Costume Institute of the Metropolitan Museum of Art,
Gift of Mr. Henry Frankel, 1949.

decorations of the fabrics were those of lace or accessory objects, instead of embroidery stitches. The one great exception to this was the extensive use of whitework techniques, a style that the empress Eugénie consciously established in emulation of the taste of Marie Antoinette. Whitework decorated cuffs, collars, hems, handkerchiefs, and all sorts of linens. The entry on embroidery in an encyclopedia of 1867 lists five different kinds in this category: "broderie de feston," which is the main stitch of "broderie anglaise"; "broderie en reprise," for lightweight fabrics; "broderie de dentelle," made on net or gauze or other fabrics by pulling threads of the fabric and by complicated appliqué work; and "broderie au plumetis."[86]

Another woman who had an influence on embroidery styles was Marie Louise (1791–1847) who at the fall of Napoleon I was made duchess of Parma, where she created most of her masterful needlework compositions. During the restoration she commissioned splendid banners in her favorite colors, sky blue and silver. Although it is possible that she embroidered some of these herself, the heavy silver ornamentation was probably applied by a person of greater physical strength.[87] Marie Louise's most important works date from the 1840s, and the table cover illustrated here represents her finest accomplishment (figure 91). Stitched onto a black wool foundation fabric, the delightful floral and bird pattern is done with silk threads in satin stitch, double running backstitch, chain stitch, knots, and appliqué. The cover is edged on all four sides with a hand-knotted fringe that she also made.[88]

Although Marie Louise designed most of her embroidery pieces, she also purchased patterns, which were distributed by firms such as Vallardi, Dubreuil, and Corplet in Paris, as well as from Vienna and Berlin, the latter having emerged as a major center for a type of canvaswork still called *Berlin work*. But like many women of the day she also looked to the plethora of ladies' magazines for embroidery designs. Publications such as *Sajou* and *Journal des Demoiselles* included pictures and directions for the fabrication and decoration of wool slippers, cushion covers, chair seats, napkin rings, and a wide variety of purses. Most of these magazines advocated canvaswork techniques, and the vast majority of the designs were to be carried out with all-wool or wool and silk threads. Unfortunately, these designs were rarely of an outstanding quality, and the extant body of domestic needlework from the Second Empire indicates how urgent was the need for new ideas and for a new vocabulary of forms.

By far the most exciting embroidery of the third quarter of the nineteenth century was not that of Paris or other cities but that of the provinces, where regional traditions flourished, particularly in the north and south. With a limited repertory of stitches provincial needleworkers created sophisticated compositions that remained virtually the same throughout the entire second half of the nineteenth century and the first decades of the twentieth century. A young woman's jacket from Pont l'Abbé in Brittany (figure 92) illustrates a powerful geometric design in satin stitch and chain stitch. The various lengths and positions of these stitches give the appearance that many different embroidery techniques have been utilized.

The Midi is another area rich in regional needlework traditions, especially quilting. But this technique was also employed as far north as Normandy, as can be seen in a woman's cap (figure 93) from the Metropolitan Museum of Art. The simple elegance of this cap is a result of both quilting and openwork techniques.

Embroidery in France followed a continuous path of development from the Middle Ages until the close of the Second Empire, at which point the traditions of the past were no longer adequate to provide artists and designers with the means to express their contemporary views.

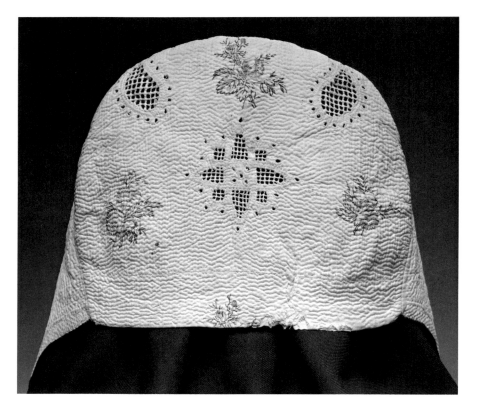

93 Woman's cap. Normandy, late eighteenth or early nineteenth century. Cotton, quilting and openwork; printed cotton ground. Costume Institute of the Metropolitan Museum of Art, Gift of Mrs. Edna G. Duschnes, 1942.

Notes

The bibliography for this essay starts on page 186.

1 The term "gold and silver thread" is used throughout this essay to refer to the presence of one of any combination of the following techniques: vellum or another skin coated with gold leaf and then wrapped around a silk or linen thread; flat gilt or silver gold wire; wavy or looped silver and/or gold strips. At different times, particularly after the Middle Ages, other metals were mixed with gold and silver. For a thorough discussion of metallic threads in general, see the technical appendix, "Analysis of Precious Metal Threads," in Peggy Stoltz Gilfoy, *Fabrics in Celebration from the Collection*, Indianapolis Museum of Art, 1983.

2 *Trésors des eglises de France* (1965), p. 52.

3 Brel-Bordaz, *Broderies d'ornements liturgiques XIII–XIVe siècles* (1982), p. 16.

4 Young, "Opus Anglicanum" (1971), p. 291.

5 Christie, *English Medieval Embroidery* (1938), p. 3.

6 Lespinasse, *Histoire générale de Paris* (1892), II: 162–163.

7 The French provenance of these embroideries is the subject of a forthcoming article by Monique Toury-King and Donald King; information communicated by letter, 8 June 1982.

8 Both Troyes and Montieramey are in the department of the Aube in the Champagne region of France.

9 Geijer, "Medieval Textiles in the Cathedral of Uppsala, Sweden" (1954), pp. 4–5.

10 Lespinasse, II: 163.

11 Christine de Pisan, *Oeuvres poétiques*, vol. 2; cited in Laigle, *Le Livre des trois vertues de Christine de Pisan* (1912), pp. 189–190.

12 Laigle, p. 208 n. 1.

13 Huizinga, *The Waning of the Middle Ages* (1954), p. 249.

14 Quicherat, *Histoire du costume en France* (1879), p. 254.

15 Labarte, *Inventaire du mobilier de Charles V, roi de France* (1879), p. 392.

16 Farcy, *La Broderie du XIe siècle jusqu'à nos jours* (1890), I: 75.

17 Laigle, p. 356.

18 See Beaulieu and Bayle, "La Mitre épiscopale en France" (1973), p. 76; *Les Fastes du gothique* (1981), p. 399; and Meiss, *French Painting in the Time of Jean de Berry* (1967), p. 100.

19 See Beaulieu and Bayle, "La Mitre épiscopale en France," p. 76.

20 For an illustration of this miter the reader is referred to Schuette and Muller-Christensen, *The Art of Embroidery* (1963), pls. 219–220.

21 Other important aumônières or fragments of aumônières are in the collections of the Metropolitan Museum of Art, New York; the Musée Historique des Tissus, Lyons; the Musée de Cluny, Paris; the Museum für Kunst und Gewerbe, Hamburg; and the Cathedral Treasury at Sens.

22 Laborde, *Glossaire français du Moyen Age à l'usage de l'archéologue et de l'amateur des arts* (1874), p. 144.

23 Ibid.

24 Information from telephone conversations and meetings with Laila Gross, Department of English and Comparative Literature, Fairleigh Dickinson University, Teaneck, New Jersey.

25 Ledit, "Le Trésor de la Cathédrale" (1975).

26 Guiffrey, *Inventaires de Jean duc de Berry* (1894–1896), I: lxxii.

27 *The Waning Middle Ages* (1969), pp. 92–93.

28 Two are at the Cloisters, New York; two at the Cooper-Hewitt Museum, New York; one at the Walters Art Gallery, Baltimore; four in the Robert Lehman collection, Metropolitan Museum of Art, New York; one in the collection of Alastair Bradley Martin; and twenty at the Musée Historique des Tissus, Lyons. There are also four embroideries that deal with the same subject but differ stylistically and technically from the others; two in the Musée Historique des Tissus, one at the Cloisters, and one in the collection of Countess Margit Batthyany.

29 See Freeman, *The Saint Martin Embroideries* (1968), pp. 82–92, and Eisler, "Two Early Franco-Flemish Embroideries" (1967), p. 580.

30 Freeman, p. 72.

31 For a complete discussion of these embroideries see Freeman, *The Saint Martin Embroideries* (1968).

32 New documents have been found that point to more extensive embroidery works by Pierre de Villant, which are to be the subject of an article by Francesca Weinmann.

33 See information in the files at the Musée de Cluny, and *L'Ecole de Fontainebleau* (1972), p. 428. For an illustration of the corporal box see Bridgeman and Drury, *Needlework* (1978), p. 89.

34 Illustrations of some of these works can be found in the following publications. *The Penitent Magdalene* is reproduced in Hackenbrock, *English and Other Needlework*, (1960), pl. 169, where it is incorrectly described as Italian. The Cooper-Hewitt embroidery is pictured in Sonday and Moss, *Western European Embroidery*, (1978).

35 *Richesses tirées du trésor de l'Abbaye de Saint Denis, du Garde-Meuble de la Couronne . . . pour servir au sacre de . . . Louis XVI* (1775), pp. 3–5.

36 *L'Ecole de Fontainebleau*, p. 429.

37 For illustrations of the tapestries designed for the Galerie de François I at Fontainebleau, see ibid., figs. 443–448.

38 The inscription in the upper cartouche is not legible; that of the lower cartouche reads, "SPE ET SILENTIO."

39 *Fountainebleau. Art in France, 1528–1610* (1973), II: 10. The author does not intend to propose that this embroidery was destined for the palace at Fontainebleau, but rather simply to point out the coincidence of the dates on the panel with the date the court was not in residence.

40 Information from Michael Hall, Jr., of Michael Hall Fine Arts Incorporated, New York. A paper label attached to the wooden stretcher on which the textile is mounted reads, "Madame la Comtesse Jeanne de Castellan."

41 Standen, "A Picture for Every Story" (1957), pp. 165–175.

42 Analysis of the fiber content of these threads was carried out by the Textile Conservation Workshop in South Salem, New York. Despite variations in the hue, causing some of the background stitches to appear to be cotton, all are silk.

43 Taburet, "Les Broderies du Château d'Ecouen" (1979), pp. 38–39.

44 Ibid., pp. 39–40.

45 Bonaffe, *Inventaire des meubles de Catherine de Medicis en 1589* (1874), pp. 106–107.

46 Ibid., pp. 58–61.

47 Ibid., p. 106.

48 For a detailed account of the embroidery activity of Mary, Queen of Scots, and her debt to France, plus a bibliography of previous studies on this subject, see Wardle, "The Embroideries of Mary, Queen of Scots" (1981).

49 Lespinasse, p. 164.

50 Monique Toury-King, in Bridgeman and Drury, p. 56, and Farcy, p. 81.

51 Battifol, "Marie de Medicis et les Arts" (1906), p. 242.

52 Farcy, p. 435.

53 The prints can all be found in the albums at the library of the Union Centrale des Arts Décoratifs, Paris. A large collection of drawings by Georges Baussonet is in the Bibliothèque Municipale, Reims.

54 Guiffrey, *Inventaire général du mobilier de al couronne sous Louis XIV* (1885), II: 399.

55 Weigert, "La Retraite de Mme. Montespan" (1949), p. 214 n. 2.

56 Ibid., p. 214.

57 Coen, "The Duc de Crequy's *Primavera*" (1964), p. 23.

58 Guiffrey, *Comptes* (1881–1901), II: 100.

59 Saint-Simon, cited in Standen, "A Boar Hunt at Versailles" (1963), p. 144.

60 Aumale, *Inventaire du Cardinal Mazarin* (1861), p. 228.

61 For a complete explanation of the technique of beadwork or *broderie en jais* see Saint-Aubin, *The Art of the Embroiderer* (1983), p. 112.

62 Most French images of the Agony in the Garden are less complex than those of Italian or Northern origin. For an example of a seventeenth-century French representation of this scene, see *Abrégé de la vie de Jésus Christ et passion* (1663), pl. 12: *Jesus prie au jardin*: Cabinet des Estampes, B.N. cote: Rc.2/in 4° in. 40.

63 Cabinet des Manuscrits, B.N., Cinq-Cents Colbert, 81, fol. 341–345.

64 Delpierre, "Un Album de modèles pour broderies de gilets" (1956), p. 1.

65 *L'Ecole des maris*, 1.9 (Paris, Chez la Veuve Duchesne, 1775), p. 27.

66 Foster, *Bags and Purses* (1982), pp. 12–13.

67 Malherbes, "Lettres à Peirsec" (1862), p. 413.

68 Foster, pp. 12–13

69 A chasuble of the same period, style, and technique is in the collection of the Embroiderers' Guild, Hampton Court Palace, East Molesey, Surrey, England, no. 126.1982. Special thanks to Rosemary J. Ewles, curator, for bringing this vestment to my attention.

70 The Los Angeles County Museum of Art has published an English translation of this book, cited in the bibliography under Saint-Aubin. Readers are referred to this source for further technical information.

71 Saint-Aubin, p. 49, n. 1.

72 Scheuer, "*The Elegant Art of Embroidery*" (1983), p. 89.

73 Delpierre, "Album des modèles," p. 9.

74 Saint-Aubin, p. 41.

75 Ibid., p. 54.

76 *Le Costume traditionnel à Marseille* (1980), n.p.

77 For a history of this firm see Little, "Signed French and Spanish Chintzes" (1938).

78 Delpierre, *Uniforms civils* (1982–1983), p. 13.

79 Tassinari & Chatel was found by Camille Pernon in 1762. The major textile designers of Lyons worked for this prestigious firm, including Dugourc.

80 Letter to Marianne Carlano from Bernard Tassinari, 17 November 1983.

81 Metropolitan Museum of Art, 23.82.1 and 23.82.2.

82 Legrand, *Petit Nécessaire* (1819), p. 12.

83 *Règlement arrêté par le Roi* (1820), p. 3.

84 Ikle, *La Broderie mécanique 1828–1930* (1931), pp. 9–45.

85 This plate appears in the catalogue *Exposition de l'industrie française* (1844), without any commentary.

86 *Grand Dictionnaire universel du XIXe siècle* (1867), p. 1299.

87 Carlano, in *Curiosità di una reggia Vicende* (1979), p. 216.

88 Information from archives of the Museo Glauco-Lombardi, Parma; Marie Louise's personal papers, not inventoried.

The Lace Industry ❋ Anne Kraatz

I consider lace one of the prettiest imitations ever made of nature's fancy; indeed, lace forever evokes in me those incomparable designs which the branches and leaves of trees embroider on the sky and I believe that its invention could not have, in the human spirit, a more gracious or more precise origin.

Gabrielle Chanel in *L'Illustration*, 29 April 1939

Lace makes a relatively late appearance in the world of decorative arts, compared to weaving or embroidery, which have been practiced since earliest antiquity. It is probably not until the 1540s that *whitework* embroiderers, who may have lived in Venice or its province, realized that the technique of withdrawing threads from a woven cloth, covering the remaining ones with buttonhole stitches, and building patterns from the gridlike formation could be taken a step further. The foundation could be built "into the air" by constructing the gridlike network of threads on a temporary support, here a piece of parchment on which the design had been traced. The name *reticella*, which means literally a gridlike network, refers to the original drawnthread technique, while *punto in aria*, or "stitch in the air," applies to the further development outlined above. Real needle lace, therefore, as opposed to whitework embroidery, is executed according to this particular technique.

The development of *bobbin laces* seems to have begun at the same time as that of needle laces, in the 1540s. It is generally accepted that this development occurred contemporaneously in Italy and Flanders. Certainly the early presence of bobbin laces in Italy is attested to by numerous references found in inventories of the time, notably in Venice. Unlike needle laces, however, the invention of which must have been due to individual initiative, bobbin laces probably evolved from the traditional craft of plaiting–weaving practiced by the corporations of *passementiers*, members of which were soon to demand for themselves the privilege of bobbin lace manufacture.

The State of the Industry from the 1540s to the 1650s

The manufacture of whitework embroidery and needle laces seems at first to have been confined to the households of aristocratic ladies, who took part in it alongside their attendants and servants, and to the workrooms of convents where well-to-do young girls as well as poor ones prepared their trousseaus. No doubt some of this latter work was done for resale to the outside, but the quantities do not seem to have been significant at the beginning. That lace was a genteel occupation is obvious from the dedications of pattern-book designers to queens, noble ladies of high rank, and to "virtuous and genteel women" in general. This remained true until the end of the seventeenth century, when the making of lace fell out of favor with the upper classes. In all probability there was a needle-lace cottage industry in France from the 1550s or 1560s on, but specific traces of it are lacking.

Bobbin laces are a different matter. Designs for bobbin laces were included in pattern books such as *Le Pompe*, an anonymous publication printed in Venice in 1557, and in Cesare Vecellio's *La corona delle nobili et virtuose donne*, where in the 1617 edition the title specifies that many of the patterns "may be used for bobbin work as well."[1] However, bobbin lace was soon claimed as a privilege by the corporations involved for the following reasons. The bobbin technique was possibly more difficult to master, than that of the needle, which was at first an extension of embroidery—a skill that every woman of any condition was taught in her early years. Furthermore, bobbin lace required too many tools—a pillow, bobbins, pins. Finally, the technique had evolved from the weaving and plaiting in which the various *passementerie* makers were already engaged.

An examination of the statutes and edicts concerning the corporation of the *tissutiers–rubaniers* and of the passementiers[2] of the city of Paris reveals that the manufacture of *passements*, a word synonymous with lace at that time, must have been rather extensive in France in the late sixteenth and early seventeenth centuries, or there would have been no point in issuing such specific regulations about their manufacture. For example, the statutes of the tissutiers–rubaniers and the letters patent confirming them signed by Henri III in 1585 indicate that members of the corporation were entitled to make all sorts of passements described in specific detail such as "passemens à deux cordons cablez et non cablez . . . à dantelles . . . à carreaux."[3] Most of these passements were made out of silk thread with silver and gold *cannetillé* "fine as well as false." Indeed, the use of flax or woolen threads in combination with silk was severely prohibited.[4] The manufacture of such passements must have been lucrative, for the corporation of tissutiers–rubaniers tried several times, without success, to retain its exclusive privilege. Instead, another corporation, that of the *passementiers–boutonniers* of the city of Paris, was also granted the right, confirmed by Henri IV in 1594, to make "cordons à quatre fuzeau, passemens à jour et dentelle."[5] In 1612 the parliament of Paris reiterated that the members of the corporation could continue to manufacture not only silk laces but also "toutes sortes d'ouvrages de passements à dentelle de fil blanc, . . . et de toutes autres sortes de fil . . . de couleurs."[6]

Paris was not the only city to produce bobbin laces. In 1570 a Parisian mercer, Pierre Cramoisy, sold "dentelles à jour façon de Rouen" and "passements à cueur de Rouen."[7] according to the inventory of his goods taken after his death. From what is known of the later importance of the Normandy lace industry, it is not surprising that Rouen should have been an early producer.

The region of Le Puy, in the Auvergne, is reputed to have been one of the first in France to develop bobbin lace making on a fairly extensive scale, but to my knowledge specific records are lacking regarding the exact date at which the industry there became more than an individual pastime or a conventual enterprise of little importance. As early as the third quarter of the sixteenth century, however, Le Puy lace makers, working outside the framework of any corporation, probably manufactured sizable quantities of bobbin laces out of linen and also out of gold and silver thread. By 1640 the production occupied many hands there, for when the parliament of Toulouse, a larger city to the south, issued a prohibition against the wearing of laces "either of silk or of thread together with gold or silver ones," it caused much consternation in Le Puy and neighboring towns among the lace makers. The ordinance was eventually rescinded, thanks to Père François Regis, who went on to become the patron saint of lace makers in the area.

Aurillac, another city in the Auvergne, must also have been producing laces at an early date, both needle and bobbin, made out of silver and gold thread in particular, for its products were well known in the first half of the seventeenth century. Indeed, a royal lace manufactory was established there in 1665 rather than in Le Puy.

The innumerable sumptuary laws promulgated during the first half of the seventeenth century all make mention of passements and laces, either to prohibit their importation into France if they were foreign, or to restrict their dimension to a reasonable width of "two fingers" if they were domestic. Fortunately perhaps for the French lace industry, such laws were largely ignored.

In summary, it may be said that lace was indeed manufactured on an industrial scale in France by the mid-seventeenth century. This manufacture concerned primarily bobbin laces made of silk or gold and silver thread and produced by members of various corporations in and around Paris and by individual lace makers throughout Normandy and Auvergne, their products being destined for the time being to local or regional consumption. Needle-lace manufacture remained for a long time a widespread but unorganized occupation, which did not develop to the cottage industry stage until the second quarter of the seventeenth century.

Stylistic Aspects of Lace from 1540 to 1650

As with all other European countries, France's laces are inseparable in their early days from those of Italy. This remained true in terms of technical and stylistic developments until the second decade of the seventeenth century, when the influence of Flanders predominated for a time.

The model books for whitework embroidery, darned netting, and lace patterns that were to contribute so much to the success of lace techniques were first published in Venice in the early sixteenth century. The existence there of a well-established tradition of the sumptuary arts, and the presence of numerous artists trained in designing for the decorative arts, combined with the extensive publishing activities of the Republic to produce an extremely large number of pattern books. These were widely distributed as well as copied throughout Europe.

Federico Vinciolo, the most celebrated of these pattern designers was, not surprisingly, Venetian, but his book *Les Singuliers et Nouveaux Pourtraicts . . . pour toutes sortes d'ouvrages de lingerie* was first published in France, in 1587, by the Parisian printer Jean Leclerc.[8] In 1587 alone there were three editions of Vinciolo's book, followed until 1658 by some fourteen others, nine of them in Paris, another in

94 Franz Pourbus II. *Maria de'Medici*, detail. Ca. 1609. Oil. Louvre, Paris. The queen wears a collar and cuffs of reticella and punto in aria needle lace.

Lyons. The book was dedicated to the dowager queen of France, Catherine de'Medici who, it is said, had encouraged Vinciolo to establish himself in Paris and liked to work at needlepoint and darned netting herself.

Vinciolo's may be one of the best-known pattern books, along with Cesare Vecellio's, but its style is essentially the same as that of all the other books of this kind published at that time. The designs proposed are endless variations on a geometric theme, prismatic in the constant splitting and reuniting of their basic elements. The enclosure of these elements within a rigid frame, here a gridlike system of squares, is obviously a result of the technique. Drawn-thread embroidery could produce foundation elements crossing at right angles only. Perhaps not surprisingly, when the new punto in aria method

was developed, it was first perceived as a quicker and more rational way of achieving the same result, for it saved one the tedious step of removing threads from a piece of cloth someone had taken the trouble to weave. Hence, the delay in taking advantage of the operational freedom afforded by the new technique. Indeed, it took nearly sixty years, from the 1540s to the 1600s, before the possibilities of free-form designs of punto in aria began to be exploited in full.

Geometric elements have universal appeal; they are also almost completely devoid of personality. This makes it extremely difficult if not impossible to identify with certainty the provenance of laces produced in the style of the pattern books. This is especially true in France. There are no dated samplers of the period in French public collections to compare with finished pieces. In addition, laces in

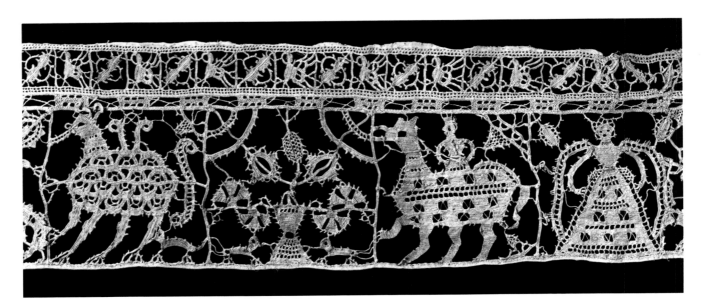

95 Lace band. Western Europe (possibly France), ca. 1590–1610. Linen. Reticella and punto in aria needle lace with bobbin-made plaiting. 3 1/2 x 57 1/2 (8.9 x 146). Private collection, Paris.

French portraits of the time do not exhibit any particular characteristics that would make them specifically and recognizably French.

It is not until the ascension to the throne of France of Maria de'Medici in 1600 that a difference becomes slightly perceptible. In her portrait painted around 1609 by Franz Pourbus II, now in the Louvre, the queen is wearing a lace collar held rigid at the back of her neck probably with the help of a brass binding-wire frame (figure 94). The pattern of the lace is here indicated with perfect exactness. Its design, at least on the inner part, can be traced to the influence of Cesare Vecellio's book *La corona delle nobili et virtuose donne* rather than to Vinciolo's Parisian patterns. The border of the collar instead makes good use of the resources of the punto in aria technique in its treatment of flowers, here daisies and fleurs de lys, which are free of any geometrically restricting frame. The gracefulness of these flowers contrasts in a novel and felicitous manner with the rigorous precision of the rest of the collar. The whole has "the dry perfection that is characteristically French."[9]

Is such a dry perfection then to be the criterion by which laces should be designated as French? Unfortunately, between 1540 and 1600 there are few other elements on which to base an opinion, in the absence of historical examples, such as dated

samplers or recorded pieces. The two largest public collections of laces probably dating back to that time are housed in the Musée des Arts Décoratifs and in the Musée de Cluny in Paris. In the first may be found the collection gathered by M. Dupont-Auberville, which has never, unfortunately, been systematically studied (inv. no. 6988bis). Although I was able to see the collection and to trace it back to M. Auberville, I did not have the opportunity of establishing valid rules for a classification of the pieces within a stylistic or technical system that could be defined as French. As for the Musée de Cluny collection, a detailed catalogue is planned for publication in the near future.

The band of reticella and punto in aria shown here (figure 95) could have been made in France around 1600, even though its technique is the classical one used throughout Europe. The supposition that it may be French rests chiefly on stylistic elements. The figure of the woman in particular is treated with a combination of restrained elegance and grace. She has neither the naive awkwardness of Flemish figures, the compact and overdressed stiffness of comparable embroidered English compositions, nor the highly stylized and sometimes crudely drawn appearance of southern productions. Her tight-waisted bodice, narrow sleeves with puffed-up shoulders, and her skirt—still trapezoidal in shape but with a hint of paniers on either side—all suggest the latest fashion of the day. The shape of her head indicates that the lady wears her hair, or perhaps a cap, in a peaked or "butterfly" manner rather than in the extremely characteristic two-horned Venetian coiffure such as may be seen in Vecellio's models. A similar figure with peaked cap, tight waist, and a dress draped at the sides appears several times on a coverlet of reticella and punto in aria datable to the same period or slightly earlier, from the Louvre (deposited at the Musée des Arts Décoratifs; inv. no. LI 10).

Another essential difficulty in determining the origin of laces of the period is their almost total lack of stylistic correspondence with other decorative productions of the time. The mosaiclike use of triangular, square, or circular motifs proposed by the pattern designers has a direct link to the so-called Moresque decors in vogue a century earlier such as could be seen on damascened metalwork produced by oriental craftsmen (some of whom were established in Venice), on fabrics decorated with strapwork such as had been woven in Moorish Spain, and on the carpets and rugs of Anatolia.[10] Therefore, at the height of their popularity, between 1540 and 1615, these geometric laces were the latest manifestations of a style that had been prevalent in other forms of decoration as long as one hundred fifty years before.

To conclude this summary of the stylistic aspects of lace in France up to 1650, a certain crisp elegance coupled with a graceful simplicity can sometimes be detected in laces of that time extant in French collections, especially when human or animal figures are involved. However, in regard to laces worked in abstract designs, neither technique nor style permit us to affirm that we are dealing with a French production.

Lace Making during the Reign of Louis XIV

Lace making on a sizable scale became established in the early years of Louis XIV's reign (1653–1715). The young king fluctuated at first between the desire to keep people from spending too much on laces and other finery, especially foreign goods, and the need to promote existing industries. In a proclamation dated 27 November 1660, he recognized that sumptuary laws against luxury in dress reduced "a great number of poor artisans who draw their subsistence and that of their family from the manufacture and making of silk bobbin laces to a state of dire necessity." Stricken with compassion, he desired, therefore, his subjects to be allowed to "wear any and all sorts of passements and laces, and others made out of thread, so long as they are manufactured and produced within our kingdom."[11]

Jean Baptiste Colbert, Louis XIV's minister for finance and commerce, undertook accordingly to make France capable of competing effectively with its rival neighbors, Italy and Flanders, in the field of lace making. The loosely structured, geographically widespread, and stylistically undefined lace industry then existing in France formed the almost ideal challenge to Colbert's administrative talents. His method was simple: centralize all decisions into his own hands and appoint "civil servants" to run local manufacturing centers; provide designs for laces to be furnished by court artists; offer incentives for workers such as exemptions from tax and from the obligation to house billeted soldiers. Products from these manufactories were to enjoy free passage throughout France (it must be remembered that goods traveling from one French province to the other were subject to duty on entering each different administrative district) and were to be exempt from taxes.

The well-known declaration establishing royal lace manufactories was registered at parliament on 14 August 1665.[12] "In the interest of commerce, which brings abundance to the people, and in order to prevent the flow of very considerable sums of money out of the kingdom," the king designated eight cities as the future sites of manufactories "of laces, both bobbin and needle, which are henceforth to be known as *point de France*." These cities were Le Quesnoy, Arras, and Sedan in the north; Reims, Château-Thierry, and Loudun in the east; Alençon in the west and Aurillac in the center. In order to manufacture laces "with as much abundance and perfection as is now done in the cities of Venice, Genoa, and elsewhere in foreign lands," the declaration specified that thirty mistresses from Venice and two hundred of the best Flemish workers should be brought into France where they would teach French lace makers their skills. These foreigners were offered immediate French citizenship, if they wished to accept it, and the guarantee that their children would be able to inherit their property.

It is not clear whether in fact so many ever came. However, the presence of one Italian mistress, a Madamoiselle Rati, is confirmed in Auxerre by a letter dated 29 November 1667 from Madame de Voullemin, director of the royal manufactory there.[13] In Reims, where Colbert's aunt, Madame de Mesvilliers-Colbert, and his sister Agnes, who had taken religious vows, directed the manufactory, there were as many as twenty-four Flemish workers in 1667.[14]

Colbert's interest in the lace manufactories he had established never waned, even after the original subsidy granted Jean Pluymers and Catherine de Marcq—two of the civil servants mentioned above —could not be renewed because of the state of the economy. His correspondence on the subject is extensive, for the stakes were important indeed. Not only did the creation of a national lace industry permit France for a while to reverse its position from that of an importer to that of an exporter of laces in a very short time, but it had a political impact as well. It demonstrated to competitors, particularly Venice, that point de France laces could become successful in the very center of the production that they originally sought to imitate. The frequent mentions of French laces in Venetian inventories of the time illustrate just how well Colbert's plan had succeeded.

The difficulties encountered in the new establishments were another reason for Colbert's concern. Many laceworkers resented having to work for the royal manufactory. Those who wished to continue their practice on an individual basis were theoretically allowed to do so. In reality, though, they were continuously exhorted to join the manufactory, and parents were threatened with fines and other punishments if they failed to send their children into apprenticeship there. Merchants were forbidden to copy designs provided to the official establishment, which effectively cut them off from many of their noble customers who had been strongly advised to wear only point de France. Nevertheless, there were numerous instances of

fraud, particularly in convents where the police could not penetrate.

Two of the eight cities mentioned in the declaration, Sedan and Alençon, were specified as already having a considerable number of workers. On the other hand, Le Quesnoy, Arras, Château-Thierry, and Loudun never figured afterward in Colbert's correspondence at all. Instead, a number of other cities not previously associated with the lace industry became involved in the production of point de France and affiliated with the royal manufactories. These were Bourges, La Flèche, Le Mans, Riom, Sens, Issoudun, Montargis, Beauvais, Auxerre, and others. Some of these, such as Auxerre, did well enough. On 23 August 1672, for example, Madame de Voullemin sent Colbert a list of the laces manufactured in her establishment. Among them are several *rabats*, or bib-front collars, which she describes as handsome.[15] Other locales did not fare equally well, and Montargis was one of them. On 21 November 1668, after several years of effort to establish the lace industry, a memorandum to Colbert suggest levying an added tax on wine sold at the local cabaret to pay lace workers while they learned![16] But in Reims, Colbert's relatives sent him a complete list of the lace workers there, praising them and suggesting that the best among them be given cash bonuses.[17]

Such documents, of which there are several among Colbert's papers, bring the production of lace in France singularly and movingly to life with their long lists of names such as Marie Daumet, Anne Bonin, or Perette Bonon, who might each have made a meter of point de France and received one livre for it, or the Bernadine nuns who, together and anonymously, furnished the manufactory with "three meters of point de France and two handkerchieves, mounted and finished" for the sum of twenty-four livres.[18]

The king and his entourage were the foremost customers of the manufactory's laces, although Louis XIV reserved for himself the right to wear foreign laces for a number of years after he forbade their importation. In July 1666, the king paid Monsieur Mausy "of the Royal Manufactory of point de France established in Paris"—in reality an outlet for the manufactory's products—some 18,491 livres for the delivery of "26 neck kerchieves, 8 bib-front rabats, 8 cravats, 32 *ells* of 'other' laces for two arm bands, 18 ells for *rhingraves*, etc."[19]

There were other attempts at establishing royally sponsored manufactories of other laces besides point de France, notably toward the end of the century, when Flemish bobbin laces from the great centers of Brussels, Binche, and Malines had become more fashionable. One such attempt was made at Villiers-le-Bel, a small city northwest of Paris, where in 1691 a privilege for the manufacture of Malines-like laces was granted to a Pierre de Chars and his sisters.[20]

Besides these establishments, lace continued to be produced in centers where a tradition of lace making had been established since the latter part of the sixteenth century. One of these areas was that of Le Puy, of course; another was Normandy where from Honfleur to Dieppe much bobbin lace, presumably of a coarser type, was being made. In 1666 the inventory of a Parisian mercer included "88 pieces of white thread laces from Le Havre, Flanders, Dieppe, and Honfleur."[21] That these laces were also appreciated is evident from a contemporary engraving showing an elegant gentleman of the day shopping for laces (figure 96). Behind the salesgirl, on the top shelf, is a box clearly labeled "P[oint] de Dieppe," among others.

As for the manufacture of Brussels-type lace, known as *point d'Angleterre*, it had been prohibited in France. The official reason given was that such lace was of inferior quality, being made in separate pieces and not according to the continuous thread method. In fact, this was an attempt to discredit it by branding it as less durable and to stop the ever-growing demand for it to the detriment of French needle laces. In Calais the municipal council nevertheless requested permission from the king on 12 July 1691 to manufacture Angleterre laces in spite of the prohibition, as they occupied a number of families in the area.[22]

By then, however, the requirements of fashion and those of a declining economy in France combined with the death of Colbert in 1683 to make the lace industry in its specifically French manifestations a much less financially viable enterprise. The laces of *Alençon* and of neighboring *Argentan* continued to be manufactured after Louis XIV's death and throughout the eighteenth century and to retain their reputation for unostentatious elegance

Marchande Lingere en sa boutique

a Paris chez Gerard Jollain, rue S. Iacques a l'Enfant Iesus auec priuil. du Roy 1688.

96 *Marchande lingere en sa boutique.* 1688. Engraving. Bibliothèque Nationale, Paris. The salesgirl wears an elaborate headdress known as "fontages" after Louis XIV's mistress, who started the fashion. On the shelves at her back are boxes of lace and cloth labeled as point de Dieppe, point d'Espagne, point d'Angleterre, Havre, Malines, etc. She is obviously attempting to convince the young novice to wear a lace collar rather than a plain one.

and class, but they were not to be made again into such prestigious objects as the great flounces of the period 1665–1685, which played an integral part in the public relations scheme devised for the greater glory of the French king.

The revocation of the Edict of Nantes in 1685 dealt a severe blow to the industry, for a considerable number of Huguenots were involved in either the commerce or the manufacture of lace. Many of them left France to exercise their skills elsewhere; but paradoxically their departure had the positive effect of exporting French taste as well. From that time until the French Revolution it may be said that most of the laces manufactured in the rest of Europe followed the dictates of French fashion in all its varied forms.

Stylistic Aspects of French Lace
under the Reign of Louis XIV

There is little doubt that the royal manufactories at
first produced chiefly Venetian-style *gros point*,
which French lace workers were already imitating.
Indeed, many were reluctant to work at anything
else. As a letter to Colbert dated 7 September 1665
from the administrator of Normandy, Duboulay-
Favier, indicates, "a number of people are not
capable of working on the new sort of point . . .
because they are accustomed to gros point, which
sells very well."[23] This letter is important because it
implies that the new point de France genre was
already taking shape, technically and stylistically,
even as it admits the existing skill of the workers in
producing the *Venetian gros point*. In regard to a lace
worked in the heavily padded style characteristic of
gros point, therefore, it is a difficult task indeed to
ascribe its manufacture to its city of origin, Venice,
or to one of the French royal manufactories. Once
again, neither the thread used—linen imported more
often than not from Flanders—nor the technique—
which is identical—supplies reliable information to
help in this task. Stylistically, however, the well-
known French taste for order and clarity does
manifest itself in these productions.

The scrolling Venetian designs of the period,
punctuated with heavy fleurons and pomegranates,
seem to unfold in unending volutes very oriental in
their resolutely impersonal way, whereas French ones
tend to be placed on either side of a median line, with
the fleurons and pomegranates strategically placed to
achieve greater plasticity. Even when this is not the
case, French scrollwork never seems to have the
sensual abandon of the Italian style but to strive instead to impose on an essentially luxurious baroque
form a certain French classicism (see figure 97).

The heyday of gros point may be placed between
1650 and 1670, although it did not completely
disappear from the fashionable scene until the end of
the seventeenth century. Very rapidly, however, the
new point de France became the rage. This new lace,
a low-relief needle lace with decorative motifs
equally distributed on a background of regular,
hexagonal meshes, took on its final appearance as
early as the year 1665, judging from the contents of
the letter to Colbert quoted above.

97 Antoine Masson. *André Le Nôtre*. Engraving, late seventeenth
or early eighteenth century, after the painting by Carlo Maratta,
ca. 1665. Private collection, Paris. Le Nôtre wears a bib-front
collar and cuffs of heavy, padded, Venetian-style gros point lace
with an ordered symmetry of design that suggests a French
manufacture.

The king's official painters had been designated in
the declaration of August 1665 as responsible for the
design of the point de France laces. Chief among
those was of course Charles Le Brun, also director of
the Gobelins manufactory and of the Mobilier
National. Since his appointment in 1662, his influence could be felt in every branch of the decorative
arts: furniture marquetry, carved wood panels,
stuccowork, wrought-iron balconies, tapestries,
etc., all of which could be found in the palace at
Versailles then being completed.

Examples abound of such flounces of point de
France, made to conform in their decor to the officially devised court style. Numerous allusions to the
king himself—his emblem the sun, sunflowers,
fleurs de lys, royal crowns, etc.—are present in most
of the large pieces produced between 1665 and 1680.
Thereafter, they tend to disappear, leaving room for

98 Furnishing or ecclesiastical flounce, detail. Most probably Alençon, ca. 1670–1680. Linen. Punto in aria needle lace of the point de France type with characteristic ground of hexagonal meshes. 24½ x 134½ (62.2 x 341.6). Private collection, Paris.

99 Detail of figure 98.

less image-oriented compositions. Some of these latter laces, said to have been designed by Jean I. Bérain (figures 98–100), who had replaced Le Brun as court painter in 1690, are decidedly airier, and their composition includes naturalistically drawn elements; but what they gain in charm and understated elegance, they lose in grandeur and sense of national statement.

From around the end of the century until approximately 1720, a form of point de France known as "point de Sedan" seems to have predominated (figure 101). Its chief technical characteristic is the placement of relief work in strategic locations on the motifs, where it is likely to increase the plasticity of the whole, instead of being used systematically to underline contours. The motifs used are more often than not great vases filled with very naturalistic flowers, the whole on a scale almost too large for its lace medium. The technical virtuosity of these point de Sedan pieces is superb. Each flower, each decorative element, is treated in a profusion of diaper patterns, zigzags, chevrons, etc. The influence here is clearly foreign, for the French did not tend at that time to subordinate the effect of a whole to the technique of its parts.

Sedan is located in the Ardennes, close to Flanders. Thus it is probable that its lace industry, which was very active at least until the middle of the eighteenth century, was to some extent influenced by that of its neighbor. Indeed, one may well ask whether some of the flounces traditionally attributed to Sedan were not actually made in Brussels where, according to some authors, there existed a needle-lace industry qualitatively if not quantitatively on a par with the bobbin one at the time.

Alongside this style, another type of lace made its appearance. It is variously known as *point de rose* or *point de neige*, a terminology dating back only to the nineteenth century. Its chief characteristic is its accumulation of minute picots, or small decorative loops, sometimes two or three layers high on each motif. Some of the pieces were produced in France, others in Venice. They are difficult to distinguish from one another, although here as always the French tendency is to treat this lace vertically and to include by then truly indistinguishable symbolic elements into its decor, whereas the Venetian pieces completely lose the viewer in a maze of the tiniest curlicued volutes.

Fashion abandoned point de France as rapidly as it had embraced it, even though large flounces continued to be used as furnishings, notably around toilette tables, and on ecclesiastical garments (figure 102). But as early as 1678 *Le Mercure Galant*, the news magazine of the day, noted that a skirt of Angleterre, or Brussels bobbin lace, was now the latest fashion. In 1687 the royal bathtubs at the palace of Marly, near Versailles, were lined with cotton *damask* trimmed with "a tall flounce of Angleterre lace, pleated all over on the top, a medium flounce of the same in the middle, and a smaller one at the side!"[24]

Not only were bobbin laces such as Angleterre less costly than point de France ones because they could be made more quickly; they were also more versatile. They could be pleated or gathered to achieve a frothy effect and, although more delicate, they could be washed more easily than needle laces. All of these factors combined to make point de France laces after the 1680s less objects of fashion than of prestige. They were to retain this aura throughout the eighteenth century and even during the following one, but it can be argued that they never again reached the artistic and social pinnacle they had attained during the heyday of the Sun King's reign.

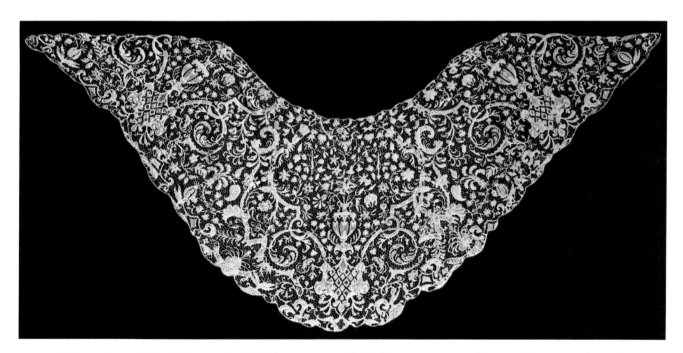

100 Collar made out of a furnishing or ecclesiastical flounce. Most probably Alençon, ca. 1690; collar mount late nineteenth or early twentieth century. Linen. Punto in aria needle lace of the point de France type. 15 x 48 (38.1 x 121.9). Wadsworth Atheneum, Gift of Mr. and Mrs. Erving Pruyn, 1965.445.

101 Jean-Marc Nattier. *Isabelle de Bourbon*. Ca. 1745. Oil. Musée de Versailles. The child is wearing a stomacher, quintuple sleeve cuffs, bodice trimming, and gathered apron of needlepoint lace of the point de France/point de Sedan type. The ensemble may have been cut out of a previously made large flounce, for the style of the design seems to predate that of the period at which the portrait was painted. The young lady's dress is further trimmed with two flounces of gold lace at the bottom.

102 Jacques-Nicholas Tardieu. *Pierre de Langle, Bishop of Boulogne*. Engraving, ca. 1675, after a portrait probably painted in the seventeenth century. Musée des Beaux-Arts et de la Dentelle, Alençon. The prelate is wearing an alb flounce and matching cuffs of point de France similar in their decorative treatment to figures 100 and 101.

The Lace Industry in the Eighteenth Century

Even before Louis XIV's death in 1715, French borders had been reopened to foreign lace imports, or at least the prohibitions were no longer enforced. Belgian laces—Brussels, Malines, and Binche—had developed a characteristic style and technique easily recognizable by all. This was true of the French needle laces too, but the same could not be said for her bobbin laces. Unfortunately, bobbin laces were in great demand and, for reasons not completely understood, French bobbin lace makers never seemed able to match the technical or aesthetic standards of their Flemish counterparts. Bobbin laces manufactured in France in the eighteenth century, except for silk and metallic ones, were coarser or technically inferior.

Jacques Savary des Bruslons's *Dictionnaire universel du commerce* (1759–1765) confirms that bobbin and needle laces were still extensively manufactured in France then, perhaps even more so than in the preceding century. However, if we are to believe him the quality of the needle lace had decreased. He goes so far as to say that Alençon lace is "inferior in taste and delicacy of execution. . . . Its chief disadvantage is the padded thread around the flowers, which is thick indeed and becomes even thicker when wet. . . . We are in addition justified in asking Alençon manufacturers for greater variety in their fillings."[25] Such an exceedingly severe judgment appears exaggerated, in the face of the Alençon pieces which have come down to us from that period (figure 103). Savary des Bruslons generally considered thread laces from "Spanish Flanders" to be the finest and most beautiful, but he did not concede that "real Valenciennes," as he termed it, might be ranked with distinction.

The stylistic and technical development of *Valenciennes lace* in the 1740s constitutes in fact one of the most important elements in the French lace industry at the time. Lace had been manufactured in Valenciennes ever since the technique was introduced in 1644 by Françoise Badar, who had studied it

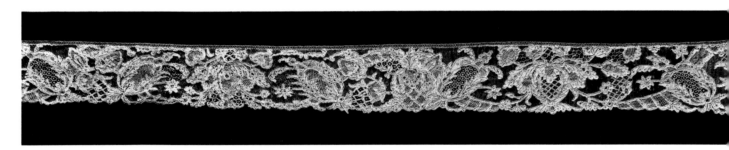

103 Border. Most probably Alençon, ca. 1725–1735. Linen. Punto in aria needle lace of the Alençon type with characteristic ground of small meshes and ornamental stitches or "modes." 2½ x 51 (6.3 x 129.5). Wadsworth Atheneum, 1923.492.

104 and 105 Matching trimming length and lappet. Valenciennes, ca. 1755. Linen. Continuous thread bobbin lace of the Valenciennes type. Fig. 104: 2½ x 23 (6.35 x 58.4). Fig. 105: 4½ max. x 55½ (11.25 max. x 140.9). Wadsworth Atheneum, Gift of Mrs. George Nichols, 1969.136 and 135.

105

in Antwerp. However, the city did not become French until 1678, after the conclusion of the war with Holland, and for a long time it remained under the aesthetic influence of the Low Countries. Then in the 1740s Valenciennes lace really came into its own; a rigorously square mesh was developed, as opposed to the round one used heretofore not only in Valenciennes itself but also in other centers where similar lace was produced, notably Antwerp. The designs lost the touching awkwardness that characterized so many of the lesser Belgian productions, and took on a sophistication that was truly French (figures 104 and 105).

Because this lace became very fashionable at court and in elegant circles, the industry in Valenciennes entered into an era of great prosperity. In 1767 one ell of real Valenciennes, so named to distinguish it from imitations manufactured outside the city limits or elsewhere, cost one hundred ninety livres, according to a bill submitted by a M. Vanot, supplier to Louis XV and a member of the Valenciennes lace merchants' corporation.[26] By comparison, the average yearly wage of a Valenciennes lace maker for the period 1748 to 1774 was 156.6 livres, or less than the price of one ell of her own lace.[27]

Numerous attempts were made throughout the century to revive the industry in traditional centers where it had died down, or to create new centers altogether. More often than not such attempts were linked with charitable institutions from which one could obtain cheap labor, such as former prostitutes or orphaned children of both sexes. In particular, it seems as if the manufacture of *Blonde* silk bobbin laces, very much in fashion from the 1750s on, attracted all sorts of entrepreneurs.

One M. Ducoin had established such a manufactory in Sassenaye en Dauphiné, near Grenoble, which occupied "more than two hundred pupils, orphaned or abandoned children." M. Ducoin had received a subsidy, but in 1785 he required another for the upkeep of the children, which he estimated at six sols a day (approximately the price of two loaves of bread). This request was turned down by the authorities on the ground that "six sols a day for children who are old enough to work seems infinitely too much." The children involved had been specified as "all the girls below the age of seven

106 Trimming length. Most probably Paris area, ca. 1775. Silver "filé" over a silk core. Continuous thread bobbin lace of the Blonde type with characteristic five-hole mesh ground. 6½ x 48 (15.87 x 121.9). Wadsworth Atheneum, Costume and Textile Purchase Fund, 1985.5. The decor is as elaborate as the stiffness of the material will permit. This is a rare example of a type of lace produced in large quantities but now seldom found. Most metallic-thread laces were melted down to recover the precious metal with which they were made.

and above the age of five . . . who are to stay five years."[28]

Silk and metallic Blonde laces were manufactured in their traditional centers to the west of Paris as well, and in Caen and Rouen in Normandy (figure 106). French Blonde laces were evidently renowned and appreciated, for other lace manufacturers, notably the Venetians, sought to rival them by producing their own. In 1762 the establishment of one Gabrieli, for example, who had received a subsidy from the Venetian senate, along with another partner who later dropped out, was producing an average of three hundred meters of "silk, silver and gold, or polychrome Blonde laces" a month,[29] which he claimed were as good as those of the French. Toward the end of the monarchy in France, Blonde lace seems to have been the only fashionable one. The general state of the economy was disastrous, but fashion not finance had been the decisive factor here, for it had decreed that lace was no longer desirable. Needle laces were particularly hard hit because their severe, and by then rather skeletal elegance corresponded less and less to the romantic look then in fashion.

In 1780 Olivier de Saint Vast, a member of the Alençon municipal council, moved by the miserable state in which many of his lace making constituents found themselves, wrote to Queen Marie Antoinette begging that she "wear Alençon once a week." Presumably others then would follow suit, thereby "saving 50,000 people from misery." On 18 September 1780 an anonymous civil servant replied to M. de Saint Vast that "it has been observed that it is with needlepoint as with many other things, they are subject to the rule of fashion, therefore submitted to revolutions . . . that such changes are unfortunate for the merchants and manufacturers . . . but that it cannot be sufficient reason to interfere with the taste of the consumer and even less with that of the queen."[30]

The revolutionary government showed itself more responsive toward the lace making population. A report dated from the 11 Pluviose, year III of the Republic (2 February 1794), indicated that lace was by nature "frivolous and costly" but that the country needed export goods and, further, that "lace makers cannot so soon have forgotten the skills on which the reputation of the manufacture is based." The report

is in answer to a request for subsidies made by the Alençon municipal council. The subsidy seems to have been granted, although it was accompanied with recommendations to switch over to the manufacture of toiles, presumably a less frivolous industry.[31]

Stylistic Aspects of Lace in the Eighteenth Century

The most important stylistic as well as technical development in lace, namely the appearance of a true mesh ground in needle laces, took place in fact before the beginning of the eighteenth century. Madame Despierres dates it around 1700.[32] However, it could predate 1700 by as much as twenty years or more, given the facts that a true mesh ground on a larger scale had been developed in point de France probably as early as 1665, and that bobbin laces à réseaux or with a mesh ground, as opposed to those with à brides, or with connecting bars, were well known at the same time.

At any rate, lace styles in the eighteenth century are best described as consisting of many meshes, ornamented at first with fancy "modes" or fillings, then plainer and plainer ones, with the decorative elements proper playing an ever-decreasing role.

During the Régence (1715–1723) and the early years of Louis XV's reign, lace style was affected by the general movement away from contrived decors toward ever more naturalistic ones. Naturalistic is here understood not as a faithful rendering of nature; that would not come until later in the century. Instead designers improved upon nature by redistributing its elements into the most pleasing manmade combinations. Thus we find realistically drawn flowers, often carnations or peonies, much larger than the vases in which they are put, huge pinecone shapes surrounded with minute flowers, or Chinese pagodas smaller than the butterflies fluttering around them.

Besides Chinese porcelainlike decors, there was also a perceptible Indo-Persian influence on lace designs of the time. Trilobed medallions enclose buta or leaves, the whole often distributed along a broken diagonal similar to those found on bizarre silks at the beginning of the century—themselves,

107 Trimming ribbon. Lyons (?), ca. 1765. Silk warps, wefts, and pile; velvet weave, cut and uncut pile; dusty rose ground, white pile. 4 x 23 (10.16 x 58.4). Wadsworth Atheneum, Gift of Mr. and Mrs. William J. Robertson in memory of Adolf Loewi, 1984.29. The decoration imitates lace with its meshlike background and scalloped medallions.

108 Trimming length. Argentan or Alençon, ca. 1740–1745. Linen. Punto in aria needle lace of the Argentan type. 3 x 48 (7.6 x 121.9). Wadsworth Atheneum, 1968.134a. The pinecone and artichokelike shapes of the decor were originally found in dress and furnishing silks of some thirty to forty years earlier, notably in the so-called bizarre and lace-pattern silks of the late Louis XIV period. When no longer as fashionable on fabrics, these motifs migrated over to the lace field for a time.

it is thought, of oriental inspiration. Bobbin lace makers, particularly those of Brussels, Malines, and Binche, excelled in these representations.

The makers of needle laces, which were still France's forte, intelligently attempted to compete with them not so much by producing the same kinds of design. Technically speaking, it can be done and sometimes is, but stylistically, the possibility for relief inherent in the needle technique almost invariably gives such laces a stiffer look. So French needle-lace makers developed the series of variegated fillings mentioned above, the "modes." These are minute ornamental devices in the shape of stars, squares, hexagons known as "partridge eyes," etc. Even when similarly conceived designs are present in bobbin laces, because of the technique they result in an altogether different appearance.

In the 1740s Valenciennes lace became very fashionable. Its characteristic square mesh, plaited

on all sides, played in a sense the same role as did the great hexagonal mesh devised almost a century earlier for the point de France. It formed a rigorous grid against which realistically drawn elements were set off. The great shift toward true naturalness, as opposed to the manmade one mentioned above, had now taken place. Flowers are ever more recognizable in all their botanical detail—a reflection of the scientific mania that took hold after the publication of Diderot's *Encyclopédie* began in 1751, an interest in wild herbs and plants developed, and products from the farm, such as wheat ears and bunches of grapes, made their appearance.

Figures 104 and 105, a Valenciennes lappet and matching flounce of about 1755, show just such recourse to the use of wheat ears, here bunched and tied with a ribbon or arranged in sprays along the border. The ribbon, merely suggested, soon became ubiquitous in almost all forms of lace, as indeed in fabrics of the period. Whether it meandered in lazy curves or was broken up into half medallions, it served for a good thirty years as an indispensable element in lace decors.

Even while lace lost some of its specific qualities, attempting as it did to integrate itself into the general decorative scheme of the day, it became more indispensable than ever as an accessory. Wearing lace automatically gave one a touch of class, the reverse of how it functioned in the Louis XIV years when one had to have class to wear it! Lace motifs entwined with multicolored ribbons, stripes, or flowers were woven into the silk fabrics of the day, many examples of which have survived. Even *velvet* pile was trimmed or looped into lace motifs, as in the dusty rose and white velvet here (figure 107).

Around the time of Madame de Pompadour's death in 1763, the decorative elements drawn from nature began to migrate from lace to embroidery. From that time on, the mesh ground became the chief element against which spare, Japanese-like plum or cherry boughs were finely traced, the only other adornments being strings of pearl-shaped medallions, as in figure 108.

Stimulated by the discoveries of Herculaneum and Pompeii and by the publication of such books as *Antiquities of Athens* (1762) by the Englishmen James Stuart and Nicholas Revett, the taste for Hellenic art began to influence every branch of art and literature. In April 1764 Horace Walpole wrote from Paris, "Everything must be à la Grecque, accordingly the lace on their waistcoats is copied from a frieze."[33] Although portraits of the period show that lace worn by the sitters was not always so Greek, his observation suggests that some laces with a design of palmettes or urns generally thought to have been produced in the 1790s or 1800s may in fact date back to the 1760s, some thirty years earlier.

Since the middle of the century Blonde laces had also become very important. The term is a generic one for various sorts of bobbin laces made out of gold or silver thread or of blonde-colored silk. In the eighteenth century, with the demand for laces of all kinds much stronger than in the preceding century, Blonde laces, which were quick to make because of their entwined, unplaited meshes and their summarily drawn motifs, literally flooded the market. A chenille thread was more often than not threaded in afterward around the contours of the motifs, with the help of a needle. Artificial flowers or ribbons were often inserted as well into their large-size meshes. A portrait of Sir Humphrey Morice by the Italian painter Pompeo Batoni (figure 109) shows the sitter wearing shirt and sleeve ruffles of Blonde lace, the diamond-shaped meshes and chenille threads of which are clearly recognizable.

Few examples of these eighteenth-century Blonde laces have survived, for they were exceedingly fragile, even though their production was extensive in several other countries besides France, notably in Spain and Italy.

Stylistically, lace was already dead when the French Revolution came in 1789. All graphic invention and originality had gone out of its designs. It continued to be made and worn, of course, but it had become a fabric, used like one, and accorded no greater consideration.

109 Pompeo Batoni, detail. *Sir Humphrey Morice.* Ca. 1762. Oil. Wadsworth Atheneum, The Ella Gallup Sumner and Mary Catlin Sumner Collection, 1936.43. The sitter is wearing a shirt trim and matching cuffs of silk bobbin lace of the Blonde type with a velvety chenille thread contouring the motifs.

The State of the Industry from 1800 to 1870

Even before the French Revolution, laces were no longer fashionable. There was an additional psychologically important, development: laces were being worn next to the skin, something that had never happened before. Even when laces had been used to trim morning robes or nightcaps, they were always meant to be seen, not to be hidden. It follows that lace that was not visible required less elaborate designs and techniques. Soon the centers still active were all producing similar-looking laces, usually in very narrow widths, with boringly repetitive motifs.

Napoleon I, who was as keen as Colbert had been to develop industries in the French empire, promoted French laces by making them a required part of court attire for men and women. He placed a number of orders with Alençon lace makers for the trousseau of his second wife, Empress Marie Louise of Austria. Unfortunately, the empress also patronized the Belgian industry—the country was under France's domination—and ordered quantities of Brussels and Malines.

If the needle laces of Alençon survived thanks to imperial commissions, the bobbin laces of Valenciennes did not fare so well. Lace making had definitely stopped in the city after the fall of the Ancien Régime. A neighboring city, Bailleul, had taken it up but most Valenciennes-type laces would henceforth be made in Belgium, notably in Ypres and Ghent.

The silk bobbin-lace industry, on the other hand, was perhaps holding its own better than the others. As early as 1803 an exhibition of such laces took place in Caen,[34] a traditional center of production. Pierre-Aimé Lain, its organizer, indicated in his report that "the laces exhibited by our manufacturers compare favorably for beauty and quality with those of other more celebrated manufacturers." Another exhibit was organized there in 1806, at which one Louis Horel showed a large square shawl. The object had taken three lace makers six months to make and, we are told, had required three thousand bobbins and eighteen thousand pins.

As in other lace centers, the prosperity these exhibits seem to indicate ceased for a time with the fall of the emperor in 1812. The appearance on the market of machine-made net dealt another blow to the industry in general. The technology had been imported from England around 1809. On 31 January 1812, only three years after its introduction in France, M. de Rens, president of the Association of Lace Manufacturers, wrote a letter to the imperial authorities requesting that "machine-made nets not be tolerated any longer for ordinary wear nor for court dress."[35]

In fact, machine-made tulle or net was being constantly perfected; as a result production increased tremendously and prices soon fell, making the product a cheap one, undesirable in the eyes of the public. Paradoxically, this development, which took place in the 1820s, combined with the renewed fashionableness of lace, ushered in an era of unprecedented prosperity for the handmade lace industry that was to last almost forty years.

Modern methods of production, management, and distribution, coupled with the manufacturers' keen understanding of the requirements of the market, notably in matters of design, made France, unlike in the preceding century, the best-organized lace producing country in Europe, as Patricia Wardle indicates in her *Victorian Lace*.[36]

The "point de raccroc," an invisible stitch used to sew strips of bobbin lace into large flounces or shawls, had been perfected in 1833, at precisely the time when such objects were in demand. Auguste Lefébure, who was to become the most important and celebrated lace manufacturer in France, won his first silver medal at the Paris exhibition of May 1834 for just such a shawl.

Lefébure had established himself in Bayeux, where his lace makers worked primarily on silk Blonde laces and on a bobbin lace made out of flax or cotton known as "point de Bayeux," a cross in technique between Chantilly and Lille which are described below. He soon branched out in Alençon, however, there taking up the manufacture of the celebrated points again and largely contributing to the renewed favor and prestige these laces were beginning to enjoy in the 1840s. The Parisian firm of Videcoq et Simon had preceded him there, however, and its first Alençon laces were exhibited in Alençon itself in 1842 to great acclaim.

Alençon lace was at last coming back to the forefront, a little later, it is true, than other laces. From then on, and especially after 1855, when

Lefébure and others had taken over, no aristocratic trousseau in Europe could be complete without Alençon laces. Among other factors, this was perhaps due to the fact that Alençon point could not be satisfactorily imitated by machines, as could Chantilly and other laces, until the end of the century.

The intensive training and strict discipline to which Alençon lace workers were subjected made possible any technical feat. When in 1854 Empress Eugénie herself ordered a set composed of tiered flounces of Alençon lace, sleeve ruffles, and a shoulder bertha comprising altogether several dozen meters of lace, the set was ready in less than a year, in time to be shown at the Exposition Universelle in Paris in 1855.

Even the modest laces of the Lorraine region in the east benefited in the general euphoria. Mirecourt had been a center of production since the seventeenth century; its laces then were mostly exported outside of France, notably to Italy as the inventory of a Venetian lace merchant taken in 1671 testifies.[37] A large pool of bobbin lace workers was therefore available, so that from the 1840s onward these were engaged in the very prosperous manufacture of Duchesse–like laces, application motifs, and heavy laces for furnishings made in part with a thick silk cordonnet and called "guipure arabe."

The Lorraine lace workers, apparently working under intelligent management, responded quickly to the demands of fashion and produced good quality laces at low prices. In his report on the Exposition Universelle of 1867, Félix Aubry, himself an important manufacturer in Le Puy, does not hesitate, to his credit, to designate the Mirecourt manufacturers as "the most fecund . . . the indefatigable avant-garde that stimulates innovations, traces the way to be followed and gives a salutary and energetic impulsion to all its rivals."[38]

Lille and Arras in the north were also producing large quantities of "Lille à fond clair," a bobbin lace with a simple, unplaited ground and small motifs contoured with thicker thread. It is a relatively simple lace to make, similar to Bucks Point in England, and a good worker is able to make a yard or more a day. Laces had been made in the north since the late seventeenth century but had never been especially prestigious. In the first part of the nine-

teenth century their extremely transparent look became fashionable, and production was high. During the Second Empire they did not compare as favorably with the richer laces then appreciated, and their manufacture began to decline as early as 1850.

In terms of number of workers, Le Puy was probably the most important lace making center in France in the second half of the nineteenth century. In 1867 it was estimated that one hundred thousand young girls and other women were engaged in bobbin lace making in the surrounding area. They made all sorts of laces including linen or cotton "torchon," a sort of coarse lace with shell and other

110 Anonymous photograph. Ca. 1860. Bibliothèque Nationale, Paris. The lady is draped in a black silk Chantilly shawl.

simple motifs; "Cluny," a lace supposedly derived from sixteenth-century samples housed in the Musée de Cluny in Paris; "silk Chantilly," gold-thread lace; and especially a *guipure lace* of black mat silk thread much used by matrons and widows.

The large lace shawls made of Chantilly, which were universally appreciated from the early 1840s to the 1870s, were by then no longer manufactured in their namesake city of the same name, northwest of Paris (figure 110). It has often been said that Chantilly lace workers were beheaded during the French Revolution for having served the aristocracy, but some undoubtedly survived, for in the 1820s a number of manufacturers were still located there. It is true that they were beginning to suffer from the competition of similar manufacturers in Caen and Rouen as well as from the appearance of machine-made laces. In 1826 the Chantilly firm of Moreau Frères had to ask the government for help in saving from bankruptcy their 120-year-old enterprise, which employed more than two thousand workers. The authorities' response, in March 1827, was discouraging. It stated dryly that "the introduction of machines in the manufacturing of this article makes it possible to produce such laces at infinitely lower cost."[39] The harsh realities of the mechanical era had killed the lace industry in Chantilly more surely than had the French Revolution.

Possibly because the Normandy workers were better organized, as witness the numerous exhibitions organized there since the beginning of the century, the Normandy silk bobbin-lace industry took up the production of Chantilly in the 1830s, in addition to its traditional output of Blonde laces.

111 Parasol. Most probably Bayeux, ca. 1855. Black silk. Continuous thread bobbin lace of the Chantilly type; ivory handle and finial. Diam. 25½ (64.77). Wadsworth Atheneum, Gift of Mr. and Mrs. James Lippincott Goodwin, 1952.30.

112 Triangular shawl, detail. Most probably Bayeux, ca. 1855. Black silk. Continuous thread bobbin lace of the Chantilly type with needle-made joining. 56 x 120 (142 x 304.8). Wadsworth Atheneum, Gift of Dieter and Anne Kraatz, 1984.70. This large shawl was probably manufactured in Bayeux, judging by its charcoal-colored silk, as opposed to the jet black one used in the rival manufacturing center of Grammont, Belgium, and by the uniformity of its "grillé" or open stitch.

From then on the best and the most beautifully designed Chantilly shawls, parasols, flounces, and fans came from that area, specifically from Bayeux (figures 111 and 112). Auguste Lefébure's legendary firm received one gold medal after another for its Chantilly products, and M. Lefébure himself was awarded in 1855 the Grand Cross of the Legion of Honor for his activities.

By then there were many other lace manufacturers of both bobbin and needle laces in Normandy, among them the house of Verdé-Delisles Frères & Cie, Lefébure's most serious competitor, also known as La Compagnie des Indes because of its business in Kashmir shawls.

By the year 1870 the French lace industry had reached an economic pinnacle from which it would inevitably soon begin to descend. As early as 1862 French laces exhibited in London did not receive as much praise as before, and in 1867, in spite of such a brilliant exhibition that "the memory of it will never be forgotten by all who saw it,"[40] the laces shown were so perfect as to be considered "véritable objets d'art." By attaching this label to handmade lace, members of the jury perhaps unconsciously recognized that it had ceased to function as a usable object. Lace was becoming divorced from its lifeline, fashion, and was thus ultimately destined to be put under glass and exhibited rather than worn.

Lace Styles from 1800 to 1870

Lace styles in the nineteenth century followed perhaps more closely than ever before the evolution of the general decorative schemes of the day.

As we have seen, Napoleon I took a personal interest in the promotion of the lace industry in Alençon and other cities. For his coronation he ordered from the firm of Mesdames Lolive, de Beuvry & Cie. two pairs of cravats, a pair of cuffs, and a collar of "superfine *point à réseau* with wolf's teeth border," for four thousand francs. The lace may be seen in the painting by Jacques-Louis David commemorating this ceremony, now at Versailles. The tooth edge constituted the most novel stylistic development in lace since about 1785 (figure 113), for almost all laces produced in the eighteenth century had had straight edges. The fashion lasted until approximately 1815, the sharply pointed "teeth" then becoming rounded and eventually turning into broad scallops. These wide scallops were better adapted than triangular ones to the bobbin technique. In particular they were well suited to Blonde laces, with their large-scale flowers.

Empress Marie Louise's wedding trousseau reflects her personal preference for such laces with a dress of Blonde and gold chenille worked in ivy-leaf motif typical of the period. It is interesting to note that the dress cost twenty-four hundred francs (in 1810), or only half as much as the Alençon lace set Napoleon had worn.

The empress had other Blonde lace dresses, a dress of Lyons tulle—mechanical silk net—priced at six hundred francs, several made entirely of Brussels point valued at five thousand to six thousand francs, as well as dozens of others trimmed with Malines, Belgian-made Valenciennes, and more Brussels. Among her many lace shawls, there was one of Brussels needlepoint and bobbin lace with a decor of "rose buds, scattered leaves, stars and dots, poppies and tulips"; next to such an impressive list of Belgian laces we find only one entry for an Alençon lace shawl, without further description, at a cost of three thousand francs.[41]

The laurel wreaths and fasces modeled after those of imperial Rome did not survive the fall of the French empire in 1812 any more than did Napoleon's emblems of bees and beehives. All political allusions were banished for the time being from the field of lace designs, and flowers become the sole components of its decor.

From the 1820s on, however, a new style developed, which was due largely to the influence of

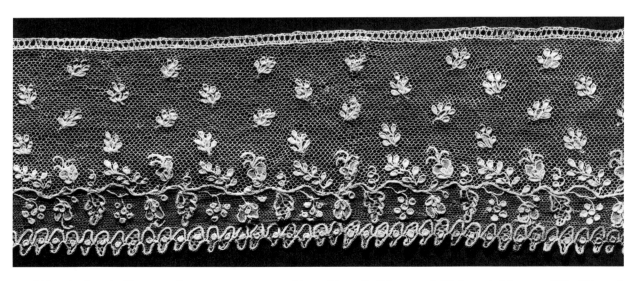

113 Trimming length. Alençon or Argentan, ca. 1795–1805. Linen. 3½ x 52½ (8.89 x 133.4). Wadsworth Atheneum, Gift of Mr. and Mrs. Thomas H. Truslow, 1977.178.

114 Square shawl. Most probably Bayeux, ca. 1830. Linen. Continuous thread bobbin lace of the Blonde type with needle-made joining stitch. 72 x 72 (182.8 x 182.8). Wadsworth Atheneum, Gift of Mrs. George Nichols, 1969.139. The material used here is not the traditional silk but instead extremely fine flax thread; this strongly suggests a Bayeux production rather than one of Caen.

Kashmir shawls, much in vogue since the late eighteenth century. Blonde lace motifs in particular were often derived from Kashmir-style designs, even if they were not always in vogue on lace at the same time at which they were on shawls; such is often the case in the adaptation of a given motif to another medium.

Figure 114, for example, a square of Blonde silk bobbin lace, exhibits above a dentate edge a large border of buta sprays surrounding a field with rows of single carnations. But whereas the corresponding Kashmir shawls may be dated to the early 1800s, this

type of lace did not appear until the 1820s and lasted into the 30s.[42]

At the Paris Exposition of 1839, however, a new feeling was apparent in the designs proposed. The house of Violard, for example, of Paris and Caen, manufacturers of silk Blondes, wool, and Kashmir-thread laces, showed airier, pyramidal flower arrangements with numerous tendrils issuing from them as from a climbing vine. Curiously, these were juxtaposed with formal cartouches reminiscent of the Louis XIV era.[43] The house of Violard was awarded a bronze medal at the exhibition and received the commendations of the jury "for its contribution to the immense vogue enjoyed by silk laces."[44]

Seemingly unimpressed by M. Violard's efforts, the chronicler for the *Journal des Demoiselles* in her report on the exhibit had high praises for the laces of Mirecourt and Le Puy instead and candidly indicated that such productions made it no longer necessary to obtain "one's laces by removing them from the garments of religious statues in country churches."[45]

The style introduced by M. Violard ushered in a period of an uninhibited mélange of decorative references to previous eras. Pyramidal bouquets arranged in formal seventeenth-century fashion were composed of such contemporary flowers as cabbage roses, lilacs, and hydrangeas.

After 1842 the railroad, which was introduced relatively late in France, captured everyone's imagination, including that of lace manufacturers. Thus it is that especially on Chantilly shawls may be seen railroad track motifs—ties and rails—following a serpentine course through ribboned "tunnels" surmounted by a Pompadour bow, amid flowers and ferns.

As usual, needle laces showed a little more restraint in their decor. Alençon laces especially, try as they might, never managed to shed completely their rigid and somewhat brittle elegance. Precisely because of that, however, they rarely fell into the excesses sometimes committed by their bobbin-made counterparts and thus were able to maintain a very prestigious image.

115 Rectangular stole. Most probably Maison de Lefébure, Bayeux, ca. 1860. Linen and cotton. Punto in aria needle lace of the Argentan type with modified mesh ground. 30 x 110 (76.2 x 279.4). Wadsworth Atheneum, Costume and Textile Purchase Fund, 1985.6.

116 Detail of figure 115.

A good example of this uncompromising rigor is seen in figures 115 and 116. It is a large stole of Argentan lace—a slightly modified form of Alençon—seemingly typical of the work of the famous Lefébure house. Datable to circa 1855–1860 by the shading of its flowers, a process reputably introduced for the first time at the Paris exhibition of 1855, the stole is executed with a great variety of ornamental stitches. However, these are intelligently confined to the outer edges and do not interfere with the composition of the field. There a skinny ribbon meanders among flower sprays, some of which are made out of the "imperial crown," a flower much used in decoration since Napoleonic times.

Whether it is because too many hands, trained to be perfectly alike, worked on this piece, thus giving it a paradoxically mechanical look, or because its rich decor was treated in a prudishly static manner, this perfectly executed lace object is strangely devoid of personality. Perhaps this very remoteness is what keeps it from looking cheap, giving it instead the

class that was expected of Alençon or Argentan needle laces.

But competition from the mechanical industry was growing stronger every day. By 1861 there were 2,020 mechanical looms in France, 790 of them in Calais alone and 350 in Lyons.[47] Valenciennes, Blonde, and Chantilly laces were particularly successful imitations even if, in the case of Chantilly, workers had to hand thread the cordonnet around the motifs, something that could not be done mechanically at that time. One of the leading houses in the manufacture of mechanical silk laces was Dognin & Cie., of Calais and Lyons, whose productions received much favorable attention at the London Exhibition of 1862, and again in Paris in 1867 and in Vienna in 1873. The house of Dognin, founded in 1805, closed its doors in 1984.

Conclusion

Although Alençon lace is as celebrated as Brussels point or Honiton, there has perhaps been too little awareness of the extent of the lace industry in other regions of France from Paris and its northwestern suburbs (silk and metallic thread laces) to the west, in Normandy (needle and bobbin laces, linen and silk), the center, especially Le Puy and its area (silk, thread and metallic bobbin laces), and Lyons (silk and gold and silver laces); back to Reims (royal manufactory) and the Lorraine area in the east (Mirecourt and its bobbin laces); and lastly to the north, all along the Belgian border, to Valenciennes, Sedan, Lille, and Arras (needle and bobbin laces). Only in the south of France, with a few scattered exceptions, was lace making never fully developed, though it was no doubt practiced there in homes and convents.

It is no exaggeration, therefore, to say that the French lace industry occupied at certain given times more hands, especially female ones, than any other finished products trade, with the possible exception of cloth weaving. Its laces did not always rise above mediocrity. But when they displayed in their technique and decor that sureness of taste nurtured by a long-established sense of national identity, they were without peer. At their best such laces contributed in no small measure to the charming yet decisive elegance that has come to be associated with everything French.

Notes

The bibliography for this essay starts on page 189.

B.N.: Bibliothèque Nationale, Paris
A.N.: Archives Nationales, Paris
A.S.V.: Archivio di Stato Veneto, Venice

1 I.e., "possono servire ancora per opere a mazette."
2 René de Lespinasse, *Les Métiers et corporations de la ville de Paris*, III: 32.
3 Ibid., III: 36: "passements made with two strings of plied or unplied yarn . . . passements in the manner of laces, . . . with square holes."
4 Ibid., III: 36.
5 Ibid., II: 148: "four-bobbin braids . . . passements in the manner of laces."
6 Ibid., II: 153: "all sorts of work in the manner of passements and laces made out of white thread . . . or any and all other sorts of thread . . . including colored ones."
7 Béatrix de Buffévent, "La Fabrication de la dentelle dans les campagnes parisiennes sous Louis XIV" (Thèse de Troisième Cycle, Université de Paris, 1979), p. 125: "open-work laces in the manner of Rouen" and "heart-shaped Rouen passements."
8 In her introduction to the facsimile of Vinciolo's book (Bergamo: Istituto Italiano d'Arti Grafiche, 1909), Elisa Ricci suggests that there existed a previous edition printed in Italy prior to 1587. Her argument rests on a mention in the dedicatory epistle of "patterns found earlier in Italy." Considering that all such patterns originated in Italy, her point fails to carry weight. Vinciolo's is a French book in the sense that it was first published in France.
9 Joan Evans, *Pattern: A Study of Ornament in Western Europe from 1180 to 1900* (New York: Da Capo, reprint, 1976); Vol. II: *The Renaissance to 1900*, p. 24.
10 Cf. Donald King, *The Eastern Carpet in the Western World* (London, 1984, exhibition catalogue), for examples of Anatolian rugs.
11 Jacob le Bibliophile (Paul Lacroix), *Receuil curieux de pièces originales* (n.d.), p. 105.
12 B.N., Actes Royaux, Imprimés 37, p. 1141.
13 B.N. MSS. 146, f. 217.
14 B.N. MSS. 145, f. 142.
15 B.N. MSS. 161, f. 233.
16 B.N. MSS. 149, f. 544.
17 B.N. MSS. 146, f. 100.
18 B.N. MSS. 148bis, f. 437.
19 B.N. MSS. 274, f. 21.
20 A. M. de Boislisle, *Documents inédits sur l'histoire de France* (Paris: Imprimerie Nationale, 1881), I: 606.
21 A.N., Minutier Central, X136, 2 April 1666.
22 A. M. de Boislisle, *Correspondance des contrôleurs généraux des finances avec les intendants des provinces* (Paris: Imprimerie Nationale, 1874), I, no. 9981.
23 Laprade, *Le Poinct de France* (1905), p. 72.
24 Jules Guiffrey, *Inventaire du mobilier de la couronne* (Paris: J. Rouen, 1886), II: 379–380.
25 Jacques Savary des Bruslons, *Dictionnaire universel du commerce* (Paris, 1741, new ed.), III: 262.

26 A.N. O1830, f. 676.
27 Philippe Guignet, "The Lace-Makers of Valenciennes in the 18th Century: An Economic and Social Study of a Group of Female workers under the Ancien Regime," *Textile History* 10, no. 96 (1979): 113.
28 A.N., F121430–1431, f. 1741/2.
29 A.S.V., Cinque Savii alla Mercanzia, B. 455.
30 A.N., F12561, f. 5.
31 A.N., F121430–1431, f. 49.
32 Despierres, *Histoire du point d'Alençon* (1886), pp. 81–84.
33 Evans, I: 108.
34 Charles Colas, *Rapport sur l'exposition de dentelles organisée à Caen à l'occasion de l'exposition de 1875* (Caen: Imprimerie Le Blanc-Handel, 1876), p. 32.
35 A.N., F122459, f. 4.
36 Wardle, *Victorian Lace* (1982, 2d ed.).
37 Anne Kraatz, "The Inventory of a Venetian Lace Merchant Dated 1671," in *Bulletin de Liaison du Centre International d'Etude des Textiles Anciens*, no. 55–56, Lyons, 1984, pp. 127–134.
38 Félix Aubry, *Exposition universelle de 1867 à Paris: "Dentelles"* (Paris, 1867), p. 11.
39 A.N., F122459, f. 1.
40 Colas, p. 50.
41 Maze-Sencier, *Les Fournisseurs de Napoléon Ier et des deux impératrices* (1893), pp. 321–322.
42 For a history of the Kashmir shawl in France see Monique Lévi-Strauss, Odile Valansot, Gabriel Vial, and Pierre Fayard, *Le Châle cachemire en France au 19e siècle* (Lyons: Musée Historique des Tissus, 1983).
43 *Souvenir de l'exposition de 1839* (Paris: Chavant, n.d.).
44 Colas, p. 45.
45 *Journal des Demoiselles*, 7th year, 2d series, no. 1 (Paris: Imprimerie de Veuve Dondey-Dupré, 1839), I: 188.

Printed Textiles ❖ Jacqueline Jacqué

Origins

Sumptuous silks have been the most valued and sought-after textiles throughout history, but their expense has always kept them a luxury item available mainly to the upper classes. The vast majority of the population has made do with piece-dyed woolens, cottons, and linens, which provide serviceable clothing and furnishings but which usually appear drab next to their silk cousins. One of the biggest problems Western textile manufacturers struggled with over the centuries was the difficulty of obtaining dyes that did not fade and were not fugitive when subjected to the repeated cleanings that functional textiles require.

Various attempts at printing patterns onto fabric with woodblocks were made in Europe throughout the Middle Ages and later, with the designs often derived from contemporary silk weavings.[1] However, no real technical progress was made in this field until Indian printed and painted cottons began to appear in Europe, brought back by those engaged in the recently established East Indian trade. By the late sixteenth century these curiosities, with their brilliant, wash-resistant colors, were capturing Europe's attention.

If the Western world was enamored with the new colors and exotic patterns available in these cottons, it was less than enthusiastic about the dark grounds that the Indians traditionally used.[2] The various companies controlling trade with the East—among them the Compagnie des Indes, founded in France in the seventeenth century—eventually acted to have cottons produced in India that were more to the European taste, keeping the exotic floral motifs but decreasing the scale of the pattern elements and placing them on predominantly white backgrounds in keeping with the general shift from baroque ornamentation to that of the rococo. To achieve this end, the Europeans frequently produced the designs themselves, which the Indian manufacturers translated into beautifully colored cotton goods destined for the ever-growing Western market.[3]

The techniques of textile printing that so intrigued Europe at this time had been practiced for centuries in the East, although the oldest extant Indian printed cottons date from only the fourteenth century, products of trade to Egypt that have been excavated at Fostat, outside Cairo.[4] Elaborate steps were taken to obtain the various colors, combining the techniques of mordant dyeing with resist dyeing and direct printing and painting onto the fabric. It is not surprising that, as these goods became more popular and more lucrative objects of trade in Europe, the desire grew to imitate them locally. Numerous reports were made on the Indian practices of dyeing and printing, one of the most complete being that of the ship captain de Beaulieu (1669–1764), of the Compagnie des Indes. Complete with samples of fabrics from each of the successive stages of production, de Beaulieu's manuscript of 1734 gives a very precise report of the techniques used in the Indian province of Pondicherry at that time.[5]

The first European workshop to attempt its own version of these printed textiles was established in the seventeenth century in Marseilles, the French port most in contact with the East. It was followed later in the century by manufactories in England, the Netherlands, Germany, and Switzerland. These early workshops produced mediocre textiles, however, and they provided no real competition for the trade goods. A second reason for the difficulties encountered by these early factories was the intense opposition they drew from both the silk and woolen industries and from the various East India companies, which could hardly expect to welcome competition from a European printed cotton or chintz market.

In France this opposition culminated in October 1686 with a decree issued by Louis XIV prohibiting the manufacture or sale of painted cloths. Moreover, the Edict of Nantes had been repealed in the previous year, which resulted in a mass exodus of Huguenots from France to other parts of Europe. As the majority of chintz makers were Protestant, their departure dealt a severe blow to the infant printing industry in France. No prohibition could stem the ever-increasing infatuation for chintz, however, and efficient enforcement was impossible. Nevertheless, France was to lag behind its European competitors in the production of these fabrics until well into the eighteenth century. Throughout this time printed fabric manufacture in France was maintained chiefly in the free ports and in certain privileged regions such as Chantilly.[6]

117 Detail of figure 123:
"Works of the Jouy
Manufactory."

Popular opinion favoring the rescindment of the prohibition of French-produced printed fabrics grew continually in the eighteenth century, culminating in 1759 with a report by Abbé Morellet, titled *Reflexions sur les avantages de la libre fabrication et de l'usage des toiles peintes en France*. On 5 September 1759 the ban on fabric printing in France was lifted, followed in 1760 by an edict requiring that all cloths painted or printed in the realm be stamped at the top and bottom with a red label (known as the "chef de pièce") indicating the manufacturer's name, the date of fabrication, and the designation of the use of "fast" or "commercial" dyes.[7] With these actions, France entered into an era of intense activity in the field of printed fabrics. Produced in important centers throughout the nation, ultimately they were rivaled only by England's printed textile industry.

The Jouy Manufactory (1759–1843)

Undoubtedly the best known of all French printed fabric manufactories is that of Jouy.[8] This reputation was well earned, as the Jouy factory was blessed with an able and innovative director, talented designers,

and a knack for producing fabrics that answered the needs and tastes of its varied markets. Jouy's activities throughout its history mirror those of other French factories, and by studying its production one can gain an understanding of the technical progress and stylistic trends of the field as a whole.

Christophe Philippe Oberkampf (1738–1815), director of the printed fabric works at Jouy from 1760 until his death, was the single most important force in the manufactory's leading position. Coming from a family of Protestant dyers in Württemberg, Germany, he learned his trade from his father and added to that education in Basel, Lörrach, and Aarau. For a long time he worked as an engraver in Mulhouse at Koechlin Dollfus & Cie., before settling in Paris where he worked in the privileged enclosure of the arsenal of the Clos Payen. At the time the ban on printed fabrics was lifted, a Swiss, A. Guerne, called Tavanne, noticed the young Oberkampf's talents and took him on as an associate. The result was the establishment of a small factory in the village of Jouy-en-Josas, near Versailles, on the banks of the Bièvre. The river was famous for the purity of its water, an important consideration in obtaining dyes of high quality.

118 Two-part dress. Jouy-en-Josas, Oberkampf Manufactory, end of the eighteenth century. Tabby weave, cotton warp and weft. Copperplate printed: alumina mordant, madder dye; carmine red. H. of overdress: 52³/₈ (133); H. of petticoat: 35¹/₂ (90). Musée de l'Impression sur Etoffes, Mulhouse, 983.405.1 and 2.

119 Furnishing fabric. Jouy-en-Josas, Oberkampf Manufactory, ca. 1775. Tabby weave, cotton warp and weft. Copperplate printed: alumina mordant, madder dye; pink. H. of repeat: 36¹/₂ (93). Musée de l'Impression sur Etoffes, Mulhouse, 977.177.1.

The first fabrics produced in this factory were printed by woodblocks in a manner illustrated in a later textile design, "Works of the Jouy Manufactory" (figure 117). Here the printer stands behind a table several yards long, which is covered with a thick flannel padding that is in turn covered with the white cloth on which the printing will be done. The large vat to the right of the table contains the dye.

The printer, having permeated with dye his block, on which the pattern has been carved, places the block on the cloth and beats it with a mallet to facilitate the penetration of the dye. Often several blocks were used for a single textile, carrying different pattern elements or a succession of different dyes.[9] The designs of these wood-block prints were most often floral (such as that shown on the textile of figure 117), and frequently bear a striking resemblance to those of their Indian cousins.

A second textile technique, copperplate printing, which was perfected in the eighteenth century, was to revolutionize the industry and eventually provide a totally new design vocabulary for printed fabrics. As early as 1752 the engraved copperplate was adapted to continuous textile printing in Ireland, and in 1770 Oberkampf introduced it to France through his Jouy factory. At first the patterns he used were

120 Furnishing fabric:
"Chinoiseries."
Jouy-en-Josas, Oberkampf
Manufactory, ca. 1780.
Tabby weave, cotton warp
and weft. Copperplate
printed: alumina mordant,
madder dye; red. H. of repeat:
39 (99), incomplete. Musée de
l'Impression sur Etoffes,
Mulhouse, 954.450.1.

similar to those of the wood-block prints. The graceful floral motifs of roses, daisies, and sweetbriar on
the dress in figure 118 could have been produced by
either method, although here they have been printed
by copperplate.[10] However, the designs were to
become more and more scenic in nature, quite
possibly due to their close technical relationship to
prints executed on paper. A furnishing fabric featuring various game birds (figure 119), printed in Jouy
around 1775, shows a step in this progression. One
of the challenges of the copperplate was the production of designs that were balanced and did not
give jarring evidence of the beginning and end of the
repeat. In these matters, the fabrics of Jouy excelled.

The printed fabric "Chinoiseries" (figure 120)
demonstrates the frequent dependence on print
sources for designs. Here the designer has incorporated six vignettes by the French artist Jean

121 One of the six engravings by Jean Baptiste Pillement entitled
Collections of Several Chinese Children Playing Games.

122 Furnishing fabric: "Chinoiseries." England, Nixon and Co.,
ca. 1775. Musée de l'Impression sur Etoffes, Mulhouse,
976.209.1.

Baptiste Pillement (figure 121) into his scheme,
connecting them with graceful branches and garlands of flowers. A comparison of this treatment of
Pillement's original design with another printed in
England by Nixon and Co. (figure 122) is instructive
in its affirmation of the superiority of Jouy's textiles.
The French design sways gracefully from one scene
to the next, with no hint of a break in its rhythm. The
English example, on the other hand, stacks one scene
on top of the other with an awkward break in the
pattern between the two. The printing of the English
example is very skillful, admittedly, with every
engraved detail visible. This technical virtuosity
seems to have been the chief concern here, however,
while the Jouy scenes transcend their origin as
separate prints, to form a unified design better suited
to use as a continuous length of cloth.

Jean-Baptiste Huet (1745–1811) was surely the

most talented of Jouy's designers. He worked there
for many years as principal cartoonist, and his
distinctive style was copied by other cotton printing
factories throughout France. Whether adapting
earlier prints to the textile medium or creating totally
new designs, he succeeded in turning out beautifully
balanced scenic compositions skillfully distributed
on cloth. One of his most famous designs, "Works
of the Jouy Manufactory" (figure 123), was the first
order that Oberkampf placed with him. This textile
was intended to celebrate the granting of letters of
patent of 19 June 1783 that made Jouy a royal manufactory. Its scenes trace the various steps required to
create a finished printed fabric. The activity is rather
idyllic, however, with the looms, dye vats, and
other machinery placed across a landscape instead
of within the factory walls. Huet himself makes a
cameo appearance as the man seated at his drawing
table in the center of this activity, while to his back
Oberkampf and his son are taking a stroll. The
buildings presented in the vistas are those of the
village of Jouy. The overall effect, punctuated by
romanticized foliage, would have surprised a factory
worker of the time, however, as it appears more
appropriate to a fête galante than an industrial
activity.

Copperplate printed fabrics of the late eighteenth
and early nineteenth centuries, because of their
pictorial possibilities, were frequently used to depict
or reflect upon contemporary events; and with political and social revolutions occurring around the
world there was no lack of potential subject matter.
One of Huet's designs in this vein is "America's
Tribute to France" (figure 125), executed about 1783
or 1784, in which the new country thanks France for
help provided during its victorious fight for independence from England. The main scene shows a
seated crowned woman, representing France,
holding a scepter and resting her left hand on a globe
decorated with a fleur de lys. Behind her a soldier in
armor holds a flag that also bears fleurs de lys. The
exotic contingent from America that she greets
includes an Indian, a woman symbolizing liberty, a
soldier carrying the American flag, and a kneeling
black man. This party is circled with secondary
scenes of loaded ships prepared to depart for the new
country, an allusion to the freedom of the seas, with
the towers of the French harbor La Rochelle in the

123 Jean-Baptiste Huet, design. Furnishing fabric: "Works of the Jouy Manufactory." Juoy-en-Josas, Oberkampf Manufactory, 1783. Tabby weave, cotton warp and weft. Copperplate printed: alumina mordant, madder dye; pink. H. of repeat: 36¼ (92). Musée de l'Impression sur Etoffes, Mulhouse, 858.344.1.

background. As was frequently the case with Jouy's textiles, this design was copied elsewhere in France. At least two other versions of it are known: a polychrome example produced in Nantes,[11] and a more primitive version thought to have been printed in Alsace.[12]

The romanticism of these copperplate printed textiles frequently joined with popular rococo decorative elements, the result of which were designs such as "The Four Elements," printed about 1790 in Jouy (figure 124). Here the unknown designer based his scenes directly on a series of four engravings of the same subject executed by Charles Dupuis (1685–1742) and Louis Desplaces (1682–1739) after the Parisian artist Louis de Boullogne le Jeune (1654–1733).[13] While the figures chosen by the designer appear virtually unaltered from their earlier counterparts, the whole effect of the printed fabric is

much lighter. Many figures have been dropped completely, and the background is white, with no suggestion of sky or clouds. The most notable innovation, however, is the compartmentalization of the scenic elements, quite different from the continuous landscapes of earlier printed fabrics. The delicate scrolling borders include garlands and trophies associated with the elements depicted within the scenes. This idea of gathering scenes in medallions or cameos was to reach its fullest realization in the designs of the early nineteenth century (see figure 133, for example).

It would be incorrect to assume that only scenic copperplate printed fabrics were produced in Jouy or elsewhere in France in the late eighteenth century, as the handkerchief of figure 126, printed by woodblocks, shows. Floral prints never ceased to be popular, especially for costumes and accessories, and

124 Furnishing fabric: "The Four Elements." Jouy-en-Josas, Oberkampf Manufactory, ca. 1790. Tabby weave, cotton warp and weft. Copperplate printed: alumina mordant, madder dye; red. H. of repeat: 39³/₈ (100). Musée de l'Impression sur Etoffes, Mulhouse, 961.284.1.

125 Jean-Baptiste Huet, design. Furnishing fabric: "America's Tribute to France. Jouy-en-Josas, Oberkampf Manufactory, ca. 1783–1784. Tabby weave, cotton warp and weft. Copperplate printed: alumina mordant; red. H. of repeat: 38¹/₂ (98), incomplete. Musée de l'Impression sur Etoffes, Mulhouse, 961.320.1.

126 Thierry, design. Hand-kerchief. Jouy-en-Josas, Oberkampf Manufactory, 1795–1800. Tabby weave, cotton warp and weft. Wood-block printed, with wood and metallic relief printing: two reds, black, blue, and yellow. H.: 38 (96.5); W.: 37 (94). Musée de l'Impression sur Etoffes, Mulhouse, 954.573.1M.

they were especially coveted by the middle classes throughout France. However, the flowers tended more and more to be local varieties rather than those of the first Indian-inspired chintzes, and here they are naturalistically rendered tulips, carnations, roses, and daisies.[14] Often dyed, as here, the backgrounds for these textiles became darker toward the early 1800s, popular because they showed wear and soil less. These floral handkerchiefs were especially desirable in the late eighteenth and early nineteenth centuries, when they were worn by women as small shawls crossed at the bosoms of their otherwise unpatterned empire-style dresses.

In 1783 an Englishman named Thomas Bell perfected printing with an engraved copper cylinder, and this innovation eventually dramatically changed the textile printing industry—technically, economically, and in terms of design. By 1797, when Oberkampf introduced copper-roller printing on the European continent, a single machine could produce over five thousand yards of printed fabric a day, which dramatically speeded up production and reduced the cost of the finished fabrics. Moreover, he soon brought back from England a three-roller machine that could print different colors at the same time. The economic advantages of roller printing are obvious, but the technique caused certain design problems. Because the copper cylinders were continuous, the occasional awkward break that could occur between impressions of copperplates was eliminated. However, the diameter of the cylinders was seldom more than twenty inches and often as little as fourteen, so that a repeat of the pattern occurred much more quickly than before.

Even the most talented designers had difficulty adjusting to this new limitation, as one can see in the

127 Jean-Baptiste Huet, design. Furnishing fabric: "Paul et Virginie." Jouy-en-Josas, Oberkampf Manufactory, 1802. Tabby weave, cotton warp and weft. Copper-roller printed: brown. H. of repeat: 20 (51). Musée de l'Impression sur Etoffes, Mulhouse, 961.359.1.

128 Set of bed hangings in twelve parts. Jouy-en-Josas, Oberkampf Manufactory, 1812. Tabby weave, cotton warp and weft. Copper-roller printed: sepia. H. of repeat: 19¼ (49). Musée de l'Impression sur Etoffes, Mulhouse, 961.333.1–3.

printed fabric "Paul et Virginie," designed by Huet in 1802 (figure 127).[15] Based on a popular novel of the day, the scenes deal with events leading up to a shipwreck in which Virginie dies, to be mourned by Paul. The skilled engraving of Huet is present everywhere, but the whole design lacks the space, the room to breathe, that characterize his earlier compositions. This should not be surprising in that the total height of the pattern repeat here is only one-half that of the typical copperplate print.

A more successful means of employing the roller printer, and one that suited the neoclassical design vocabulary, was the placement of scenes on a ground with an endlessly repeating pattern element. In Jouy's design of 1812 celebrating the arts (figure 128) this element is scallops joined at the intersections with stars. Even here, however, there is a certain imbalance and crowding, which is not helped by the placement of trophies in the junctures of the scenes. The scenes themselves demonstrate the popular fascination with classical subject matter, in their depiction of the four arts. At top center Orpheus and Eurydice, exiting Hades, represent music. To either side a young couple tracing their silhouettes on a wall represent art. In the center left sculpture is honored by Pygmalion finishing his Galatea. The remaining scene, symbolizing architecture, shows Anaxagoras presenting Alexander with the draft of a triumphal arch.

Throughout his lifetime Oberkampf kept his manufactory in Jouy in the forefront of French art, reaping numerous awards. In 1806 he received the gold medal of the exposition of industrial products; in 1812, the grand decennial prize for scientific works rewarding the best performance by a French manufacturer. Napoleon, who came to visit him twice, in 1806 and 1810, awarded him the Legion of Honor. After Oberkampf's death in 1815, the factory continued its successful production until finally closing its doors in 1843.

Nantes

Jouy is undoubtedly the best known of the textile printing factories in France, but this village had many important compatriot rivals, ranging from the port city of Nantes to the Alsace region located on the French-German border. Each of these regions made its own special contribution to the art of printed fabrics, and any general study of this field must not overlook them.

Nantes, a Breton port on the Loire River, had all the necessary elements for the development of textile printing. It was a rich city due to its thriving business community, and was in fact one of the leading importers of Indian printed cottons. As a port, Nantes had numerous foreign technicians and attracted many Protestant workers seeking to settle or emigrate from there. Finally, there was a large local work force and an abundance of clean water. As early as 1758 printing factories began to spring up and prosper, and by 1785 there were nine, employing twelve hundred workers.

Among the Nantes manufacturers, Pierre Dubern (1789–1813) and the Gorgerat brothers

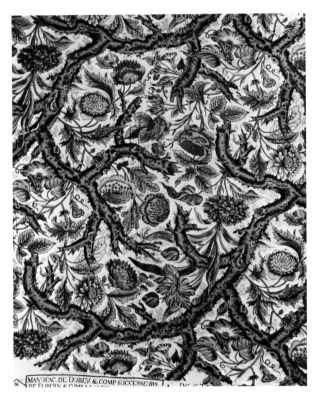

129 Furnishing fabric. Nantes, Manufactory Dubey & Cie. [mark], ca. 1810. Tabby weave, cotton warp and weft. Woodblock printed: vegetable mordants; eight colors. H. overall: 40½ (103). Musée de l'Impression sur Etoffes, Mulhouse, 954.445.1.

(1760–1815) deserve mention, but the most important factory was that founded in 1770 by the Petit-pierre brothers from Neuchâtel, Switzerland. At the factory's peak in 1790 its printed textiles supplied clients throughout France, as well as in Italy, Switzerland, and Germany.

The productions of the Nantes manufactories most often cannot be distinguished from one another without the existence of a trademark. However, as a group they can often be distinguished stylistically from the textiles of Oberkampf's factory at Jouy. Their design is often more naive, and the scale of the patterns from one scene to another often does not take perspective into account. The city's proximity to England may account for the regular occurrence of elements drawn from that country's parks and gardens, and its existence as a port explains frequent references to shipping, exotic vegetation, and a fascination with subjects drawn from distant lands. Although textile printing was to thrive here for a long time, the factories began to close one after another in the second quarter of the nineteenth century due to competition from Rouen and Alsace.

The floral print in figure 129 is not the earliest of the Nantes examples illustrated here, as it is believed to date from about 1810. Its relatively late date is important, however, in demonstrating the persistence in Nantes of earlier technical and design practices. The pattern is executed by means of woodblocks in no fewer than eight colors, a range infrequently encountered during the height of copperplate and roller printing. Moreover, the floral motifs look back to their Eastern origins, possibly due to Nantes's continuing trade with these regions. They evoke much of the exoticism of flowers appearing in Indian chintzes and are certainly far removed from the blossoms on the more or less contemporary handkerchief produced in Jouy (figure 126).

Figures 130, 131, and 132, all produced by the Petitpierre factory in Nantes, are prime examples of copperplate printed fabrics of latter eighteenth-century France. Their varied subjects are typical of the production as a whole, but each has characteristics peculiar to Nantes. "The Chariot of Dawn," produced between 1785 and 1789, again shows the great interest in classical mythology and architecture awakened at this time (figure 130).[16] Here the main

130 Furnishing fabric: "The Chariot of Dawn." Nantes, Petitpierre & Cie., ca. 1785–1789. Tabby weave, cotton warp and weft. Copperplate printed: alumina mordant, madder dye; red. H. of repeat: 39 (99). Musée de l'Impression sur Etoffes, Mulhouse, 954.455.1.

element, the chariot grouping, is derived from the famous *Aurora* fresco by Guido Reni (1575–1642) at the Casino Rospigliosi in Rome. Closer to home, Le Brun (1616–1690) had also used this same model for the central sculpture of the Apollo basin at Versailles. Other scenes have identifiable progenitors, among them that of Daphne turning into a tree just as Apollo catches her, reminiscent of Bernini's grouping in the Borghese Gallery in Rome, and a temple of music inspired by the Temple of the Sybil in Tivoli. This textile is not lacking for visual excitement, with its many scenes and vistas. However, the design as a whole suffers from the huge scale of the chariot grouping in relation to the many smaller scenes around it. Moreover, the foliage of the independent motifs seems to serve no other purpose than to provide visual interest and to fill otherwise empty

131 Furnishing fabric: "The Inauguration of the Port of Cherbourg by Louis XVI." Nantes, Petitpierre & Cie., ca. 1787. Tabby weave, cotton warp and weft. Copperplate printed: alumina mordant, madder dye; red. H. of repeat: 38³/₄ (98.5). Musée de l'Impression sur Etoffes, Mulhouse, 859.4.1.

spaces. The balance and rhythmic movement from one scene to another, so important in the best of Jouy's designs (see figure 123, for example), is missing here.

A Nantes treatment of an historical event may be seen in "The Inauguration of the Port of Cherbourg by Louis XVI," printed about 1787 (figure 131). The popularity of this nautical subject in Nantes can be easily understood, especially in light of its historic significance. The king's journey to Cherbourg in June 1787 marked his only official trip away from the French court until his ill-fated trip to Varenne in 1792. The building of the harbor jetty, begun in 1783

and not completed until 1858, was achieved by the sinking of huge cones, which then served as foundations. The act of placing these cones must have been spectacular, and one suspects that the novelty of the feat was as important as any political or ceremonial consideration the king may have had in wishing to be present on one such occasion.

The king appears several times in the textile's scenes: standing with his party in a royal barge positioned in the harbor, greeting subjects on the land, and riding in a carriage. The port of Cherbourg is also depicted, as well as several of the jetty cones. The scale of these motifs is in better balance than in

"The Chariot of Dawn," but one does notice the designer's tendency to avoid any open space, preferring instead to fill it with ships of random size.

"Panurge dans l'île des lanternes" (Panurge on the Island of Lanterns) offers another expression of the chinoiserie so popular throughout Europe during most of the eighteenth century (figure 132). The title, found on a banner held in one of the textile's scenes, refers to a popular comedy of the day, which had music by Crety and a libretto by the Count of Provence and Morel. The story was inspired by Rabelais, and Panurge is a character from his *Pantagruel* who arrives after many misadventures on the Island of Lanterns near China. Here the unknown designer has taken delight in providing exotic costumes and landscapes for the charming

132 Furnishing fabric, quilted, "Panurge dans l'île des lanternes," Nantes, Petitpierre & Cie., ca. 1785–1790. Tabby weave, cotton warp and weft. Copperplate printed: alumina mordant, madder dye; red. H. of repeat: 41 (104). Wadsworth Atheneum, Healy Fund, 1943.111.

133 Furnishing fabric, quilted: "Homage to Love." Nantes, Favre, Petitpierre & Cie., ca. 1815. Tabby weave, cotton warp and weft. Copper-roller printed, with wood-block and copperplate details: alumina mordant, madder dye; red with yellow and dark red. H. of repeat: 18³/4 (47.5). Musée de l'Impression sur Etoffes, Mulhouse, 961.688.1.

134 Furnishing fabric: "The Country Wedding." Nantes, Favre, Petitpierre & Cie. [mark], ca. 1820. Tabby weave, cotton warp and weft. Copperplate printed: iron pyrolignite mordant, madder dye; purple. H. of repeat: 41³/8 (105). Musée de l'Impression sur Etoffes, Mulhouse, 954.453.1.

action taking place. Once more the visual interest is derived mainly from the individual vignettes rather than from the design as a whole.

A later printed fabric from the Favre, Petitpierre factory, "Homage to Love" (figure 133), shows a typical fully developed roller printed design with scenic medallions against a background of extremely stylized leaf patterns. These patterns and the medallion borders themselves were popular elements of the empire style, recurring again and again in architectural details, on furniture ornament, and in silk weavings of the early nineteenth century.[17] This textile is technically more complex than many in that, while the main red of the medallion scenes was roller printed, a yellow was then added with woodblocks and a darker red with copperplates. Virtually

none of Nantes's designers are known to us today. However, it is worthy of note that the manufacturer of this printed fabric—Favre, Petitpierre & Cie. —has apparently left us its initials "FP" on a small rock in one of the medallions.

A final example of Nantes's production, "The Country Wedding," is also by Favre, Petitpierre & Cie. (figure 134). This copperplate print, dating from around 1820, boasts an extremely unusual design layout. The four scenes, directly inspired by prints of Jazet from *Hippolyte Lecomte*,[18] show the proposal, wedding ceremony, procession, and banquet. Here no attempt has been made to give any space to the individual scenes, nor have they been staggered. Rather they are lined up side by side and one on top of another, which promotes an uneasiness in trying to read the perspective of the whole. This textile may have been popular at the time, for it was copied,[19] but it is not surprising that this peculiar arrangement of scenes is extremely rare.

Alsace

Of the many locations in Alsace where textile print-ing was established in the eighteenth century, none was more important than Mulhouse. In 1746 four young men launched a small cloth printing factory there, Koechlin Schmalzer & Cie., which was to alter the history of the city.[20] Others, attracted by their success, followed their example. By 1768 Mulhouse had fifteen textile printing factories, and by 1787 nineteen. The whole Alsatian province was affected by this new activity, which generated work in related fields as well, such as spinning and weaving. Among the factors favoring Mulhouse as a printed fabric center were, of course, plentiful sup-plies of clean water and of cotton cloth from nearby Switzerland. But equally important was its situation along a trade route reaching from Basel, Switzer-land, a financial center, to the Lorraine in France. At its peak in the nineteenth century, the printing industry in Alsace employed as many as fourteen thousand workers.

Mulhouse always dominated the Alsatian printed textile field, but the situation was one of constant change as different factories gained prominence and then subsided. In the second half of the eighteenth century the industry branched out to other parts of Alsace, among them enterprises in the upper Rhine-land, in particular in the Vosges valley. Haussmann, at Logelbach near Colmar, was founded in 1775 by a chemist who had worked with Schule d'Augsbourg, a famous German printer. The Hartmann factory in Münster was established by J. J. Schmalzer in 1777, reaching the peak of its fame in the first quarter of the

135 Dujardin, design. Furnishing fabric: "The Horse Cart and Village Dance." Alsace, Wesserling Manufactory, ca. 1785. Tabby weave, cotton warp and weft. Copperplate printed with wood-block details: brown red, blue and yellow. H. of repeat: 35½ (90.5), incomplete. Musée de l'Impression sur Etoffes, Mulhouse, 858.64.1.

nineteenth century. The Wesserling manufactory was also started in 1777, and later it was granted the title of royal manufactory by Louis XVI.[21]

"The Horse Cart and Village Dance" (figure 135) is an accomplished fabric from the Wesserling factory, dating from about 1785. Here one sees an excellent example of a copperplate print supple-mented by wood-block printing to obtain a polychrome textile. The bucolic scenes are quite different from those of contemporary fabrics from Jouy or Nantes. They have an earthy vitality, featuring robust figures, rather than a more subdued elegance of line. The textile is no less accomplished technically, but rather it is aimed at giving a more direct and less intellectual pleasure. While the Alsatian printers could, and often did, imitate their city cousins, this piece shows their delight in por-traying simple but vivacious activities. The figures take over the cloth, with what landscape elements there are receding into the background. Yet the

136 Dujardin. Watercolor study for "The Horse Cart and Village Dance." Musée de l'Impression sur Etoffes, Mulhouse.

137 Dujardin. Wash study for "The Horse Cart and Village Dance." Musée de l'Impression sur Etoffes, Mulhouse.

whole design has a grace and balance that is a tribute to the designer. The artist for these scenes was apparently one Dujardin, whose watercolor and wash drawing for these two scenes (figures 136 and 137) have survived in the Wesserling factory's archives.

Another outstanding textile from the Wesserling factory is illustrated in figure 138. Apparently intended for use as wall paneling, it features a bust of Benjamin Franklin in an almost architectural setting,

with decorative elements popular at the time of Napoleon. Here again a copperplate was employed for the major part of the printing, with added details and colors introduced through wood-block printing. The bust is part of a still life, resting on a drapery covered with fruits and flowers. This bust is visually set into a wall panel, with a second panel above featuring a sunburst and clouds with an eye at their center, a rectangular panel below patterned in imitation of marble, and finally a border along the

138 Jean Koechlin, design. Furnishing fabric: "Benjamin Franklin." Alsace, Wesserling Manufactory, ca. 1800. Tabby weave, cotton warp and weft. Copperplate and wood-block printed: black, brown, yellow, red, blue. 98 x 48½ (248.9 x 123.2). Musée de l'Impression sur Etoffes, Mulhouse, 863.1.1.

139 Cape. Alsace, Haussmann Manufactory, ca. 1780. Tabby weave, cotton warp and weft. Wood-block printed: five colors. H.: 48⅞ (124). Musée de l'Impression sur Etoffes, Mulhouse, 954.492.1.

bottom reminiscent of woven silk trims of the period. Thus a single textile gives the effect of several different media.

The elegance of this textile shows the extreme sophistication of furnishing fabrics that Alsatian printers could achieve. At least as important in their production, however, were textiles meant to be used as clothing and accessories, and fortunately a large number of these have survived (figures 139–143).

The cape of figure 139 is a type that was extremely popular in the latter eighteenth century. The flowers strewn over the dark ground show an affinity to their Indian prototypes, but they are now westernized and less exotic. The dark background itself, which became known as "ramoneur" (literally, chimney sweep), enjoyed a great vogue at the same time, no doubt partially because it would show little dirt even after repeated wearings.

The man's waistcoat in figure 140 is an extremely elegant example of a printed design intended for wear. Uncut, it closely resembles contemporary embroidered examples, and shows the care that went into the production of every detail, down to the dyeing of circles along the center vertical axis, intended to cover the garment's buttons when cut out. Produced in the Hartmann factory in Münster in the late 1790s, it was designed by Marie Bonaventure Lebert. She makes reference to objects of this type, with their Wedgwood-like pocket decorations, in her diary: "My diary includes drawings of various kinds with prints on fabrics . . . from the eighteenth century for articles of clothing, waistcoats with antique cameo subjects on the pockets."[22]

The Kashmir or paisley shawl was as popular and elegant an article of woman's clothing in the late eighteenth and early nineteenth centuries as was the man's neoclassical-style waistcoat. Any Frenchwoman who could afford a genuine shawl woven from the fine hair of highland Kashmir goats had one. Indeed one needs only to look at female portraiture of Europe and America from the early nineteenth century to understand just how common

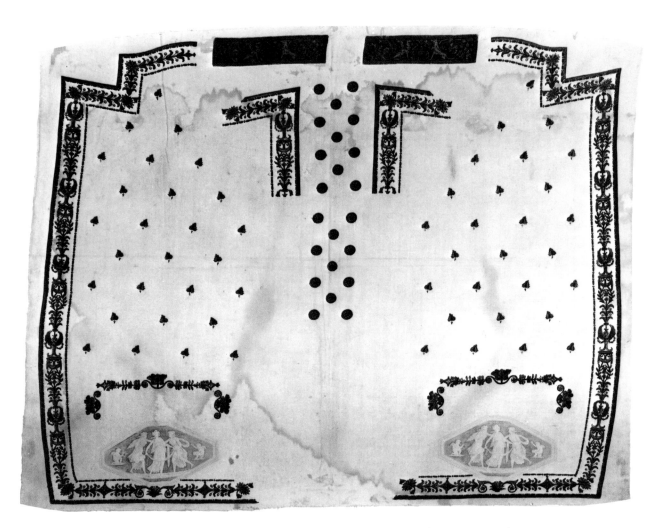

140 Marie Bonaventure Lebert, design. Man's waistcoat. Alsace, André Hartmann Manufactory, ca. 1797. Serge weave, cotton warp and weft. Wood-block, copperplate printed and painted: charcoal, yellow, two blues. 25½ x 31½ (65 x 80). Musée de l'Impression sur Etoffes, Mulhouse, 858.333.1.

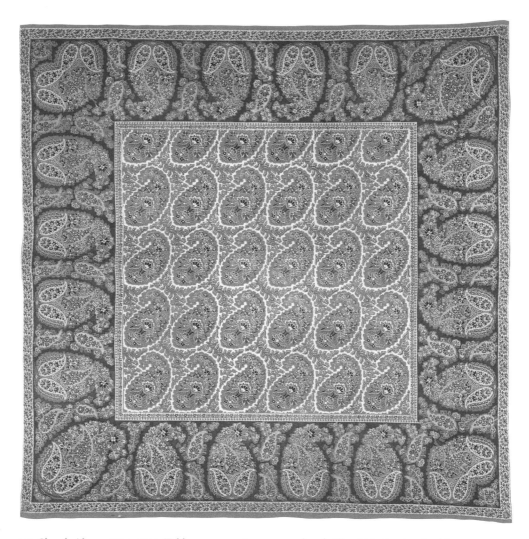

141 Shawl. Alsace, 1800–1825. Tabby weave, cotton warp and weft. Wood-block printed: white, yellow, blue, black, red. 44¹/₂ x 42¹/₁₆ (113 x 107). Wadsworth Atheneum, Gift of John G. Greene, 1956.352.

a luxury item the shawls must have been. Aside from their exotic designs, they were practical—lightweight but still quite warm, an advantage at a time when fashionable dresses were thin garments of muslin with few underpinnings.

Of course, not everyone could afford the real thing, and European woven copies began to be made in the nineteenth century for broader consumption. For those women who could not afford or did not feel it necessary to own either an original or a woven

imitation, printed fabrics such as the shawl in figure 141 began to be produced. This textile, made in Alsace, probably dates from the first quarter of the nineteenth century. Here the cone-shaped buta flower is not yet elongated, and the various blossoms that make up its body are more realistic than those of a later date. While from close-up this printed fabric would not have the feel or look of an authentic Kashmir shawl, from a distance it would have produced the desired exotic effect.

Most of the printed textiles that have been preserved are of the more sophisticated scenic designs, meant for furnishing upper-class homes. However, they were surely not a majority of what was produced in printing factories. With the advent of printed fabrics, patterned textiles for the first time were affordable for the middle and even lower classes as well, and patterns such as that of the petticoat of figure 142 were turned out in vast quantities. This type of floral pattern was apparently extremely popular in the south of France, judging from the number of examples preserved in the regional museums of Provence. In the eighteenth century many small regional factories produced goods such as these, but by the turn of the century their production was eclipsed by similar examples that poured forth from the larger factories of Jouy and Alsace. This petticoat features a particularly charming wood-block pattern of floral sprays, printed in six colors on a yellow ground.

Flowers were ever-popular motifs for dress and accessories, as a handkerchief manufactured in Alsace between 1836 and 1841 attests (figure 143). The dark background here provides an excellent contrast to the realistic peonies, roses, and sweet-briar distributed across the field.

Scenic painted fabrics maintained their popularity as furnishing fabrics throughout the first half of the nineteenth century. Their overall appearance underwent a metamorphosis, however, as can be seen in figure 144, produced in Alsace about 1840. Here the roller printed design organizes scenes in medallions, a style established in the early nineteenth century (cf. figure 133). However, the small-scale geometric background has given way to virtual jungles of floral wreaths that are in danger of over-powering the children fishing and playing with geese. A common stylistic device at this time, it indicates the increased massing of design elements that was to become characteristic of the decorative arts in the Victorian era. With regard to printed fabrics, flowers did indeed succeed in overtaking scenes, and few figural depictions occur in these objects after the middle of the century. This textile is especially significant, as preparatory studies for it exist in two stages. Figure 145 shows the scenes outlined but not filled in, while figure 146 shows a completed rendering of the figures in tinted colors.[23]

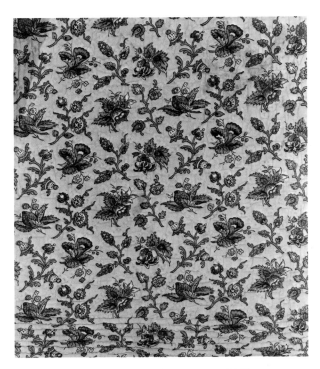

142 Petticoat, detail, quilted. Alsace, ca. 1830. Tabby weave, cotton warp and weft. Wood-block printed: six colors on yellow. 36½ (92). Musée de l'Impression sur Etoffes, Mulhouse, 981.395.1.

143 Handkerchief. Alsace, Eck, Dollfus & Huguenin Manufactory [mark], 1836–1841. Tabby weave, cotton warp and weft. Wood-block printed: five colors on brown. 44½ x 44½ (113 x 113). Musée de l'Impression sur Etoffes, Mulhouse, 859.26.1.

144 Furnishing fabric. Alsace, Dollfus Mieg(?), ca. 1840. Tabby weave, cotton warp and weft. Roller printed: brown. H. of repeat: 18⅜ (46.5). Musée de l'Impression sur Etoffes, Mulhouse, 978.45.1.

145 Preparatory drawing for figure 144. Musée de l'Impression sur Etoffes, Mulhouse.

146 Preparatory drawing, tinted, for figure 144. Musée de l'Impression sur Etoffes, Mulhouse.

Other Centers of Textile Printing

The factories of Jouy, Nantes, and Alsace were joined by those of many other French regions at various times throughout the latter eighteenth and early nineteenth centuries, but less is known of their production. Little documentary or archival material has survived for these manufactories, and attributions can be made only infrequently to one or another of these regions. When a textile does permit such an attribution, it most often gives clues to the relative obscurity of its place of origin. The majority of these examples are of mediocre technical quality and less skillful design. These factors, perhaps combined with a weaker financial base and less sophisticated promotion, could explain why the textiles from these areas did not manage to compete successfully with their better-known counterparts for any length of time.

This does not mean that certain regions did not have major factories at one time. Rouen, for example, was one of the oldest textile centers in France, and textile printing was introduced there in 1763 by Frey. By 1786 the city had twelve factories, and there were more than ten others in the surrounding countryside. Nevertheless, the preserved examples from Rouen are rarely exciting. The copperplate prints are often copies from the factories of Jouy and Nantes. Wood-block prints frequently show an endearing naiveté, but the technical quality is seldom first-rate.

The range of wood-block patterns that may have been available in Rouen toward the close of the eighteenth century may be seen in figure 147, a sampler of patterns. This sampler is unique, the only known instance where the various patterns remain on the length of fabric rather than having been cut up and placed in a sample book. It bears a Rouen trademark on a small fabric stitched to its back (figure 148). While not of one piece, the trademark and the sampler are printed on an identical ground, which reinforces the theory that this printed fabric may have been manufactured in Rouen.

The handkerchief in figure 150 is probably more typical of production in Rouen. On the whole the city tended to specialize in more ordinary products of this kind. In addition to floral designs such as this one, Rouen had a phenomenal success with anecdotal handkerchiefs depicting military, political, and everyday themes. This particular example is of note for its light, graceful design and for its monochromatic purple color, suitable for women in half mourning.

One other floral furnishing fabric of about 1800 deserves notice (figure 149), as its trademark identifies it as having been printed in the Meillier factory in Beautiran near Bordeaux. This woodblock printed fabric is unusual for its smoothness of contour in the framing elements and in the leaves and petals of the flowers themselves. These outlines produce stylized shapes quite unusual for this time.

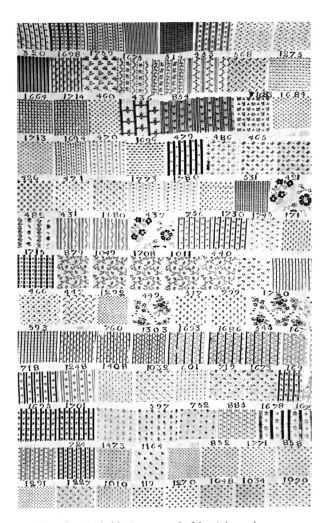

147 Sampler. Probably Rouen, end of the eighteenth century. Tabby weave, cotton warp and weft. Wood-block printed: black, blue, red, and purple. 78 x 32³/4 (198.1 x 83.2). Philadelphia Museum of Art, Purchase, Art in Industry Fund, 37.11.12.

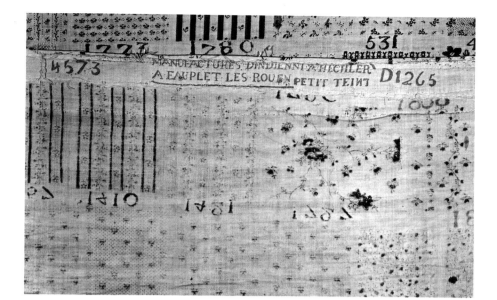

148 Detail of figure 147, reverse, showing chef de pièce stitched to back.

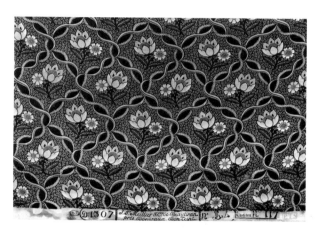

149 Furnishing fabric. Beautiran near Bordeaux, Meillier Manufactory, ca. 1800. Tabby weave, cotton warp and weft. Wood-block printed: black, beige, red. H. of repeat: 9½ (24). Musée de l'Impression sur Etoffes, Mulhouse, 954.466.1.

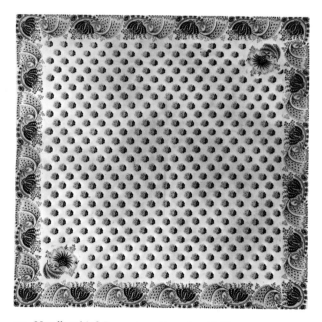

150 Handkerchief. Rouen, ca. 1830–1840. Tabby weave, cotton warp and weft. Wood-block printed: purple. 36⅝ x 35½ (93 x 90). Musée de l'Impression sur Etoffes, Mulhouse, 954.589.1.

Printed Cottons after 1850

Two last floral textiles show the direction of cotton printing at the time of the Second Empire. The first features a pattern of wisteria designed by Charles Ruffly about 1856–1857 and produced in the Schwartz–Huguenin factory in Dornach (figure 151), intended as a companion to wallpaper of the same design produced by Jean Zuber & Cie. (figures 152 and 153). The collaboration of Jean Zuber with various textile factories in Alsace began in 1845 and continued throughout the Second Empire.

The goal of the design here is apparently to produce the most realistic flowers possible and, moreover, to shade them in a successful attempt at three-dimensionality. They seem to float on the surface of the textile, rather than to be an integral part of it. In an era becoming familiar with the ideas of indoor plants and winter gardening, this floral

151 Furnishing fabric. Dornach, Schwartz-Huguenin Manufactory, design by Charles Ruffly, ca. 1856–1857. Tabby weave, cotton warp and weft. Wood-block printed: white, gray, H. of repeat: 29³/₈ (74.5). Musée de l'Impression sur Etoffes, Mulhouse, 980.328.1.

152 Charles Ruffly, design. Wallpaper. Rixheim, Jean Zuber & Cie., 1856–1857. Musée du Papier Peint, Rixheim, 856.4850.1.

153 Charles Ruffly. Sketch for wallpaper of figure 152. Musée du Papier Peint, Rixheim, 856.4850.1.

style enjoyed a great vogue. While these textiles could be used for dress, the major market was for furnishing fabrics, and, in combination with matching papers covering the walls and occasionally the ceilings as well, their effect must have been striking indeed.[24]

Technical virtuosity came to play an even more important role in nineteenth-century fabrics, as can be seen in figure 154, a wood-block print on cut *velvet*, in twelve colors. Printed velvets first appeared in Alsace in 1810 in the George Dollfus factory, and for the visit of Charles X to Mulhouse in 1828 superb printed velvets with turkish red backgrounds were presented. The tradition continued in the nineteenth century, although few examples produced before 1900 survive today. This example was printed by the Steiner factory in Belfort in 1876.

The very deep superimposed reds found here were a specialty of this factory. The realistic and sumptuous treatment of plants and fruits remains in the great tradition of the Mulhouse workshops during the Second Empire, a look destined to fall from favor with the advent of the arts and crafts movement and the proto-modernism of the late nineteenth century.

154 Furnishing fabric. Belfort, Steiner Manufactory, 1876. Velvet weave, cut pile, cotton warp and weft. Wood-block printed: twelve colors. H. of repeat: 31 1/2 (80). Musée de l'Impression sur Etoffes, Mulhouse, 982.182.2.

Notes

The Bibliography for this essay begins on page 190.

1 Many of the extant European printed textiles dating from the Middle Ages are reproduced in Donald King, "Textiles and the Origins of Printing in Europe," *Pantheon* 20 (January–February 1962): 23–30.

2 In the early seventeenth century the following advice was sent by the English East India Company to their merchants in India: "Those [cloths] which hereafter you shall send we desire may be with more white ground, and the flowers and branch to be in colours in the middle of the quilt as the painter pleases, whereas now most part of your quilts come with sad red grounds which are not equally sorted to please all buyers." Quoted in Alice Beer, *Trade Goods* (Washington, D.C.: Smithsonian Institution Press, 1970), p. 31.

3 See Irwin and Brett, *Origins of Chintz* (1970), pp. 16–21, for an excellent discussion of this design development.

4 See John Irwin and Margaret Hall, *Indian Painted and Printed Fabrics* (Ahmedabad: Calico Museum of Textiles, 1971), pp. 1–6, cat. nos. 1–14, for examples of these early printed textiles.

5 This manuscript is in the Museum d'Histoire Naturelle in Paris (ms. 193). It is reproduced and translated in Irwin and Brett, pp. 36–41.

6 "La Fabrique d'indiennes du Duc de Bourbon" (1966).

7 National Archives, Paris, F12, 1405A, f 10195, art. 1.

8 So famous was this printing center that all printed cottons came to be referred to as "toile de Jouy," literally, "cloth from Jouy."

9 The Musée d l'Impression sur Etoffes, Mulhouse, has the Rÿhiner (1766) and the Rupied (1786) manuscripts, which give in detail the wood-block printing techniques in practice at that time.

10 This attribution to Jouy is based on stylistic grounds, especially the close relationship of the pattern to similar English ones. For a discussion of this relationship see Chassagne, *Oberkampf* (1980), pp. 119–122.

11 Royal Ontario Museum, Toronto, 934.4.82.

12 Musée de l'Impression sur Etoffes, Mulhouse, 858.220.1.352.

13 Discussion of the modifications made in transferring these prints to the textile medium can be found in *In Memoriam: Nancy Graves Cabot* (1973), pp. 39–42.

14 A sample of the ground motif is in the museum of Jouy-en-Josas, letter 424, Reims, 1804. The print used for the border design is in the Musée des Arts Décoratifs, Paris, no. 2241–525, and is signed "Thierry."

15 The original drawing for this textile is in the Union Central des Arts Décoratifs, Cabinet des Dessins, Paris, no. 9763.

16 The Lambinet Museum, Versailles, has the copperplate used to print this fabric. The Musée des Arts Décoratifs, Nantes, has another example of this textile with the chef de pièce of Beautiran, France. This could be possible for a design made and first used in Nantes, as factories occasionally bought plates from others after their initial use.

17 These scenes may have been inspired by work of the British painter Angelica Kaufmann. They are similar in design to those of a printed cotton "Cupid and Psyche," for which Alice Zrebiec of the Metropolitan Museum of Art, New York, has identified Kaufmann print sources.

18 These prints are in the Bibliothèque Nationale, Paris.

19 One of the numerous variations on this textile design, printed in Rouen, is in the Musée de l'Impression sur Etoffes, Mulhouse, 954.368.1.

20 The founders were Jean-Henry Dollfus (1704–1802), Samuel Koechlin (1719–1776), Jean-Jacques Schmalzer (1721–1797), and Jean-Jacques Feer (1717–1780). Their success was immediate, and after twelve years they split to launch, in turn, other factories.

21 For a history of the Wesserling manufactory see Jean-Marie Schmitt, *Aux origines de la révolution industrielle en Alsace* (Paris, 1912), p. 193. A coverlet in the Wadsworth Atheneum, Hartford (W A 1977.37), has appliqués of printed cottons, one of which, showing children climbing a tree in search of birds' nests, comes from this factory.

22 This diary is kept in the municipal library of Colmar.

23 These preparatory sketches were given to the Musée de l'Impression sur Etoffes, Mulhouse, by Daniel Koechlin-Ziegler, who also deposited there a number of similar fabrics.

24 Mulhouse artists at this time shared an affinity with Flemish flower painters who had settled in Paris at the end of the eighteenth and beginning of the nineteenth centuries, and who continued to imitate the style of Jan Van Huysum. One of these painters, Joseph Laurent Malaine, came to Mulhouse in 1793 and prepared designs for printed textiles and wallpapers. Many young Mulhouse artists in the early nineteenth century went to Paris to study flower drawing, before returning to draw for the Alsatian workshops. The establishment of a school of industrial design in Mulhouse in 1829, and the importance it gave to flower drawing, made this a lasting tradition.

Glossary and Bibliography for Technical Terms

This glossary gives brief explanations for technical terms in the essays. Those seeking additional information may wish to consult the following bibliography.

Alençon lace	A French needle lace with a background mesh made up of looped stitches twisted around with thread.
applied work (appliqué)	The technique in which pieces of fabric or embroidered ornaments (as in *guipure* embroidery) are applied to a ground fabric. These pieces can stand alone or can be joined to cover completely the surface, as in some appliquéd quilts.
Argentan lace	A needle lace with a mesh ground, each side of which is worked over with several minute buttonhole stitches.
aune	An early form of French measurement. In Paris it measured 3 feet, 7 inches, and 10 5/6 lines (1.1884 meters).
	In Metz, in the Lorraine, it was 0.677 meter; in Bourg-en-Bresse, 0.808 meter; and in Bordeaux, 1.191 meters. In fact, each city and each province possessed its own measurement. In 1812 France adopted a metric or common *aune* equaling 1.20 meters. This system was finally replaced in 1837 by today's metric system.
baguette	Here, a straight stem with a row of leaves on either side (see border of embroidery in figure 86).
Berlin work	A type of nineteenth- and twentieth-century canvaswork embroidery, usually worked in wools following a colored pattern drawn on a graphed chart. One of the first major suppliers of these charts and the wools with which to work them was Berlin; hence, the name Berlin work has become applied to this technique in general.
Blonde lace	Bobbin laces of gold or silver thread, or of blonde-colored silk, or black or even polychrome silk yarns. These form a distinctive group, as the metals or silk yarns give the finished lace a shine that is absent from their linen cousins.
bobbin lace	The category of laces built up by the intertwining of numbers of threads held on spools or bobbins. Macramé is a simple form of bobbin lace.
bonnes grâces	Borders for furnishings, wider than *passsementeries* and usually made of lace.

bourserie en lisse	A type of bag or purse woven on a loom in a technique similar to that of knitting. *Bourserie en lisse* makers were the forerunners of stocking manufacturers.
boutis	A Provençal word referring to a type of embroidery associated with Marseilles and maritime Provence since the late eighteenth century in which two pieces of cotton fabric of the same size are placed one on top of the other and then sewn together. Cotton wick wrapped around a stalk of flexible metal is then inserted between the layers of fabric. The cotton wick forms areas of relief between the stitching, which makes the design stand out.
à brides	Bobbin laces held together with connecting bars or *brides*.
brocatelle	A weaving with a silk warp-faced pattern in high relief to a weft-faced ground. The weft is often a coarse linen or a less shiny silk.
broderie en jais	Embroidery in which glass cylindrical beads are inserted on the embroidery yarn as the stitches are made.
buratto	A technique bordering between lace and embroidery. The design is worked in a *darning stitch* on a woven open-mesh ground.
button loom	Hand-operated loom with the weave and color controlled by hand pulls or buttons located in front of the weaver above his head.
calque	A pricked paper pattern, used for tracing.
camelot	A simple textile, similar in weave to a *tabby*. Associated more with lower classes of textiles than with high-quality silk weavings.
camisole	A woman's bodice or jacket. Later a woman's sleeveless underbodice.
cannetillé	A weave with short ribs on the surface arranged to give the appearance of small monochrome checks.
canvaswork	Embroidery, usually in *tent stitch*, which completely covers the ground fabric. This technique was especially popular in the Renaissance for the creation of sturdy table covers, bed valances, and wall hangings.
carrez de gaze	A type of needlework lace (see *buratto*).
cartoon	The design, usually full scale with colors indicated, from which a textile is executed. This term is used especially in connection with tapestry weaving, but is also used in reference to other weavings and to embroideries.
cendal	During the Middle Ages *cendal* or *sendal* was a lightweight fabric often used for banners, curtains, and dress. Florence Lewis May, in *Silk Textiles of Spain*, (New

York: Hispanic Society of America, 1957), p. 62, has suggested that *cendal* was a generic word for any silk fabric.

chain stitch (*point de chainette*)	Chain-stitch embroidery produces a row of interlocked circular stitches on the surface. In chain stitch a needle is used to bring the thread through to the surface, to make a loop, and is then returned by the needle to the back of the ground fabric. The next stitch is positioned to hold this loop in place against the ground fabric.
chaperon	Hood or hooded cape.
chiné a la branche	Process in which the warp is painted or printed before weaving.
corsage	Woman's bodice, similar to a close-fitting sleeveless jerkin or jacket.
couched work	In couched-work embroidery a thread is laid along the surface and caught to the fabric by small stitches that encircle the couched thread at intervals which may be close together or far apart. This technique is especially useful in holding down metallic threads, which are difficult to work through a tight or delicate fabric. *Or nué* (shaded gold stitch) is a form of couching. *Underside couching* is produced in the same manner as couched work, but the securing stitches are pulled through to the back of the textile and are, therefore, not visible from the face. This type of couching is the main distinguishing characteristic of true *opus anglicanum*.
cutwork	The removal of warp and/or weft yarns from a fabric to create an open space then filled in with needle embroidery. A forerunner of lace techniques.
damask	A self-patterned weave in which the pattern is formed by a contrast of binding systems. A true damask textile is reversible.
darning stitch	Basically a long running stitch, often used to build up a design on lightweight muslin, mesh, or filet grounds.
deflected element	Any embroidery technique in which the position of yarns of the ground fabric is altered, as in openwork and drawnwork.
double running backstitch	One of the favorite stitches for producing outlines in quilting, or for sewing layers of material to each other. In this technique the stitches are worked in a line with each successive stitch being returned or brought "back" to touch the last stitch at the point it is worked through the ground fabric.
Dresden work	A type of *whitework* embroidery most often worked in cotton yarns on a lightweight muslin ground. The ground is often drawn open in patterns that resemble lace.
ell	An English measure equal to 45 inches.

en broderies	A term used to denote an object or setting rendered in embroidery.
en rapport	A term used to denote the assembling of embroidered sections, often similar to *guipure* embroidery, and the application of them to a ground fabric. This technique is especially effective in producing spectacular embroidery on velvet, which is often so stiff and dense that working on the fabric itself can be extremely difficult.
engageantes	Cuffs or ruffles for the sleeves of a woman's dress.
façonné	Patterned fabrics.
frisé	Frisé velvet is uncut velvet. Frisé silk may have meant a yarn that was looped or crimped, then woven into a fabric.
gaufrure	The couching of parallel rows of yarns, often gold or silver threads, to produce a wafflelike pattern.
Genoa velvets	Velvets with many colors used for the pile, often both cut and uncut. The design of these velvets was usually floral, and they were a specialty of the Italian city of Genoa.
grand broché	An informal term referring to any particularly spectacular brocaded silk weaving.
à la grande tire	Loom for weaving fabrics of regular width, from one-half to three-fourths *aune*.
gros de Tours	A *tabby* weave with a weft of much larger diameter than the warp.
gros point	A *tent stitch* worked over two or more horizontal yarns of a canvas ground.
guipure	The application of gold or silver threads over shaped pieces of parchment, which are then applied to a ground fabric to give a slightly raised, sculptural effect.
guipure lace	Bobbin lace worked in sections, with the separate pattern parts held together by *brides* rather than by a mesh.
knots	Embroidery yarns coiled and looped above the surface fabric to form slightly raisèd knots.
lacis	Literally, "network." Usually associated with *cutwork*. The English word "lace" is derived from this word.
long and short stitch	Worked in the same manner as *satin stitch*, but adjacent stitches are always staggered, rather than being worked in uniform rows.
loom à la tire	Draw loom. See also *à la grande tire, à la petite tire*.

lustering	Lustering is the process of giving more brilliance to silk (most often *taffeta*), by pulling silk threads moistened with water. Legend has it that Octavio Mey, an Italian of whom little is known, discovered the lustering technique by chance, while chewing silk threads in his mouth (Cf. Henri Clouzot, *Le Métier de la soie en France, 1466–1815*, Paris, p. 55.)
la marche	Treadle loom, foot operated.
Marseilles embroidery	A *whitework* technique with knotted stitches filling the ground, with the pattern created by quilting or embroidering around a cotton roving.
mise en carte (charting)	The drawing of a design for silk weaving on a graph, each square of which denotes the intersection of a single warp and weft yarn.
moiré	A watered or rippled effect given to weavings by pressing them to flatten sections in a random pattern.
opus anglicanum	This type of embroidery is chiefly associated with ecclesiastical vestments of the Middle Ages. The distinguishing characteristic of opus anglicanum is *underside couching*. Other stitches employed for this work are *split stitch*, *satin stitch*, and regular *couched work*.
or nué (shaded gold stitch)	The simultaneous surface *couching* of two parallel rows of gold thread with polychrome silk yarns. A shaded effect is achieved by a graduation from the sparse use of silks to allow the gold to show through, to the virtual covering of the gold threads with couching silks to highlight a specific color.
paillettes	A large variety of metallic decorative spangles, usually formed from a cut-metal coil and pressed to produce flattened disks. The forerunner of sequins.
pannes	*Velvets* with a much higher pile than normal.
passementerie	Any of a broad variety of trims used for furnishing fabrics and dress.
passementier	Maker of decorative trims for furnishing fabrics and dress.
passementier–boutonnier	Maker of decorative trims and buttons.
passements	Trims, of which lace is a type.
peinture à l'aiguille	Literally, "painting with the needle." Usually refers to pictorial embroideries of the Middle Ages that strove to give the appearance of paintings. Almost always worked in silk embroidery yarns, these textiles feature small *stem* and *satin stitches*, and especially *split stitches*, worked in contours similar to brush strokes and great tonal ranges that allow for careful shading of colors.

persienne	A lightweight silk fabric with both printed and woven patterns.
petit point	A *tent stitch* that passes over only one horizontal yarn of a canvas ground. Used to create fine details.
à la petite tire	Loom for weaving ribbons or trims.
point à réseau	Needle lace worked on a mesh ground.
point d'Angleterre	A fine bobbin lace, actually made in Brussels, not England.
point de chainette	See *chain stitch*.
point d'Espagne (Spanish stitch)	A variation of *chain stitch*, with the pattern that is built up forming a zigzag chevron motif.
point de France	A term given to the laces of France, both bobbin and needle, in the declaration establishing the royal lace manufactories in 1665. These laces are usually characterized by relatively small-scale designs on delicate, sometimes elaborate, grounds.
point de Hongroie	Also known as Florentine stitch, flame stitch. A *canvaswork* stitch, usually worked in flamelike patterns in wool or silk yarns on a linen ground. Especially suitable for furniture covers and window and bed draperies.
point de neige	A needle lace similar to *Venetian gros point*, but the motifs are quite small and the cordonnets feature elaborately built-up picots.
point de rose	A needle lace similar to *Venetian gros point*, but here the flowers are smaller and often tiered. The connecting *brides* of rose point tend to be much more elaborate.
point fendu	See *split stitch*.
point satiné	See *satin stitch*.
punto in aria	Literally, "stitch in the air." The category of lace created on a structure of yarns held on a temporary support, typically parchment, on which the designs have been traced.
rabat	A type of bib-fronted neckwear for men, similar to that worn by some clerics and judges.
raised work	This term refers to stitches (or to a fabric held down with stitches), which cover an area raised with vellum or parchment strips, cotton padding, or carved wood or wax. In the late nineteenth century the term "stumpwork" began to be used to identify this technique.

à réseaux	Bobbin laces worked on a mesh ground.
reticella	A type of cutwork embroidery or lace, the stitches of which are built up on the remaining yarns of the ground fabric.
rhingraves	A sort of ornamental skirt for men covering the top of the knee when high-heeled shoes were worn.
satin	A weave with long passes of either warp or weft yarns to give a shiny, smooth surface appearance.
satin stitch (point satiné)	A technique in which successive embroidery stitches are worked side by side, with the needle returning on the back side of the embroidery to the starting point of the last stitch.
sergé	A twill weave of diagonal pattern, or, by reversing direction, a herringbone or chevron pattern.
sortes	A term frequently used in the seventeenth century, and on occasion in the eighteenth century, to denote fabrics decorated with flowers or other ornamentation.
split stitch (point fendu)	Virtually always worked with untwisted silk thread, this stitch is well suited to fine embroidery details because of its potential for close shading. The stitches are worked in lines, with each successive stitch coming through and splitting or parting the fibers of the previous one.
stem stitch	An outline stitch used mainly to produce lines or outlines. The stitches are positioned touching each other and parallel to each other, with each successive stitch advancing in the direction one desires the line to go.
tabby	The basic binding system for the simplest weavings. Also known as plain cloth, cloth weave.
taffeta	A fine, tightly woven silk fabric of *tabby* weave.
tambour work	Originally done in Europe with the aid of a round embroidery frame or "tambour" (drum). Tambour embroidery produces a row of interlocked circular stitches identical on the surface to those produced in *chain stitch* with a needle. In tambour work, however, the yarn is pulled through to the face by a hooked tool, similar to a very small crochet needle.
tapisserie	Literally, "tapestry," a weaving executed in the tapestry technique. Throughout the Renaissance this term was often applied to large *canvaswork* hangings, usually worked in *tent stitch* (also referred to as *tapisseries à l'aiguille*, or "needle tapestries").

tapisserie de broderie	An embroidered wall hanging.
tapisserie de petit point	A wall hanging worked in *petit point* embroidery stitches.
tent stitch	A stitch used in *canvaswork* that creates a pattern built up of uniform stitches embroidered diagonally through the canvas itself.
à la tire	See *loom à la tire*.
tissutier–rubanier	Maker of weavings, trims, and ribbons.
underside couching	See *couched work*.
Valenciennes lace	A bobbin lace made in one piece with a round mesh or, especially after the early eighteenth century, a rigorous square mesh.
velvet	A weave characterized by a pile produced by a warp raised in loops above a ground weave. The loops may be left as loops or cut, thereby creating "uncut" or "cut" velvet.
Venetian gros point	A needle lace with floral motifs as large as two inches across, with wide padded cordonnets. This is among the most three-dimensional of all laces.
whitework	Any of a variety of embroidery techniques in which the ground fabric and the embroidery yarns are white. The creation of a design depends, therefore, on the stitches used and the texture of the materials.

Bibliography for Technical Terms

Embroidery

Bath, Virginia Churchill. *Embroidery Masterworks*. Chicago: Henry Regnery, 1972.

Clabburn, Pamela. *The Needleworker's Dictionary*. New York: William Morrow, 1976.

Enthoven, Jacqueline. *The Stitches of Creative Embroidery*. New York: Van Nostrand Reinhold, 1964.

Saint-Aubin, Charles Germain de. *The Art of the Embroiderer*. Translation of *L'Art du brodeur*, 1770, with facsimile. Los Angeles County Museum of Art, 1983.

Thomas, Mary. *Dictionary of Embroidery Stitches*. New York: William Morrow, 1935.

Lace

Bath, Virginia Churchill. *Lace*. Chicago: Henry Regnery, 1974.

Earnshaw, Pat. *The Identification of Lace*. Aylesbury: Shire Publications, 1980.

Levy, Santina M. *Lace: A History*. London: Victoria and Albert Museum, 1983.

Palliser, Mrs. Bury. *History of Lace*. New York: Charles Scribner's Sons, 1902.

Powys, Marian. *Lace and Lace-Making*. Boston: Charles T. Branford, 1953.

Printed Textiles

Clouzot, Henri, and Morris, Frances. *Painted and Printed Fabrics*. New York: Metropolitan Museum of Art, 1927.

Montgomery, Florence. *Printed Textiles, 1700–1850*. New York: Viking Press, 1970.

Jacqué, Jacqueline, ed. *Chef Oeuvres de Musée de l'Impression sur Etoffes, Mulhouse*. 3 vols. Tokyo: Gakken, 1978.

Storey, Joyce. *The Thames and Hudson Manual of Textile Printing*. London: Thames and Hudson, 1974.

Woven Textiles

Burnham, Dorothy K. *Warp and Weft*. Toronto: Royal Ontario Museum, 1980.

Emery, Irene. *The Primary Structures of Fabrics*. Washington, D.C.: The Textile Museum, 1966.

Vocabulary of Technical Terms (English edition). Lyons: Centre International d'Etude des Textiles Anciens, 1964.

Bibliography

Woven Textiles and The Art of Silk

Achard. *Notice sur la création, les développements et la décadence des manufactures de soie à Avignon.* Apt, 1874.

Adrosko, Rita J. "The Invention of the Jacquard Mechanism," *Bulletin de Liaison du Centre International d'Etude des Textiles Anciens,* no. 55–56 (Lyons, 1984), pp. 89–117.

Algoud, Henri. *Gaspard Grégoire et ses velours d'art.* Paris: Société Française d'Imprimerie et de Librairie, 1908.

———. *Les Arts de la soie: Les Velours.* Paris: Charles Massin, 1912.

———. *Grammaire des arts de la soie.* Paris: J. Schmidt, 1912.

———. *La Soie: Art et histoire.* Paris: Payot, 1928.

———. *Le Décor des soieries françaises de l'origine à 1815.* Paris: G. Van Oest, 1931.

Audin, Marius, and Vial, Eugène. *Dictionnaire des artistes et ouvriers d'art du Lyonnais.* Paris: Bibliothèque d'Art et d'Archéologie, 1918–1919.

Aynard, Edouard. *Lyon en 1889. Introduction au rapport de la section d'économie sociale.* Lyons: Mougin-Rusand, 1889.

Beaulieu, Michèle. *Les Tissus d'art.* Paris: Presses Universitaires de France, 1965. In the series Que sais-je?, 566.

Beauquis, A. *Histoire économique de la soie.* Grenoble: Imprimerie Générale, 1910.

Bertholon, Abbé. *Etude sur le commerce et les manufactures de la ville de Lyon.* Montpellier: n.pub., 1787.

Bezon, M. *Dictionnaire général des tissus anciens et modernes.* Lyons: Th. Lepagnez, 1856–1867.

Bosseboeuf, L. *La Fabrique des soieries de Tours des origines au 19e siècle.* Tours: P. Bousrez, 1900. Extract from *Mémoires de la Société Archéologique de Touraine,* vol. 49.

Boucher, François. *Histoire du costume en occident de l'antiquité à nos jours.* Paris: Flammarion, 1965. U.S. edition, *20,000 Years of Fashion.* New York: Harry N. Abrams, 1967.

Boulnois, Luce. *La Route de la soie.* Paris: Arthaud, 1963. In the series Signe des Temps.

Bouteville, Jacques de. "Ce qu'il en coûtait à M. Van Robais pour fabriquer une pièce de drap." *Bulletin d'Emulation Historique et Littéraire d'Abbeville* 22 (1967–1970).

Bréghot du Lut, F. *Le Livre de raison de Jacques-Charles Dutillieu.* Lyons: Mougin-Rusand, 1886.

Cayez, Pierre. *Métiers Jacquard et hauts fourneaux aux origines de l'industrie lyonnaise.* Lyons: Presses Universitaires de France, 1978.

Chabaud, L. *Marseille et ses industries, les tissus, la filature et la teinturerie.* Marseilles: n. pub., 1883.

Chaplain, Jean-Michel. "L'Organisation spatiale de la production industrielle en France pendant la période de transition du mode de production féodal au mode de production capitaliste, 1660–1830. Etude du cas de trois centres textiles: Abbeville, Roubais, Louviers," Mémoire de D.E.A., Université de Paris VIII-Vincennes. Paris, 1978.

Clément, Pierre. *Jean-Baptiste Colbert. Lettres, instructions et mémoires.* Paris: n.pub., 1861–1882.

Clouzot, Henri. *Le Métier de la soie en France, 1466–1815.* Paris: n.pub., n.d.

Colbert, Jean-Baptiste. *Règlemens et statuts généraux pour les longeurs, largeurs, qualitez et teintures des draps, serges, et autres étoffes de laine et de fil.* . . . Paris: n.pub., 1669.

———. *Instruction générale donnée aux commis envoyez dans toutes les provinces du royaume pour l'exécution des règlements généraux des manufactures et teintures* . . . *1664.* Paris: n.pub., 1670.

Coural, Jean, and Gastinel-Coural, Chantal. "La Fabrique lyonnaise. La Commande royale de

1730." *Revue de l'Art* 62 (1983): 49–64.

Coural, Jean; Gastinel-Coural, Chantal; and Muntz de Raissac, Muriel. *Inventaire des collections publiques françaises: Paris, Mobilier National, Soieries Empire*. Paris: Réunion des Musées Nationaux, 1980.

Courtecuisse, Maximilien. *La Manufacture de draps fins Van Robais aux 17e et 18e siècles*. Paris: n.pub., 1920.

Cox, Raymond. *L'art de décorer les tissus d'après les collections du Musée Historique des Tissus de la Chambre de Commerce de Lyon*. Paris: P. Mouillot, 1900.

———. *Musée rétrospectif de la classe 83. Soie et tissus de soie*. Saint Cloud: Belin Frères, 1900.

———. *Les Soieries d'art depuis les origines jusqu'à nos jours*. Paris: Hachette, 1914.

Custodero, Jacqueline. "Antoine Berjon, peintre lyonnais (1754–1843)." Mémoire de Maîtrise es Lettres, Université de Lyon II. Lyons, 1971–1972.

Devilliers, Alexandre. *Nouveau Manuel complet de la soierie*. Paris: Librairie Encyclopédique de Roret, 1839. In the series Manuels Roret.

Devoti, Donata. *L'arte del tessuto in Europa*. Milan: Bramante, 1974.

Diderot, Denis, and Alembert, Jean d'. *Encyclopédie, ou dictionnaire raisonné des sciences*. Paris: Braisson, David, Le Breton, Durand, 1751–1777.

Dumonthier, Ernest. *Le Mobilier National. Etoffes et tapisseries d'ameublement des 17e et 18e siècles*. Paris: Ch. Massin, n.d.

———. *Etoffes d'ameublement de l'époque napoléonienne*. Paris: C. Schmid, 1909.

———. *Etoffes d'ameublement style Empire, Mobilier National*. Paris: Ch. Massin, 1914.

Dutil, L. "L'Industrie de la soie à Nîmes jusqu'en 1789." *Revue d'Histoire Moderne* 10 (1908).

———. *Etat économique du Languedoc au 18e siècle*. Paris, 1911.

Extrait des registres de l'Académie des Sciences de Paris, du 29 juillet 1775. Lyons, An. 10 [1803].

Fagniez. *Economique sociale sous Henri IV*. Paris: n.pub., 1897.

Falke, Otto von. *Kunstgeschichte der Seidenweberei*. Berlin: E. Wasmuth, 1913.

Fenaille, Maurice. *Etat général des tapisseries de la manufacture des Gobelins depuis son origine jusqu'à nos jours, 1600–1900*. Paris: Hachette, 1903–1912.

Fischbach, Friedrich. *Die Geschichte der Textil-Kunst*. Hanau: n.pub., 1883.

———. *Die wichtigsten Webe-Ornamente bis zum 19. Jahr*. Wiesbaden: Selbst Verlag, 1901.

Flouquet. *Establissement à Rouen d'une manufacture de soieries*. Rouen: Académie des Sciences, Belles-Lettres et Arts de Rouen, 1837.

Les Folles Années de la soie. Lyons: Musée Historique des Tissus. Exhibition catalogue, 11 June–30 September 1975.

Gilonne, Georges. *Soieries de Lyon*. Lyons: Edition du Fleuve, 1948.

———; Bret, L.; and Nicout, J. *Dictionnaire practique des tissus*. Lyons: Bosc Frères & Riou, 1930.

Godard, Justin. *L'Ouvrier en soie*. Paris: A. Rousseau, 1899.

"Le Grand Broché de la Reine." *Revue l'Oeil*, no. 150 (June 1967), pp. 44–45.

Guiffrey, Jules. *Comptes des bâtiments du roi sous le règne de Louis XIV*. 5 vols. Paris: n.pub., 1881–1901.

Hardouin-Fugier, Elisabeth. *Simon Saint-Jean, 1808–1860*. Leigh-on-Sea: F. Lewis, 1980.

———, and Grafe, Etienne. *The Lyon School of Flower Painters*. Leigh-on-Sea: F. Lewis, 1978.

Harel, M. *La Manufacture de draps fins de Van Robais à Abbeville*. Paris: n.pub., 1971.

Hartmann, Simone. "Etude et catalogue raisonné des dessins de Jean-Démosthène Dugourc appartenant à la Manufacture Tassinari et Chatel de Lyon." Mémoire de Maîtrise d'Histoire de l'Art. Université de Lyon II. Lyons, 1974–1976.

———. "Précurseur de l'Empire: L'Ornemaniste Jean Dugourc." *Revue l'Estampille*, no. 98 (June 1978), pp. 30–35.

Havard, Henri. *Dictionnaire de l'ameublement et de la décoration depuis le XIIIe siècle jusqu'à nos jours*. Paris: Quantin, 1887–1890.

Hennezel, Henri, comte d'. *Claude Dangon*. Lyons: A. Rey, 1926.

———. *Catalogue des principales pièces exposées*. Lyons: A. Rey, 1929.

———. *Pour comprendre les tissus d'art*. Paris: Hachette, 1930.

Heyd, Wilhelm von. *Histoire du commerce du Levant au Moyen-Age*. Leipzig: n.pub., 1885–1886; new ed., 1923.

Hullebroeck, A. *L'Histoire du métier pour la fabrication des étoffes façonnées*. Paris: Librairie Polytechnique Ch. Beranger, 1934.

Joubert de l'Hiberderie, Nicolas. *Le Dessinateur pour les fabriques d'étoffes d'or, d'argent et de soie*. Paris: S. Jorry, 1765.

Lapierre, J. "La Vie et l'oeuvre de J. -M. Jacquard." In *Soierie de Lyon* (Lyons, 1925).

———, and Leroudier, Emile. "Historique de la fabrique lyonnaise de soierie." In *Soierie de Lyon* (Lyons, 1925), pp. 534–538.

Leroudier, Emile. *Les Dessinateurs de la fabrique lyonnaise au 18e siècle*. Lyons: A. Rey, 1908.

Lespinasse, René de. *Histoire générale de Paris. Les Métiers et corporations de la ville de Paris, 16e–18e siècles*. 3 vols. Paris: Imprimerie Nationale, 1892.

Lessing, Julius. *Gewebesammlung des königlichen Kunst-Gewerbe-Museums zu Berlin*. 4 vols. Berlin: E. Wasmuth, n.d.

Markowsky, Barbara. *Europäische Seidengewebe de 13.–18. Jahr.* Cologne: Kunstgewerbemuseum der Stadt, 1976. Catalogue.

Martin, G. *La Grande Industrie sous le règne de Louis XIV*. Paris: n.pub., 1899.

———. *La Grande Industrie sous la règne de Louis XV*. Paris: n.pub., 1900.

Michel, Francisque. *Recherches sur le commerce, la fabrication et l'usage des étoffes de soie, d'or et d'argent*. 2 vols. Paris: Crapelet, 1852–1854.

Migeon, Gaston. *Les Arts du tissu*. Paris: H. Laurens, 1909. In the series Manuels d'Histoire de l'Art.

Pariset, Ernest. *Histoire de la soie*. Paris: A. Durand, 1862–1865.

———. *Les Industries de la soie*. Lyons: Pitrat, 1890.

———. *Histoire de la fabrique lyonnaise. Etude sur le régime social et économique de l'industrie de la soie à Lyon*. Lyons: A. Rey, 1901.

Paulet. *L'Art du fabrique d'étoffes de soie*. Paris: L. F. Delatour, 1773–1778.

Pernetti, Jacques, dit, L'Abbé. *Recherches pour servir à l'histoire de Lyon, ou les Lyonnais dignes de mémoire*. 2 vols. Lyons: n.pub., 1757.

Poidebard, Alexandre, and Chatel, Jacques. *Camille Pernon, fabricant de soieries à Lyon sous Louis XVI et Napoléon I*. Lyons: L. Brun, 1912.

Raimon, Albert. *Exposition franco-britannique de 1908. Rapport du jury*. Saint Denis: H. Bouillant, 1909.

Razy, C. *Etude analytique des petits modèles de métiers exposés au Musée Historique des Tissus*. Lyons: A. Rey, 1913.

Rodier, Paul. *The Romance of French Weaving*. New York: n.pub., 1931.

Rondot, Natalis. *L'Industrie de la soie. Rapport de l'Exposition Universelle de Vienne en 1873*. Lyons: Pitrat, 1875.

———. *Les Soies*. 2 vols. Paris: Imprimerie Nationale, 1885.

Savary, Jacques. *Le Parfait Négociant, ou instruction générale pour ce qui regarde le commerce des merchandises de France et des pays étrangers*. Paris: n.pub., 1675.

———. *Parères, ou avis et conseils sur les plus importantes matières du commerce*. Paris: n.pub., 1688.

Savary des Bruslons, Jacques. *Dictionnaire universel de commerce*. 5 vols. Copenhagen: C. & A. Philbert, 1756–1766.

Schmidt, Heinrich. *Alte Seidenstoffe*. Braunschweig: Klinkhardt und Biermann, 1958.

Schmitter, M.-T., and Focillon, Henri. *Exposition de soieries modernes d'ameublement*. Lyons: Imprimerie Nouvelle Lyonnaise, 1934. Catalogue.

Schmitter, M.-T., and Guicherd, Félix. *Philippe de Lasalle*. Lyons: Vaucanson, 1939.

Serpantié, Anne. "Michel Dubost, dessinateur en soieries." Mémoire de Maîtrise d'Histoire de l'Art. Université de Lyon II. Lyons, 1980.

La Soierie en Touraine du 15e au 19e siècle. Tours: Hôtel de Ville, 1933.

Soierie tourangelle et costumes du 18e siècle. Tours: Musée des Beaux-Arts, 1974. Exhibition catalogue.

Suppa, Giuseppe. *Glossario italiano tessile in cinque lingue*. Turin: n.pub., 1975.

Thornton, Peter. *Baroque and Rococo Silks*. London: Faber and Faber, 1965.

Tuchscherer, Jean-Michel; Vial, Gabriel; Devoti, Donata; and Bernus-Taylor, Marthe. *Etoffes merveilleuses du Musée Historique des Tissus de Lyon*. 3 vols. Tokyo: Gakken, 1976.

Tuchscherer, Jean-Michel, and Vial, Gabriel. *Le Musée Historique des Tissus de Lyon*. Lyons: A. Guillot, 1977.

Vaschalde, Jean. *Les Industries de la soierie*. Paris: Presses Universitaires de France, 1961. In the series Que sais-je?, 975.

Verlet, Pierre. *Le Mobilier royal français.* 3 vols. Paris: Les Editions d'Art et d 'Histoire, 1945; Paris: Librairie Plon, 1955. Paris, 1961.

———. *Les Meubles français du XVIIIe siècle.* Vol. I: *Menuiserie.* Vol. II: *Ebénisterie.* Paris: Presses Universitaires de France, 1954.

———. *Versailles.* Paris: A. Fayard, 1961.

———. *La Maison du 18e siècle en France.* Paris: Baschet, 1966.

Wiebel, Adèle Coulin. *Two Thousand Years of Textiles.* New York: Pantheon, 1952.

Weigert, Roger-Armand. *Textiles en Europe sous Louis XV.* Fribourg: Office du Livre, 1964.

Wiederkehr, Anne-Marie. "Le Dessinateur pour les fabriques d'étoffes d'or, d'argent et de soie. Paris, 1765. Témoignages de Nicolas Joubert de l'Hiberderie, dessinateur à Lyon au 18e siècle." Thèse de Doctorat de 3e Cycle, Université de Lyon II. Lyons, 1981.

Embroidery

Angliviel de la Beaumelle, L. *Mémoires pour servir à l'histoire de Madame de Maintenon.* Amsterdam, 1761. Vol. III, book 8.

Art and the Courts: France and England from 1259 to 1328. Ottawa: National Gallery of Canada, 1972. Exhibition catalogue by Peter Brieger and Philippe Verdier.

Aumale, Henri Eugène Philippe Louis d'Orléans, duc d'. *Inventaire de tous les meubles du Cardinal Mazarin, dressé en 1653.* London: Whittingham and Wiltkins, 1861.

Battifol, L. "Marie de Medicis et les arts." *Gazette des Beaux-Arts* 47, part I (1906): 221–243.

Beaulieu, M. "Les Ornements liturgiques à Notre-Dame de Paris." *Bulletin Monumental* (1967), pp. 261–274.

———, and Bayle, J. "La Mitre épiscopale en France des origines à la fin du XVIe siècle." *Bulletin Archéologique du Comité des Travaux Historiques et Scientifiques,* no. 9 (1973).

———. "La Mitre de Charles de Neuchâtel au Musée de Besançon." In *Congrès des Sociétés Savantes Besançon,* 1974.

Bleton, Pierre. *La Vie sociale sous le Second Empire.* *Un Etonnant Témoignage de la comtesse de Ségur.* Paris: Les Editions Ouvrières, 1963.

Bonaffe, Edmond. *Inventaire des meubles de Catherine de Medicis en 1589.* Paris, 1874.

Brel-Bordaz, Odile. *Broderies d'ornements liturgiques XIII–XIVe siècles.* Paris: Nouvelles Editions Latines, 1982.

Bridgeman, Harriet, and Drury, Elizabeth, eds. *Needlework. An Illustrated History.* New York: Paddington Press, 1978.

Carlano, Marianne. Catalogue entries in *Curiosità di una reggia Vicende della guardaroba di Palazzo Pitti.* Florence: Centro Di, 1979. Exhibition catalogue.

Chaillot. Collection of engravings of embroidery designs. Paris, Bibliothèque Nationale, Cabinet des Estampes, Lh.70, n.d.

La Chapelle du Saint-Sacrement et ses tentures. Romans (Drôme): Collégiale Saint-Barnard, 1977.

Christie, Mrs. Archibald Grace I. *English Medieval Embroidery.* Oxford: Clarendon Press, 1938.

Cinq-Cents Colbert, 81, fol. 341–345. Cabinet des Manuscrits, Bibliothèque Nationale.

Clouzot, Henri. *Le Style Louis Philippe-Napoléon III.* Paris: Librairie Larousse, 1939.

Coen, Rena Newmann. "The Duc de Crequy's *Primavera.*" *Minneapolis Institute of Arts Bulletin* 53, no. 1 (March 1964): 17–25.

Le Costume traditionnel à Marseille. Marseilles: Musée du Vieux-Marseille, 1980.

Delpierre, Madeleine. "Un Album de modèles pour broderies de gilets." *Bulletin du Musée Carnavalet.* 9th year, no. 2 (November 1956).

———. *Uniformes civils français ceremonial circonstances 1750–1980.* Paris: Musée de la Mode et du Costume. Exhibition catalogue, 16 December 1982–17 April 1983.

Dentelles et broderies dans la mode françise du XVIe au XXe siècle. Paris: Musée du Costume, 1964.

L'Ecole de Fontainebleau. Paris: Editions des Musées Nationaux, 1972.

Eisler, Colin. "Two Early Franco-Flemish Embroideries—Suggestions for Their Settings." *Burlington Magazine* 109 (October 1967): 571–580.

Emery, Irene. *The Primary Structures of Fabrics.* Washington, D.C.: The Textile Museum, 1966.

Exposition de l'industrie française. Paris: n.pub., 1844.

Fage, René. *Les Broderies du Musée de Tulle.* Paris, 1908.

Farcy, Louis de. *La Broderie du XIe siècle jusqu'à nos jours.* 3 vols. in 2. Paris: Ernest Leroux, 1890–1900.

Les Fastes du gothique: Le Siècle de Charles V. Paris: Galeries Nationales du Grand Palais, 1981.

Fénelon, François de Salignac de la Mothe. *Education des filles.* Paris: P. Aubouin, 1687.

Focillon, Henri. *The Art of the West in the Middle Ages.* New York: Phaidon, 1963. Vol. 2: *Gothic Art.*

Fontainebleau. *Art in France, 1528–1610.* Ottawa: National Gallery of Canada, 1973. Exhibition catalogue. Vol. 2.

Foster, Vanda. *Bags and Purses.* New York: Drama Book Publishers, 1982. The Costume Accessories Series.

Freeman, Margaret B. *The Saint Martin Embroideries.* New York: Metropolitan Museum of Art, 1968.

French Folk Art. Paris: Musée des Arts et Traditions Populaires, and Washington, D.C.: SITES, 1978.

Geijer, Agnes. "Medieval Textiles in the Cathedral of Uppsala, Sweden." *Bulletin of the Needle and Bobbin Club* 38, nos. 1–2 (1954).

———. *A History of Textile Art.* [London]: W. S. Mercy & Sons, [ca. 1979].

Gilfoy, Peggy Stoltz. *Fabrics in Celebration from the Collection.* Indianapolis Museum of Art, 1983.

Göbel, Heinrich. *Wandteppiche.* Part 2: *Die romanischen Länder.* 2 vols. Leipzig, 1928.

Grand Dictionnaire universel du XIXe siècle. Paris, 1867.

Grandmaison, Charles L. *Procès-verbal du pillage par les Huguenots des reliques et joyaux de St. Martin-de-Tours en mai et juin 1562.* Tours: A. Mame, 1863.

———. *Documents inédits pour servir à l'histoire des arts en Touraine.* Tours: Guilland-Verger, 1870.

Guiffrey, Jules. *Comptes des bâtiments du roi sous le règne de Louis XIV.* 5 vols. Paris: n.pub., 1881–1901.

———. *Inventaire général du mobilier de la couronne sous Louis XIV (1663–1715).* Paris, 1885. Vol. 2.

———. *Inventaires de Jean duc de Berry.* 2 vols. Paris: E. Leroux, 1894–1896.

Hackenbrook, Yvonne. *English and Other Needlework, Tapestries, and Textiles in the Irwin Untermeyer Collection.* Cambridge, Mass.: Harvard University Press, 1960.

Havard, Henri. *Dictionnaire de l'ameublement et de la décoration depuis le XIIIe siècle jusqu'à nos jours.* Paris: Quantin, 1887–1890.

Huizinga, Johan. *The Waning of the Middle Ages.* New York: Doubleday, 1954. First published in 1924.

Ikle, Ernest. *La Broderie mécanique 1828–1930. Souvenirs et documents.* Paris: Chez l'auteur, 1931.

Jaubert, Pierre. *Dictionnaire raisonné universel des arts et métiers, contenant l'histoire, la description, la police des fabriques et manufactures de France & des pays étrangers.* Paris: P. F. Didot, 1773. New edition.

Labarge, Margaret Wade. *Court, Church and Castle.* Ottawa: National Gallery of Canada, 1972. Published in conjunction with the exhibition *Art and the Courts: France and England from 1259 to 1328.*

Labarte, Jules. *Inventaire du mobilier de Charles V, roi de France.* Paris: Imprimerie Nationale, 1879.

Laborde, Léon de. *Glossaire français du Moyen Age à l'usage de l'archéologue et de l'amateur des arts précédé de l'inventaire des bijoux de Louis, duc d'Anjou, dressé vers 1360.* Paris: Adolphe Labitte, 1874.

Lafitte, Louis. *Projet de dessins de broderies.* Paris, Bibliothèque Nationale, Cabinet des Estampes, Lh.22, folio.

Laigle, Mathilde, ed. *Livres des trois vertues de Christine de Pisan.* Paris, 1912. Bibliothèque de XVe Siècle. Vol. 16.

Latour, A. "Gloves." *CIBA Review* 61 (1947).

Ledit, Chanoine. "Le Trésor de la Cathédrale." *Zodiaque* (1975), p. 9.

Ledoux-Lebard, R. G., and C. "L'Inventaire des appartements de l'Empereur Napoléon Ier aux Tuileries." *Bulletin de la Société de l'Histoire de l'Art Français* (1952).

Lefébure, Ernest. *Broderie et dentelles.* Paris: Quantin, 1887.

Legrand, Augustin. *La Maîtresse broderie.* Paris: n.pub., 1816.

———. *Petit Nécessaire de jeunes demoiselles recueil d'examples de marque, broderie, filet, tricot, bourse en perles de couleurs.* Paris: n.pub., 1819.

Lemoisne, P. A. *Gothic Painting in France, 14th and 15th Centuries.* New York: Harcourt, Brace, 1931.

Lespinasse, René de. *Histoire générale de Paris. Les Métiers et corporations de la ville de Paris, 16e–18e siècles.* 3 vols. Paris: Imprimerie Nationale, 1892.

Little, Frances. "Signed French and Spanish Chintzes." *Metropolitan Museum of Art Bulletin* 33 (1938): 209.

Malherbes. "Lettres à Peiresc." In *Lettres*, Vol. III of *Oeuvres*. Paris: Ad. Regnier, 1862. New ed. In the series Ecrivains de France.

Maire, Alfred. "Un Versailles inconnu. Si Napoléon Ie l'avait habité." *Connaissance des Arts*, no. 206 (April 1969).

Marle, Raimond van. *Iconographie de l'art profane au Moyen-Age et à la Renaissance et la décoration des demeures*. 2 vols. The Hague: Nijhoff, 1931–1932.

Marrow, Deborah. *The Art Patronage of Maria de' Medici*. Princeton, N.J.: UMI Research Press, 1982. Studies in Baroque Art History, 4.

Meiss, Millard. *French Painting in the Time of Jean de Berry: The Late Fourteenth Century and the Patronage of the Duke*. London: Phaidon, 1967.

Nougier, Simone and Estelle. *Lou Vèsti Provencau*. Marseilles, 1980.

Pellegrin, Francisque. *La Fleur de la science de pourtraicture*. Facsimile edition with introduction by Gaston Migeon. Paris: Jean Schemit, 1908.

Prampolini, Marianna. *La Duchessa Maria Luigia. Vita familiare alla corte di Parma*. Bergamo: Istituto Italiano d'Arte Grafiche, 1942.

Quicherat. *Histoire du costume en France*. Paris, 1879. *Règlement arrêté par le Roi concernant l'habillement des grandes officiers de la couronne, grandes officiers, premiers officiers, et officiers de la maison de sa majesté, et autres personnes y occupant des places et emplois*. 10 December 1820. Paris, Bibliothèque Nationale, Cabinet des Estampes, Lh.21.

La Revolte des passemens. New York: The Needle and Bobbin Club, 1935. Old texts and explanatory notes assembled by Gertrude Whiting, with an English version by Hazel Dunning Sommerhoff.

Richesses tirées du trésor de l'Abbaye de Saint Denis, du Garde-Meuble de la Couronne et de différens artistes de Paris pour servir au sacre de l'auguste monarque de France le roy Louis XVI. Paris: Abbaye Royal de Saint Denis, 1775.

Saint-Aubin, Charles Germain de. *The Art of the Embroiderer*. Translation of *L'Art du brodeur*, 1770, with facsimile. Translated and annotated by Nikki Scheuer. Los Angeles County Museum of Art, and Boston: David R. Godine, 1983.

Savary des Bruslons, Jacques. *Dictionnaire universel du commerce 1759–1775*. Copenhagen: C. & A. Philbert, 1759–1765.

Scheur, Nikki. "The Elegant Art of Embroidery." In *An Elegant Art, Fashion and Fantasy in the 18th Century*. New York: Harry N. Abrams, and Los Angeles County Museum of Art, 1983.

Schuette, Marie, and Müller-Christensen, Sigrid. *The Art of Embroidery*. London: Thames and Hudson, 1963.

The Second Empire 1852–1870: Art in France under Napoleon III. Philadelphia: Philadelphia Museum of Art, 1978.

Sonday, Milton, and Moss, Gillian. *Western European Embroidery in the Collection of the Cooper-Hewitt Museum*. New York: Cooper-Hewitt Museum, 1978.

Standen, Edith. "A Picture for Every Story." *Metropolitan Museum of Art Bulletin* 15, no. 8 (1957): 165–175.

——— "A Boar Hunt at Versailles." *Metropolitan Museum of Art Bulletin* 22 (1963): 143–155.

Taburet, Elisabeth. "Les Broderies du Château d'Ecouen." *Revue l'Estampille*, no. 11 (October 1979), pp. 37–44.

Thibaud I, King of Navarre. *Chansons de Thibaut IV, de Champagne, roi de Navarre*. Paris: E. Champion 1925.

Thornton, Peter. *Seventeenth-Century Interior Decoration in England, France and Holland*. New Haven: Yale University Press, 1978.

Trésors des églises de France. Paris: Musée des Arts Décoratifs, 1965.

Varagnac, André. *French Costumes*. New York: Hyperion Press, 1939.

Verkhovskaia, A. S. *Western European Embroidery in the Hermitage Museum*. Leningrad, 1961.

Verlet, Pierre. *Savonnerie: The James A. de Rothschild Collection at the Waddeson Manor*. Fribourg: Office du Livre, 1982.

Vinciolo, Federico. *Renaissance Patterns for Lace, Embroidery and Needlepoint*. Reprint of *Les Singuliers et Nouveaux Pourtraicts*, 1587. New York: Dover, 1971.

The Waning Middle Ages. Lawrence: University of Kansas Museum of Art, 1969. Exhibition catalogue.

Wardle, Patricia. "The Embroideries of Mary, Queen of Scots: Notes on the French Background." *Bulletin of the Needle and Bobbin Club* 64, nos. 1–2 (1981).

Weigert, Roger-Armand. "La Retraite de Mme. Montespan." *Bulletin de la Société d'Etude du XVIIe Siècle*, nos. 1, 4 (1949), pp. 16–18, 211–220.

Wescher, H. "Textile Art in Sixteenth Century France." *CIBA Review* 69 (1948).

Young, Bonnie. "Opus Anglicanum." *Metropolitan Museum of Art Bulletin* 29, no. 7 (1971): 291–298.

The Lace Industry

Abrantes, duchesse d'. *Mémoires*. Paris: L. Mame, 1835.

Arsac, Jean. *La Dentelle de Puy*. Le Puy: C. Bonneton, 1978.

Aubry, Félix. *Dentelles, blondes, tulles et broderies, dans travaux de la Commission Française . . . de l'Exposition Universelle de 1851*. Paris: n.pub., 1854.

Bath, Virginia Churchill. *Lace*. Chicago: Henry Regnery, 1974.

Bayard, Emile. *L'Art de reconnaître les dentelles, guipures, etc.* Paris: R. Roger et F. Chernoviz, 1914.

Beaton, Cecil. *The Glass of Fashion*. Garden City, N.Y.: Doubleday, 1954.

Bibliophile, Jacob le, pseud. (Paul Lacroix). *Recueil curieux de pièces originales ou inédites sur le costume (lois sumptuaires, pièces en prose et en vers)*. Paris: Lacour, 1852.

Bandois, Paul-M. "Colbert et l'industrie de la dentelle, le point de France à Reims et à Sedan." *Revue d'Histoire Économique et Sociale*, 13th year (1925).

Carlier de Lantsheere, Antoine. *Trésor de l'art dentellier. Répertoire des dentelles à la main de tous les pays depuis les origines jusqu'à nos jours*. Brussels: G. Van Oest, 1922.

Carmignani, Marina. *Merletti a Palazzo Davanzati. Manifatture europee dal XVI al XX secolo*. Florence: Centro Di, 1981.

Delpierre, Madeleine. *Dentelles et broderies dans la mode française du XVIe au XXe siècle*. Paris: Musée du Costume, 1964. Exhibition catalogue.

Despierres, Madeleine G. *Histoire du point d'Alençon*. Paris, 1886.

Earnshaw, Pat. *The Identification of Lace*. Aylesbury: Shire Publications, 1980.

"Extraordinaire." *Le Mercure Galant*, January, April 1678.

Ferguson, S., *et fils*. *Histoire du tulle et des dentelles mécaniques en Angleterre et en France*. Paris: E. Lacroix, 1962.

Guillenot, M. "Exposition des arts de la femme." *Art et Décoration* (1911), pp. 137–156.

Henneberg, Alfred. *The Art and Craft of Old Lace*. New York: E. Weyhe, 1931.

Henon, Henri. *L'Industrie des tulles et dentelles mécaniques dans le Département du Pas-de-Calais 1815–1900*. Paris: Belin Frères, 1900.

Jesurum, Michelangelo. *Cenni storici e statistici sull'industria di merletti*. Venice, 1873.

Jourdain, M. "Venetian Needlepoint." *Connoisseur*, July–August 1905, pp. 145–241.

Kraatz, Anne. "Lace at the Court of Louis XIV." *Antiques* 119 (June 1981): 1368–1375.

———. "Francia-Italia, 1665–1715: La Guerra dei Merletti." In *Merletti a Palazzo Davanzati*. Florence: Centro Di, 1981.

———. *Dentelles au Musée Historique des Tissus de Lyon*. Lyons, 1983.

———. "The Elegant Art of Lace." In *An Elegant Art, Fashion and Fantasy in the 18th Century*. New York: Harry N. Abrams, and Los Angeles County Museum of Art, 1983.

———. "Petite Histoire de la dentelle." In *Modes en Dentelles*. Paris: Musée de la mode et du Costume de la Ville de Paris, 1983.

Laprade, Laurence de. *Le Poinct de France et les centres dentelliers au XVIIe et au XVIIIe siècles*. Paris: L. Laveur, 1905.

Lefébure, Auguste. "La dentelle à la main, la broderie ajourée, la guipure au Musée Galliera." *La Dentelle. Journal de la Dentelle à la Main*, 2d year, nos. 3 and 4 (30 March, 30 April 1904).

———. *Dentelles et guipures, anciennes et modernes, imitations ou copies*. Paris: E. Flammarion, 1904.

Lefébure, Ernest. *Histoire de la dentelle à Bayeux de 1676 à 1900*. Bayeux, 1913.

———. *Broderies et dentelles*. Paris: E. Grund, 1926.

Levey, Santina M. "Lace and Lace Patterned Silks: Some Comparative Illustrations." In *Studies in Textile History*, ed. Veronika Gervers. Toronto: Royal Ontario Museum, 1977, pp. 184–201.

———. *Lace: A History*. London: Victoria and Albert Museum, 1983.

Mabille de Poncheville, André. *La Dentelle à la main en Flandre*. Valenciennes, 1911.

Malotet, Arthur. *La Dentelle à Valenciennes*. Paris: J. Schenit, 1927.

"Mariage de Louise d'Orléans." *Le Mercure Galant*, September 1679.

"Mariage du Duc de Chartres." *Le Mercure Galant*, February 1692.

"Mariage du Prince de Galles." *Le Moniteur de la Mode*, 12 August 1893.

Maze-Sencier, Alphonse. *Les Fournissiers de Napoléon Ier et des deux impératrices*. Paris: H. Laurens, 1893.

Mezzara, Pierre. "Dessins nouveaux de filet brodé." *Art et Décoration* (1909), pp. 206–210.

Migennes, Pierre. "Les Dentelles de Suzanne Pinault." *Art et Décoration* (1933), pp. 315–318.

Mottola-Molfino, Alessandra, and Bianghi Olivari, Maria-Theresa. *I Pizzi: Moda e Simbolo*. Milan: Poldi Pezzoli Museum, 1977; Venice: Palazzo Grassi, 1977. Exhibition catalogue.

Palliser, Fanny. *Histoire de la dentelle, traduite par la Comtesse Gédeon de Clermont-Tonnerre*. Paris: Firmin-Didot, 1892.

Paulis, L. *Les Points à l'aiguille belges*. Brussels: Parc du Cinquantenaire, 1947.

———. *Pour connaître la dentelle*. Antwerp, 1947.

"Peasant Art in Italy." *The Studio*. Special number, 1913.

Pfannschmidt, Ernst-Erik. *Spitzen. Neue Ausdrucksformen einer alter Technik. Beispiele aus dem 20. Jahrhundert*. Ravensburg, 1976.

Ricci, Elisa. *Antiche trine italiane, raccolte e ordinate*. Bergamo: Istituto Italiano d'Art Grafiche, 1911.

———. *Merletti e ricami dell'Aemilia Ars*. Rome, 1929.

Risselin-Steenebrugen, Marie. *Trois Siècles de dentelles*. Brussels: Musées Royaux d'Art et d'Histoire, 1980.

Seguin, Jean. *La Dentelle*. Paris, 1875.

Tramar, comtesse de. *L'Evangile profane. Rite feminin*. Paris, 1905.

Van Overloop, E. *Matériaux pour servir à l'histoire de la dentelle en Belgique*. Brussels, 1912.

Verhaegen, Pierre. *La Restauration de la dentelle à Venise et l'Ecole de Burano*. Brussels: Goemaere, 1908.

Vermeil, M. P. "L'Art décoratif au Salon de 1905." *Art et Décoration* (1905), pp. 193–204.

Vrignaud, Germaine. *La Dentelle de Lunéville*. Lunéville, 1982.

Wardle, Patricia. *Victorian Lace*. New York: Praeger, 1968. 2d ed., 1982.

Printed Textiles

Manuscripts

Beaulieu, de. *Manière de fabriquer les toiles peintes dans l'Inde telle que M. de Beaulieu, capitaine de vaisseau, l'a fait exécuter devant lui à Pondichery*. 1734. Paris, Bibliothèque Centrale du Museum d'Histoire Naturelle, ms. 193.

Roques, P. *La Manière de négocier dans les Indes Orientales à mes chers amis et confrères, les engagés de la Royale Compagnie de France*. 1678. Paris, Bibliothèque Nationale, ms. F.R. 14614.

Rupied. *L'Art d'imprimer les toiles en Alsace*. 1786. Paris, Archives Nationales; Mulhouse, Musée de l'Impression sur Etoffes.

Rÿhiner, Jean. *Traité sur la fabrication et le commerce des toiles peintes*. 1766. Mulhouse, Musée de l'Impression sur Etoffes.

Early Publications

Delormois. *L'Art de faire l'indiennage à l'instar d'Angleterre et de composer toutes les couleurs bon teint propres à l'indienne*. Paris: Jombert, 1770.

Dollfus-Ausset, Daniel. *Matériaux pour la coloration des étoffes*. Paris: Savy, 1865.

Le Normand, Louis Sébastien. *Nouveau Manuel complet du fabricant d'étoffes imprimées et du fabricant de papiers peints*. Paris: Roret, 1856.

O'Brien, Charles. *Treatise on Calico Printing: Theoretical and Practical*. London, 1792.

Persoz, J. *Traité théorique et pratiq.e de l'impression des tissus*. Paris: Masson, 1846.

Quérelles, Chevalier de. *Traité sur les toiles peintes dans lequel on voit la manière dont on les fabrique aux Indes et en Europe*. Amsterdam: Barrois, 1760.

Schwartz, Paul R. "French Documents on Indian Cotton Painting." *Journal of Indian Textile*

History, nos. 2 and 3 (1956, 1957).

Thillaye, L. J. S. *Manuel du fabricant d'indiennes*. Paris: Roret, 1834.

General Works

Allemagne, Henri René d'. *La Toile imprimée et les indiennes de traite*. Paris: Gründ, 1942.

Bergeron, Louis. *Banquiers, négociants et manufacturiers parisiens du Directoire à l'Empire*. Paris, 1978.

Bernard-Leduc. "Sur l'Histoire de l'industrie des toiles peintes." *Actes du LIIIème Congrès Scientifique de France*, 1885.

Bigard, Louis. *Toiles imprimées à sujets maritimes du XVIIIème siècle*. N.p.: n.pub., n.d.

Braun-Ronsdorf, Margarete. *Zeitschrift für Waffen and Kostümkunde*. Munich: Deutscher Kunstverlag, 1970.

Cabot, Nancy Graves. "Some Pattern Sources of the 18th and 19th Century Printed Cottons." *Bulletin of the Needle and Bobbin Club* 33, nos. 1 and 2 (1949).

Christensen, Ruth. *Stof tryk: Historie, farver og teknick*. Copenhagen, 1975.

Clouzot, Henri. "Histoire de la toile imprimée au Musée Galliera." *Art et Tradition*, February 1908.

———. *La Marine en toile peinte*. N.p.: n.pub., n.d.

———, and Morris, Frances. *Painted and Printed Fabrics. The History of the Manufactory at Jouy and Other Ateliers in France (1760–1815)*. New York: Metropolitan Museum of Art, 1927.

Depierre, Joseph. *L'Impression des tissus, spécialement à la main, à travers les âges et dans les divers pays*. Mulhouse: Stuckelberger, 1910.

Fohlen, Claude. *L'Industrie textile au temps du Second Empire*. Paris: Plon, 1956.

Hugues, Patrice. *Le Langage du tissus*. Paris, 1983.

Irwin, John, and Brett, Katherine B. *Origins of Chintz*. London: HMSO, 1970.

Jacqué, Jacqueline, and Sano, Takahiko. *Chefs-d'oeuvre du Musée de l'Impression sur Etoffes de Mulhouse*. 3 vols. Tokyo: Gakken, 1978.

Lapadu-Hargues, F., and Rivière, G. H. "Imagerie, cartes à jouer, toiles imprimées." *Arts et Traditions Populaires*, July 1965.

Migeon, Gaston. *Les Arts du tissu*. Paris: H. Laurens, 1909.

Montgomery, Florence. *Printed Textiles 1700–1850*. New York: Viking Press, 1970.

"Musée de l'Impression sur Etoffes de Mulhouse," *Bulletin S.I.M.*, no. 761 (1975).

Pitoiset, Gilles. *Toiles imprimées XVIIIème–XIXème siècles*. Paris: Bibliothèque Forney, 1982.

Sampson-Preston, Paula. *Printed Cottons at Old Sturbridge Village*. Sturbridge, Mass.: Old Sturbridge Village, 1969.

Schommer, Pierre. *L'Art décoratif au temps du romantisme*. Paris: n.pub., 1928.

Schwartz, Paul R. *Histoire générale des techniques*. Paris: Presses Universitaires de France, 1928. Vol. 3.

Vaillat, L. *Le Décor de la vie. La Toile imprimée*. Paris: 1917.

Zuber, Claude. *Les Toiles imprimées et le costume*. Lecture delivered on 3 February 1955 under the auspices of the Union Française des Arts du Costume.

Europe

Bachman, Manfred, and Reitz, Gunther. *Der Blaudruck*. Leipzig: Hofmeister, 1962.

Berthoud, Dorette. *Les Indiennes neuchâteloises*. Neuchâtel: La Baconnière, 1951.

Bovet, Maurice. "Les Toiles peintes en pays neuchâtelois, cent ans après la fin des manufactures." *Revue Neuchâteloise*, Winter 1976–1977.

Bunt, Cyril E., and Rose, Ernest E. *Two Centuries of English Chintz: 1750–1950*. Leigh-on-Sea: F. Lewis, 1957.

Dreyer, Alice. *Les Toiles peintes en pays neuchâtelois*. Neuchâtel: Delachaux and Niestlé, 1923.

English Printed Textiles, 1720–1836: Victoria and Albert Museum. London: HMSO, 1960.

Fazy, Georges. "Notes sur l'industrie des indiennes à Genève." *Nos Anciens et Leurs Oeuvres*, 6th year.

Floud, Peter. "The Origins of English Calico Printing"; "The English Contribution to the Early History of Indigo Printing"; "The English Contribution to the Development of Copper Plate Printing." *Journal of the Society of Dyers and Colourists*, May, June, July, 1960.

Henschen, Ingegerd. *Tygtryck i Sverige, fore 1700*.

Stockholm: n.pub., 1942.

Jean-Richard, Anne. *Kattundrucke der Schweiz im 18. Jahrhundert*. Basel: Basler Druck-und Verlagsanstalt, 1968.

King, D. "Textile Printing in London and the Home Counties." *Journal of the Society of Dyers and Colourists*, July 1955.

Luze, E. de. "Jacques de Luze et l'Industrie des toiles peintes dans le pays de Neuchâtel," *Mémoires et Documents de la Société d'Histoire et d'Archéologie de Genève*, 1882.

Schwartz, Paul R. "Contribution à l'histoire de l'application du blue indigo (bleu anglais) dans l'indiennage européen." *Bulletin S.I.M.*, no. 2 (1963).

France

Dayot, A. *Les Vernet: Joseph-Carle, Horace*. Paris, 1898.

Depitre, Edgar. *La Toile peinte en France au XVIIème et XVIIIème siècles*. Paris: Rivière, 1912.

Juvet-Michel, A. "La Toile imprimée en France au XVIIIème siècle." *Cahiers CIBA*, no. 24 (1949).

Morellet, Abbé. *Réflexions sur les avantages de la libre fabrication et de l'usage des toiles peintes en France*. Geneva: Danonneville, 1758. This work was answered by: *Examen des effets que doivent produire dans le commerce de France l'usage et la fabrication des toiles peintes, ou réponse à l'ouvrage intitulé: Réflexions sur les avantages de la libre fabrication et de l'usage des toiles peintes en France*. Geneva: Delaguette, 1759.

O'Neill, Mary. "Origins of Pictorial Designs for French Printed Textiles of the First Half of the Nineteenth Century." *Burlington Magazine* 123 (December 1981): 722–735.

Saule, Béatrix. "Les Manufactures d'indiennes en France de 1759 à 1789." Mémoire pour le Diplôme d'Etudes Supérieures d'Histoire des Institutions. Université de Droit, d'Economie et de Sciences Sociales de Paris II, 1973.

Schwartz, Paul R., and Micheaux, R. *A Century of French Fabrics: 1850–1950*. Leigh-on-Sea: F. Lewis, 1964.

Jouy

Brédif, Josette. "Les Indiennes de la manufacture Oberkampf de Jouy en Josas (1760–1861)." Mémoire de Maîtrise d'Histoire de l'Art et Archéologie. Paris, 1978.

Cain, George. *Toiles de Jouy*. Paris, n.d.

Chassagne, Serge. *Un Femme d'affaires au XVIIIème siècle: La Correspondance de Mme de Maraise, collaboratrice de'Oberkampf*. Toulouse: privately printed, 1981.

———. *Oberkampf. Un Entrepreneur capitaliste au siècle des lumières*. Paris: Aubin-Montaigne, 1980.

Clouzot, Henri. "Les Toiles de Jouy." *Revue de l'Art Ancien et Moderne*, 10 January, 10 February 1908.

———. *La Toile peinte en France. La Manufacture de Jouy*. Versailles: n.pub., 1912–1914 (incomplete).

———. "La Fabrication des toiles de Jouy au XVIIIème siècle." *Renaissance de l'Art Français et des Industries de Luxe*, no. 3 (1926).

Indiennes, étoffes chinoises, toiles de Jouy. Paris: Guérinet, n.d.

Jacqué, Jacqueline. "Toiles de Jouy." *American Fabrics and Fashion*, n.d.

Jardel, Marguerite. "L'Art de la toile peinte, indiennes et toiles de Jouy." *Plaisirs de France*, no. 235 (May 1958).

Labouchère, Alfred. *Oberkampf (1738–1815)*. Paris: Hachette, 1866.

Latour, Anny. "Les Aventures de la toile de Jouy." *Revue l'Estampille*, no. 78 (June 1978).

Les Plus Belles Toiles imprimées de la manufacture de Jouy 1760–1820. Paris: Galigagni, n.d.

"La Toile de Jouy." *Connaissance des Arts*, no. 43 (September 1955).

Toiles de Jouy, anciennes toiles peintes, collection Paul Vignon, tissus et gravures de la collection de l'éditeur. Paris: A. Guérinet, 1913.

Toiles de Jouy anciennes. Paris: Chanloup, n.d.

Vieilles Toiles de Jouy. Paris: Guérinet, n.d.

Nantes

Clouzot, Henri. "Les Toiles peintes nantaises." *Gazette des Beaux-Arts*, January–March 1916.

————. "Les Toiles imprimées de Nantes." *La Renaissance de l'Art Français*, November 1924.

Orceau, R. "Les Pelloutier indienneurs." *Société Archéologique et Historique de Nantes*, 1926.

Roy, Bernard. *Une Capitale de l'indiennage: Nantes.* Nantes: Musée des Salorges, 1948.

Stany-Gauthier, J. "Faïences et toiles imprimées au Musée des Salorges à Nantes." *La Revue Française*, no. 145 (1962).

Mulhouse-Alsace

Albrecht-Mathey, Elisabeth. *The Fabrics of Mulhouse and Alsace: 1750–1850.* Leigh-on-Sea: F. Lewis, 1968.

Baumann, J. "Marie-Bonaventure Lebert: Artiste parisien (1759–1836) et sa contribution à l'iconographie de Thann." *Annuaire de la Société d'Histoire des Régions de Thann-Guebwiller*, 1961–1964.

"Bi-centenaire de l'impression sur étoffes en Alsace: 1746–1946." *Bulletin S.I.M.*, nos. 3 and 4 (1946).

Le Centenaire de la Société Industrielle: Son activité et ses créations 1826–1926. 2 vols. Mulhouse: Société Industrielle Mulhouse, 1926.

Clouzot, Henri. "La Tradition de la toile imprimée en Alsace." *Renaissance de l'Art Français et des Industries de Luxe*, no. 7 (July 1919).

Histoire documentaire de l'industrie de Mulhouse et de ses environs au XIXème siècle. Mulhouse: Société Industrielle Mulhouse, 1902.

Lebert, Henri. "Notice sur les développements du dessin d'impression des toiles peintes en Alsace." *Revue d'Alsace*, 1862.

Levy, Robert. *Histoire économique de l'industrie cotonnière en Alsace.* Paris: Alcan & Guillaumin, 1912.

Mieg, Jean. *Manufactures du Haut-Rhin: 1822–1825. 34 Lithographies avec une introduction de Georges Bischoff.* Mulhouse: Bisey, 1982. Reprint.

Schmitt, Jean-Marie. *Aux Origines de la révolution industrielle en Alsace: Investissements et relations sociales dans la vallée de Saint Amarin au XVIIIème siècle.* Strasbourg: ISTRA, 1980.

Schwartz, Raul R. "Les Débuts de l'indiennage mulhousien." *Bulletin S.I.M.*, 1950–1952.

Tuchscherer, Jean-Michel. *The Fabrics of Mulhouse and Alsace (1801–1850).* Leigh-on-Sea: F. Lewis, 1972.

Wehrlin, Alphonse. "Manuscrits Rupied et Deguingand ayant trait à la fabrication des toiles peintes à Mulhouse et en Alsace vers 1786." *Bulletin S.I.M.*, 1912.

Widmer, Samuel. *Lettres écrites d'Alsace.* Mulhouse: Suzanne Thurneyssen, 1911.

Rouen

Dardel, Pierre. *Les Manufactures de toiles peintes et de serges imprimées à Rouen et à Bolbec aux XVIIème et XVIIIème siècles.* Rouen: Desvages, 1940.

————. "Commerce, industrie et navigation à Rouen et au Havre au XVIIIème siècle." *Société Libre d'Emulation de la Seine Maritime*, 1966.

Wechser, H. "Der Zeugdruck der Normandie im 18. und 19. Jahrhundert." *CIBA Rundschau*, no. 147 (1959).

Bordeaux (Beautiran)

Dietlin, Evelyne. "Une Fabrique de toiles imprimées en Aquitaine à Beautiran (1802–1832)." *Bulletin et Mémoires de la Société Archéologique de Bordeaux*, 1980.

Petitcol, Xavier. "A propos d'une toile de Beautiran: L'Agréable Leçon ou l'art de'aimer"; "Répertoire des toiles imprimées des manufactures d'Aquitaine déjà publiées." *Visages du Pays de l'Aruan*, December 1982.

Other Regions

Azema, Xavier. "Notes sur une fabrique de toiles peintes au XVIIIème siècle, Fontcaude." *Actes du XXXVIème Congrès de la Fédération Historique Languedoc-Méditerranée-Roussillon.* Lodève, 1963.

Ballofet, Joseph. *Historique de l'indienne à Beligny, Chervinges et Villefranche en Beaujolais.* Villefranche: Auray Fils & Deschizeaux, 1913.

———."Mémoire de J. M. Roland de la Platière sur les articles qui se fabriquaient en Beaujolais à la fin du XVIIIème siècle." *Notes pour Servir à l'Histoire de l'Industrie et du Commerce de Ville-franche en Beaujolais*, 1913.

Chassagne, Serge. *La Manufacture de toiles imprimées de Tournemine les Angers 1752–1820.* Paris: Klinsksieck, 1971.

Chobaut, H. "L'Industrie des indiennes à Avignon et à Orange (1677–1884)." *Mémoires de l'Académie du Vaucluse*, 1938.

———. "L'Industrie des indiennes à Marseille avant 1680." *Mémoires de l'Institut Historique de Provence*, 1939.

Dauphin, V. "Les Toiles imprimées en Anjou au XVIIIème siècle." *Au Pays de Loire*, no. 1 (July 1919).

———. "Les Manufactures de toiles peintes en Anjour (1750–1840)." *Mémoire de la Société d'Agriculture, Sciences et Arts d'Angers*, 1923.

Fohlen, Claude. "Une Affaire de famille au XIXème siècle: Mequillet-Noblot," *Cahiers de la Fondation Nationale des Sciences Politiques*, no. 75 (1955).

Garsonnin, Docteur. "La Manufacture de toiles peintes d'Orléans." *Mémoires et Documents pour Servir à l'Histoire du Commerce et de l'Industrie en France*, 1913.

Morant, Henry de. "Les Toiles peintes d'Angers au Musée Saint-Jean." *Les Cahiers de Poncé et des Musées de la Ville d'Angers*, no. 17 (1949).

Morin, Louis. *Recherches sur l'impression des toiles dites indiennes à Troyes (1766–1828).* Troyes, 1913.

"Perrenod et Cie ou les indiennes de Melun." *Bulletin Municipal de Melun*, December 1981.

Sahler, Léon. *L'Industrie cotonnière au pays de Montbéliard et ses origines.* Montbéliard, 1903.

Schwartz, Paul R. "La Fabrique d'indiennes du Duc de Bourbon (1692–1740) au château de Chantilly. *Bulletin S.I.M.*, no. 1 (1966).

Exhibition Catalogues
(in chronological order)

La Tradition de la toile imprimée en France. Paris: Musée Galliera, 1907.

Ausstellung farbiger Dekorationen. Strasbourg: Alte Schloss, 1912.

La Toile de Jouy: XVIIIème et XIXème Siècles. Paris: Galerie P. Mayoux, 1913.

A Retrospective Exhibition of Painted and Printed Fabrics. New York: Metropolitan Museum of Art, 1927.

Toiles imprimées et papiers peints. Paris: Musée Galliera, 1928.

Ausstellung von antiken, bedruckten Stoffen, originale aus den Manufacturen von Jouy, Nantes, Melun und Anderen. Berlin, 1929.

W. and J. Sloane Collection of Toiles. New York, 1931.

Exhibition of Toiles de Jouy: Collection of Agnes J. Holden. Washington, D.C.: Cultural Division of the French Embassy, 1948:

"Exposition de l'été 1952." Mulhouse: Musée de l'Impression sur Etoffes, *Bulletin S.I.M.*, nos. 3 and 4 (1952).

Bont en blauw: Tien eeuwen bedruckte stof. Enschede Kunstichting, 1953.

"La Collection Louis Becker: Mouchoirs et tissus imprimés des XVIIIème et XIXème siècles." Mulhouse: Musée de l'Impression sur Etoffes, *Bulletin S.I.M.*, no. 3 (1954).

Design by the Yard. New York: Cooper Union Museum, 1956.

Deux Siècles d'impression sur tissus. Rouen: Musée des Beaux-Arts, 1958.

Painted and Printed Textiles. Los Angeles County Museum, 1961.

Planches anciennes imprimées par les anciens établisse-ments Charles Steiner de Ribeauvillé. Mulhouse: Musée de l'Impression sur Etoffes, 1964.

Littérature et toiles imprimées des XVIIIème et XIXème siècles. Mulhouse: Musée de l'Impression sur Etoffes, 1965.

Collection de toiles peintes d'Harry Wearne du Royal Ontario Museum. Mulhouse: Musée de l'Impression sur Etoffes, 1966.

Les Impressions de Wesserling aux XVIIIème et XIXème siècles. Mulhouse: Musée de l'Impression sur Etoffes, 1967.

Exposition rétrospective des étoffes imprimées au XIXème siècle par la manufacture Koechlin-Baumgartner et Cie à Lörrach (R.F.A.). Mulhouse: Musée de l'Impression sur Etoffes, 1970.

Le Style troubadour. Brou, 1971.

Dessins français de 1750 à 1825. Le Néo-classicisme. Paris: Musée du Louvre, Cabinet des Estampes, 1972.

The Age of Neo-Classicism. London: The Royal Academy and the Victoria and Albert Museum, 1972.

In Memoriam: Nancy Graves Cabot. Sources of Design for Textiles and Decorative Arts. Boston: Museum of Fine Arts, 1973.

Blues Traditions. Indigo Dyed Textiles and Related Cobalt Glazed Ceramics from the 17th through the 19th Century. Baltimore Museum of Art, 1973.

De David à Delacroix: La Peinture française de 1774 à 1830. Paris: Grand Palais, 1974.

Impressions sur étoffes XVIIème-XVIIIème-XIXème: Prestiges, curiosités, anecdotes. Strasbourg: Banque de Paris et des Pays–Bas, 1974.

Le Néo-classsicisme français. Dessins de musées de province. Paris: Grand Palais, 1974.

L'Amérique vue par l'Europe. Paris: Grand Palais, 1976.

Les Tissus imprimés dans le pays de Montbéliard au 19ème siècle: Manufacture Méquillet-Noblot. Montbéliard: Musee du Château, 1976.

La Toile imprimée: Une Technique, un art. Rennes: Maison de la Culture, 1976.

Toiles de Nantes des XVIIIème et XIXème siècles. Mulhouse: Musée de l'Impression sur Etoffes, 1977.

Les Indiennes à Villefranche. 200 Ans d'impression des tissus. Villefranche en Beaujolais: Centre d'Arts Plastiques, 1977.

Toiles de Jouy. Jouy en Josas: Musée Oberkampf, 1977.

Textieldruck: Evolutie en techniek. Duerne: Provinciaal Museum vor Kunstambachten, 1978.

Les Plus Belles Pièces des collections. Jouy en Josas: Musée Oberkampf, 1979.

Etoffes imprimées françaises: Musée de l'Impression sur Etoffes. Kyoto: Japan Design Museum, 1981.

L'Histoire vue à travers la toile imprimée. Jouy en Josas: Musée Oberkampf, 1981.

Visages du Pays de l'Aruan. Beautiran: Salle des Fêtes, 1982.

Les Indiennes de la manufacture Oberkampf de Jouy en Josas. Jouy en Josas: Musée Oberkampf, 1983.

Photographic Credits

Studio Basset: figs. 1, 17, 27, 30–31, 33, 81–82
Enrico Bertinelli: fig. 91
Courtesy of the Bibliothèque National: figs. 56, 59, 63, 86–87, 96, 110
E. Irving Blomstrann: figs. 38, 104–105
Jean-Luc Bureau: figs. 53, 66, 68, 70, 72, 76, 85, 95, 97–99, 109, 111, 115–116
Courtesy of the Cathedral Treasury at Troyes: figs. 49–50
Lynton Gardiner: figs. 13, 18, 92, 93
Courtesy of The Metropolitan Museum of Art: figs. 57, 60
Courtesy of The Minneapolis Institute of Arts: fig. 65
Courtesy of the Mobilier National: figs. 14, 40
Courtesy of the Monuments Historiques: figs. 46–48
Courtesy of the Musée de la Mode et du Costume de la Ville de Paris: fig. 77
Courtesy of the Musée de la Reine Mathilde, Bayeux: figs. 44–45
Courtesy of the Musée de l'Impression sur Etoffes: figs. 117–131, 133–140, 142–146, 148–154
Courtesy of the Musée de Versailles: fig. 101
Courtesy of the Musée des Beaux-Arts et de la Dentelle, Alençon: fig. 102
Courtesy of the Musée du Louvre: figs. 61–62, 94
Courtesy of the Museo del Palazzo Venezia, Rome: fig. 54
Courtesy of the Museum of Fine Arts, Boston: figs. 26, 35, 71, 83
Courtesy of the Philadelphia Museum of Art: figs. 84, 147
Courtesy of the Reunion des musées nationaux: fig. 58
Courtesy of the Museum of Art, Rhode Island School of Design: figs. 5, 11, 15, 39
Courtesy of The Saint Louis Art Museum: figs. 51, 67, 78
Joseph Szaszfai: figs. 2–4, 6–10, 12, 16, 19–20, 22–25, 28–29, 32, 34, 36–37, 55, 64, 69, 73–75, 80, 100, 103, 106–108, 112–114, 132, 141
Courtesy of Tassinari & Chatel: figs. 41–43, 78–79
Courtesy of Union Centrale des Arts Décoratifs: figs. 21, 88–90
Courtesy of the Walters Art Gallery: fig. 52

Design by Catherine Waters

Printer's negatives made
by Robert Hennessey
Composed in Bembo types,
printed and bound
by Meriden–Stinehour Press